200

Texas Outlaws and Lawmen

1835-1935

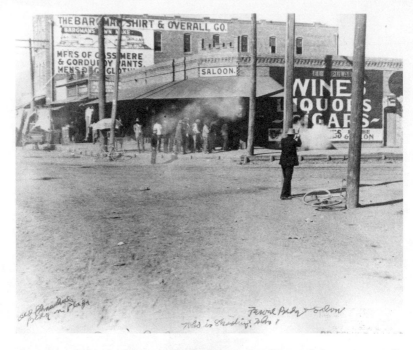

Actual gunfight. A photographer captured forever this gunfight as it actually occurred in El Paso at Seventh and El Paso streets in late 1907. (Courtesy of the El Paso Public Library, Southwest Collection)

200

Texas Outlaws and Lawmen 1835-1935

Laurence J. Yadon
with Dan Anderson

Edited by Robert Barr Smith

PELICAN PUBLISHING COMPANY
Gretna 2008

The word "Pelican" and the depiction of a pelican
are trademarks of Pelican Publishing Company, Inc.,
and are registered in the U.S. Patent and Trademark Office.

Library of Congress Cataloging-in-Publication Data

Yadon, Laurence J., 1948-
  200 Texas outlaws and lawmen, 1835-1935 / by Laurence J. Yadon,
with Dan Anderson ; edited by Robert Barr Smith.
    p. cm.
  Includes bibliographical references and index.
  ISBN 978-1-58980-514-9 (pbk. : alk. paper)
  1. Outlaws—Texas—Biography. 2. Peace officers—Texas—
Biography. 3. Criminals—Texas—Biography. 4. Texas—History—
Republic, 1836-1846—Biography. 5. Texas—History—1846-
1950—Biography. 6. Frontier and pioneer life—Texas—Anecdotes.
7. Crime—Texas—History—Anecdotes. 8. Law enforcement—
Texas—History—Anecdotes. I. Anderson, Dan, 1950- II. Smith,
Robert B. (Robert Barr), 1933- III. Title. IV. Title: Two hundred
Texas outlaws and lawmen, 1835-1935.

F385.Y33 2008
364.1092'2764—dc22
[B]
                        2007045195

Printed in the United States of America
Published by Pelican Publishing Company, Inc.
1000 Burmaster Street, Gretna, Louisiana 70053

To the men and women of Texas law enforcement

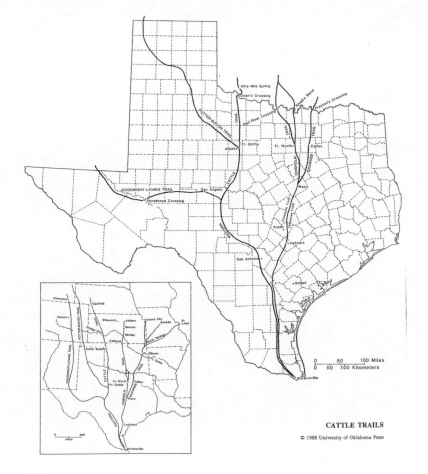

CATTLE TRAILS

© 1988 University of Oklahoma Press

Old West Texas. (Courtesy of the University of Oklahoma Press)

Contents

Preface

This popular history is an outgrowth of our previous book, *100 Oklahoma Outlaws, Gangsters, and Lawmen, 1839-1939.* Once again, we have largely relied upon the scholarship of leading Western writers for the stories told here. The principal author's lifelong interest in Texas was inspired by the frontier lives of rancher Samuel Burk Burnett and other distantly related Missouri kinsmen who settled in nineteenth-century Texas.

In this work, we have focused on notable luminaries of Lone Star outlawry and the law officers who pursued them from the opening days of the Republic to the middle years of the Great Depression. Loosely applying standards used by the eminent scholar Bill O'Neal in his seminal work *Encyclopedia of Western Gunfighters,* we have profiled the better known Texas outlaws who engaged in at least two gunfights or armed robberies in which significant gunfights occurred. Certain colorful characters, such as Judge Roy Bean, the self-appointed "Law West of the Pecos," and high-profile lawmen, outlaws, and gangsters from elsewhere who operated in Texas or who were one-time Texas residents, have also been included. These individual profiles cover the one hundred-year period beginning with the first declaration of Texas independence in assemblies in Goliad and elsewhere in 1835 and ending with the Depression-era crimes of Machine Gun Kelly and the Barrow gang. Altogether, this volume contains more than two hundred profiles featuring more than five hundred outlaws, gangsters, and lawmen, including a fistful of Texas feudists, Rio Grande border warriors, and Indian fighters.

We have also included a section identifying still accessible outlaw hideouts and locales for those who enjoy treading in the footsteps of history, as well as a Texas outlaw chronology. Usually, we have relied upon traditional narratives of events using standard sources and the works of authors generally accepted as reliable. However, in some instances we have rejected traditional narratives of events, offering alternative versions or related new interpretations based on recent scholarship or variations we deem reliable. Usually the variant theories are referenced, but not expounded, since this is a book of popular history rather than a work of academic scholarship. Generally we reviewed books, magazines, and periodicals available to us as late as January 2007.

Once again, the distinguished historian Robert Barr Smith (*Tough Towns, Outlaw Tales of Oklahoma*) took time from his own writing schedule to guide our efforts as Consulting Editor. Nevertheless the judgments we have made concerning the relative credibility of competing sources, and any errors sifting fact from mythology, have been our own.

Regrettably, but of necessity, a great many colorful, compelling Texas outlaws and lawmen have been set aside for another time. And so, dear reader, enjoy these pages with the assurance that our Texas outlaw tour has only just begun.

Laurence Yadon, Tulsa, Oklahoma
Dan Anderson, Katy, Texas
Robert Barr Smith, Consulting Editor, Norman, Oklahoma

Acknowledgments

Research for this project was performed in conjunction with our previous work, *100 Oklahoma Outlaws, Gangsters, and Lawmen, 1839-1939*. Accordingly a number of organizations assisted the authors in the research for these projects over the past four years. These institutions included but were not limited to the Flying Fingers Typing Service, Sand Springs, Oklahoma; Texas Ranger Museum, Waco, Texas; the Haley Library; Harris County Public Library; Dallas Public Library; Fort Bend County Public Library; Houston City Public Library; Young County Historical Commission; City-County Library, Tulsa, Oklahoma; Oklahoma Historical Society; Western History Collection, University of Oklahoma Library; Oklahoma Heritage Association; Oklahoma Centennial Commission; Woolaroc Museum, Bartlesville, Oklahoma; Texas Jack Association; Oklahombres, Inc.; Oklahoma Outlaws, Lawmen History Association; Tulsa Police Department; Public Library, Enid, Oklahoma; Beryl Ford Collection, Tulsa; Oklahoma Publishing Company; Lenapah Historical Society; the University of Tulsa; Kansas State Historical Society; Will Rogers Museum; National Cowboy Hall of Fame; Gilcrease Museum; Enid Public Library; Boone County Heritage Museum, Harrison, Arkansas; and the Lincoln Heritage Trust, Lincoln, New Mexico.

Individuals who assisted us in these two projects have included Bill O'Neal, Nancy Samuelson, Bob Ernst, Ron Trekell, Armand DeGregoris, John R. Lovett, Mike Tower, Michael and Suzanne Wallis, Bob Alexander, Robert K. DeArment, David Johnson, Chuck Parsons, Rick Miller, Bill O'Neal, Bob Ernst, Rod Dent, Gary Youell, Phil Edwards, Terry Zinn, Michael Koch, Diron Ahlquist, Willie Jones, Clyda Franks, Emily Lovick, Lisa Keys, Joseph Calloway Yadon (ardent researcher and author's son), Danielle Williams, Irene and Larry Chance, Glendon Floyd, Curt Johnson, Dee Cordry, Rik Helmerich, and Herman Kirkwood. Thanks are also due to Helen J. Gaines, Jim Bradshaw, Adrienne Grimmett, Beth Andreson, Jim

11

Hamilton, Dana Harrison MacMoy, Mary Phillips, Stacy M. Rogers, Rand McKinney, Jana Swartwood, Gini Moore Campbell, and Phillip W. Steele. We are especially thankful for the assistance of Mr. Dorman Holub, Chairman, Young County Historical Society, as well as Jim Bradshaw, passionate archivist with The Haley Memorial Library & History Center at Midland, Texas; Sgt. Kevin F. Foster, Fort Worth Police historian; Jane Soutner with the Texas History Division of the Dallas Public Library; and Brian Burns, Information Specialist at the Border Heritage Center of the El Paso Public Library. Special thanks also to Ashley Schmidt and Dana Brittain at the Fort Bend County Library—Cinco Ranch Branch. Thanks to the good folks at the Texas Ranger Hall of Fame and Museum at Waco.

Lastly, without the patient guidance of our Consulting Editor, Robert Barr Smith, and the patient support of our respective spouses, Martha Yadon and Julia Anderson, this book would not have been possible.

200

Texas Outlaws and Lawmen

1835-1935

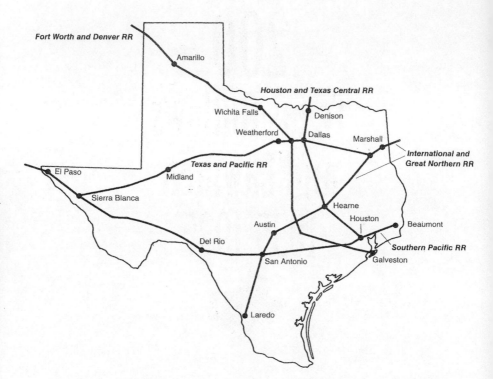

Major Railroads in Texas. (*Texas: A Modern History,* by David G. McComb, copyright 1999. Courtesy of the University of Texas Press)

Chronology of Significant Events
1835-1935

1835   Texas provisional government formed at San Felipe and independence declared by several assemblies, notably one at Goliad on December 20.

1840   Notorious Texas gunman Robert A. Clay Allison was born in Tennessee. Allison killed at least five men before his violent life ended in a wagon accident on July 1, 1887, in Pecos, Texas.

    Joseph L. Hood, first sheriff of Bexar County, was killed in a melee with Comanche chiefs within the Town Council House during the course of peace negotiations (prior to April 18).

1841   Renowned black lawman Bass Reeves was born this year or perhaps the previous year in Arkansas, then removed with the Reeves family to Grayson County, Texas. Reeves was apparently the first black deputy U.S. marshal to be appointed west of the Mississippi.

    Charles W. Jackson, a participant in the Regulator-Moderator War, was killed. A year earlier, a judge sent to try Jackson for killing Joseph G. Goodbread was himself killed near Pulaski, Texas, after fleeing for his life.

    Thomas D. Yocum, proprietor of the Yocum Inn in the Big Thicket country of East Texas, was executed by a Regulator posse on information that Yocum had murdered several people.

1843   John V. Morton, first sheriff of Fort Bend County, was killed by his former deputy, George W. Pleasants (February 7).

1844   Texas Ranger George W. Arrington was born in Alabama.

1847   Approximate birth year of Longhair Jim Courtright, probably an Illinois native who moved to Fort Worth in about 1875, then served from time to time in a series of law enforcement positions before starting his own detective service, described by detractors as nothing more than an extortion operation.

1850   Noted Texas Ranger John Barclay (Barkley) Armstrong was born in McMinnville, Tennessee.

1853   Jesse Evans, Lampasas County, Texas, cowboy and Lincoln County War participant, was born in Illinois.

1854   Texas bank robber extraordinaire Reuben Burrow was born on December 11 in Lamar County, Alabama.

1856   Road agent Texas Jack and two other bandits were confronted near Folsom, California, on September 30 by the Placer County sheriff, who killed Ned Conway. Tom Bell escaped, but was soon found by a lynch mob, leaving only Texas Jack to tell the tale in places yet unknown.

1862   Billy the Kid associate David Anderson, known as Billy Wilson, was born in South Texas. Anderson finished his career as sheriff of Terrell County, Texas.

1863   Civil War guerilla William C. "Bloody Bill" Anderson wintered in Sherman, Texas, and married a local woman before resuming his murderous career.

1865   Confederate colonel George Wythe Baylor quarreled with Gen. John Austin Wharton and killed him on April 6. Later, he became a Texas Ranger and was credited with filling El Paso jails with rustlers and thieves.

1871   Notorious bandit William T. "Black Jack" Christian was born near Fort Griffin, Texas.

Wild Bill Hickok killed his last gunfight opponent, Gonzalez County, Texas, native Phillip Houston Coe, at the Bull's Head Saloon in Abilene, Kansas (October 5).

1873   Nineteen-year-old Seldon Lindsey protected his father by shooting a vigilante out of the saddle. Later he became a deputy U.S. marshal and was credited with killing the outlaw Bill Dalton.

1874   William Sutton, supposed agitator of the Sutton-Taylor feud, was assassinated with his associate Gabe Slaughter by Taylor factionists as Sutton boarded a steamboat at Indianola, Texas (March 11).

Jim Reed and two associates from Butler, Missouri, robbed the Austin-San Antonio stage near Blanco, taking about $4,000 (April 7).

Bat Masterson, Bill Tilghman, and others were attacked by Indians led by mixed-blood Quanah Parker at Adobe Walls, in the Texas Panhandle (July 27).

1875   Former Texas Ranger Scott Cooley became an interloper in the Mason County War, whose victims included his friend and mentor Tim Williamson. Cooley killed former deputy sheriff Worley (Wohrle) on August 10, then scalped him.

Doc Holliday dueled with a Mr. Austin in a dispute over a Dallas card game. Neither was injured.

Leading Taylor factionist Jim Taylor was assassinated at Clinton, Texas, possibly with the collusion of Martin King, who carelessly allowed Taylor's horse to become loose, eliminating his chances for a quick escape (December 27).

1876   John B. Armstrong and other Texas Rangers surprised and killed three reputed cattle rustling associates of John King Fisher at Espantosa Lake near Carrizo, Texas (October 1).

Former Texas Ranger Lark Ferguson became Pete Spence following dismissal from the Texas Rangers after two questionable killings and a Seeligson bank robbery (August 24).

1877   Sam Bass and other members of the Joel Collins gang robbed a stagecoach near Deadwood, South Dakota, and killed driver Johnny Slaughter (March 25).

John B. Armstrong captured John Wesley Hardin on a train at Pensacola, Florida, and killed his associate Jim Mann (August 23).

The Joel Collins gang robbed the eastbound Union Pacific No. 4 train at Big Springs, Nebraska, taking some $60,000 (September 18).

1878   Texas impresario Kitty Leroy was killed by her jealous husband in Deadwood, Dakota Territory, when he became concerned over Kitty's real or imagined relationships with Sam Bass and Wild Bill Hickok. Kitty owned the Mint Gambling Saloon at the time of her death.

Supposed former Texas Ranger Andrew L. "Buckshot" Roberts went to Blazer's Mill, New Mexico, for mail containing the proceeds from the recent sale of his ranch, but was killed in an encounter with Billy the Kid and other Regulators (April 4).

Texas Rangers and the Wise County sheriff attacked surviving members of the Bass gang, killing associate Arkansas Johnson and all the horses, forcing the other gang members to flee on foot (June 13).

1879   Barney Mason, Lee Hall, and other Texans rode as a posse under the command of Pat Garrett in pursuit of Henry McCarty (Billy the Kid) and got their man at Stinking Springs, New Mexico (December 23).

1880　Texas possemen James East, Lon Chambers, and Louis "The Animal" Bousman, joined Pat Garrett, then pursued and encountered Billy the Kid and his Texas associates Dave Rudabaugh, Tom East, Tom O'Folliard, and Charlie Bowdre at Fort Sumner (December 19). O'Folliard was mortally wounded.

1881　Texan and deputy sheriff James W. Bell was killed while guarding Henry McCarty (Billy the Kid) at the Lincoln County Courthouse, Lincoln, New Mexico (April 28). The Kid then killed Deputy Sheriff Bob Olinger with his own shotgun from a second-story window.

Texas troublemakers Ike Clanton, Billy Clanton, the McClaury brothers, and Billy Claiborne faced former Fort Griffin, Texas, visitors Wyatt Earp, Doc Holliday, Morgan Earp, and Virgil Earp in a Tombstone, Arizona, gunfight at the O.K. Corral on October 26. Both McClaurys were killed, along with Billy Clanton.

James-Younger gang member Frank James moved to Denison, Texas, for a new start. Later, he worked as a shoe salesman at the Sanger-Harris Department Store in Dallas.

1882　James Manning, owner of the Coliseum Saloon in El Paso, killed Doc Cummings, brother-in-law of Sheriff Dallas Stoudenmire, on February 14, then killed Stoudenmire himself seven months later.

Former DeWitt County, Texas, resident and Sutton-Taylor feudist John Peters Ringo was killed, in the mountains near Tombstone, by his own pistol or otherwise (July 14).

1884　Former Dallas saloon impresario John A. Heath was hanged impromptu by a mob unhappy with the life sentence he received for planning a robbery in which several innocent citizens were killed and wounded (March 28).

1885   Williamson County, Texas, gunman Judd Roberts killed his first victim in Fredericksburg, Texas. Roberts himself was killed in July 1887 in Williamson County by lawmen Ira Aten and John R. Hughes.

1886   Texas gunman Print Olive was killed at Trail City, Colorado, by Joe Sparrow, who owed Olive ten dollars (August 16).

Notorious outlaw Dave Rudabaugh quarreled over a card game with two locals in Parral, Mexico, and lost his head—quite literally (February 18).

1887   Mannen Clements, Sr., cousin of John Wesley Hardin, was killed in Ballenger, Texas, by City Marshal Joe Townsend in an election-related gunfight (March 29).

1889   Vernon, Texas, area resident and murder suspect Boone Marlow was poisoned then shot by bounty hunters with the collusion of his young sweetheart (late January).

1890   Lawman George Scarborough was mortally wounded by cattle rustlers about twenty miles southwest of San Simon, New Mexico (April 3).

1892   "Texas Invaders" eliminated Nate Champion, a Round Rock, Texas, area native and leader of small Wyoming ranchers during the Johnson County War (April 9).

1893   Texas Ranger Frank Jones was killed by the Olguin gang at Tres Jacales, Mexico (June 30).

1894   Gainesville, Texas, native Nate Sylva and others attempted to rob a Rock Island train near Pond Creek, then a thriving community in northern Oklahoma Territory (April 9), but were captured. Sylva escaped from captivity and was never heard from again.

A bank at Longview, Texas, was robbed by men traditionally

identified as the William C. "Bill" Dalton gang (May 23).

1897   Texas gunman David Kemp mortally wounded his archenemy Les Dow on February 18 at the Carlsbad, New Mexico, post office as the unsuspecting Dow read his last letter. Predictably enough, Kemp was later acquitted on the grounds of self-defense.

1898   Rancher and former Texan John Slaughter caught the bandit Peg-Leg Finney dozing under a tree on Slaughter's San Bernardino Ranch in Arizona and settled his hash (September 19).

1900   Deputy Sheriff Ed Scarborough killed murder suspect Ralph Jenks near Silver City, New Mexico (September 3).

1901   Will Carver, former associate of Butch Cassidy and the Sundance Kid, was killed by the Sutton County sheriff (April 2).

1903   Pink Higgins killed his archenemy Bill Standifer near Higgins's Kent County, Texas, ranch then reported the incident to the county sheriff by telephone, only to be told to make sure Standifer was dead, or so the story goes (October 4).

1907   Upshur County, Texas, native Jim Stevenson killed Pauls Valley, Oklahoma, city marshal Randolph Cathey, shortly before statehood (November 3). Stevenson escaped conviction through the efforts of noted criminal lawyer Moman Pruiett, only to be beaten to death by a burglar in Tulsa forty-four years later for fifteen dollars.

1909   Notorious killer Clyde Chestnut Barrow was born near Teleco, Texas (March 24).

1922   Frank Hamer and other Texas Rangers killed Ralph "Red" Lopez and nine Lopez gang members in a gunfight.

1923   Lawmen Dave Allison and Horace Roberson were murdered on Easter Sunday in Seminole, Texas, by Hill Loftis and Milt Good, against whom they were scheduled to testify the next day.

1924   The Newton brothers, formerly of Cottonwood, Texas, robbed a Chicago, Milwaukee and St. Paul Railroad train near Rondout, Illinois, taking approximately three million dollars, the largest train robbery in American history (June 12).

1927   Marshal Ratliff, better known as the Santa Claus robber, escaped from a Cisco bank on December 23, with a large amount of cash, only to leave it behind in a stolen getaway car, after mortally wounding two lawmen. Ratliff was lynched two years later following an escape attempt.

1928   Texas native Charles Siringo, who tracked Butch Cassidy, Billy the Kid, and many others as a Pinkerton detective, died peacefully in Altadena, California, after writing six books about his exploits (October 18).

1934   Bonnie Parker and Clyde Barrow were ambushed and killed near Gibsland, Louisiana (May 23)

Town builder Asa Borger was killed at one of the towns he founded, Borger, Texas, on August 31, by his nemesis, former county treasurer Arthur Huey. Borger was finished off with his own pistol.

Wheeler County, Texas, bank robber Irvin "Blackie" Thompson was killed at point-blank range by Deputy Sheriff Roy Brewer on Route 66 in Amarillo, east of Tenth Street, while resisting arrest (December 6).

1935   Barrow gang stalwarts Joe Palmer and Ray Hamilton were executed on May 10.

Texas Outlaw Hideouts, Hangouts, and Locales

Abilene, Texas
Texas mythology says that John Wesley Hardin killed Charles Cougar here on July 6, 1871, in a hotel for snoring, although contemporary newspaper reports make no mention of such a newsworthy motivation.

Austin, Texas
Billy Thompson, younger brother of noted gunman Ben Thompson, killed his friend Sgt. William Burke after a night on the town, on September 2, 1868. Five years later he killed another friend, Sheriff C. B. Whitney, at Ellsworth, Kansas.

The Iron Front Saloon, 605 Congress Avenue, was home away from home to Ben Thompson, John Wesley Hardin, and other hard cases. During demolition of the Iron Front, a skull was reportedly founded embedded in its walls. In later times, the site was occupied by the American National Bank.

Birthplace of pioneer Texas Ranger James Gillett, November 4, 1856, and place where Texas Ranger John B. Jones died on June 19, 1881.

Austin County, Texas
Dreaded shootist Wild Bill Longley was born here on October 6, 1851, then participated in many Reconstruction-era killings before he was hanged in Giddings, Texas.

Bakersfield, California
Barney Mason, noted Texas lawman and associate of Pat Garrett, died here of natural causes on April 11, 1916.

Brown's Hole, Colorado
Isham Dart, alias Ned Huddleston, a black Texan associated with the

Tip Gault gang, was reportedly killed here on October 3, 1900, by bounty hunter and convicted assassin Tom Horn.

Brownsville, Texas
Arkansas native Nathan Reed claimed in his memoirs that he robbed a bank here in April 1891 and then was chased by Texas Rangers into Indian Territory, earning the often-claimed sobriquet Texas Jack.

Caldwell, Kansas
Texas troublemaker James D. Sherman alias Jim Talbot and fellow Texans Tom Love and Jim Martin opened fire on former city marshal Mike Meagher and his replacement John Wilson the afternoon of December 17, 1881, in violent epilogue to a disagreement between Meagher and Talbot the previous evening. Meagher was mortally wounded, while Sherman escaped, only to be assassinated himself in California fifteen years later by persons unknown, possibly his wife's paramour, or so the story goes.

Cottonwood, Texas
Hometown of the Newton brothers, perpetrators of the largest train robbery in American history (June 12, 1924).

Dallas, Texas
John Younger of the James-Younger gang killed Deputy Sheriff Charles Nichols in Dallas while resisting arrest, on January 15, 1871, according to contemporary newspaper accounts. The previous year, his better known older brother Cole Younger served as a census taker in the Dallas area during the 1870 United States Census.

The Barrow family gas station and residence is located at 1221 Singleton Road, not far from the first Dallas residence of Bonnie Parker, 2908 Eagle Ford Road. Deputy Sheriff Malcolm Davis was killed by Clyde Barrow at 507 County Avenue, West Dallas, on January 6, 1933.

Decatur, Texas
Assumed 1865 birthplace of colorful outlaw Richard "Little Dick" West, who preferred to dine and sleep outside at all times. West was

a member of the notorious Doolin gang of Oklahoma Territory, then joined the comedic Al Jennings gang, the Titanic of Oklahoma criminal organizations. Shadowy John Armstrong, later known as Milton J. Yarberry, killed a man in Decatur during an 1877 saloon brawl.

Denton, Texas
Motor Mark Garage, 311 West Oak, was burglarized by Clyde and Buck Barrow on November 29, 1929.

Dimick Township, La Salle County, Illinois
Boyhood home of Texas saloon impresario and gunfighter Rowdy Joe Lowe, who was killed in a Denver gunfight on December 1, 1899. Wild Bill Hickok grew up nearby in Troy Grove, Illinois.

Dodge City, Kansas
Former Dallas resident Mysterious Dave Mather and his brother Josiah killed young Ashland, Kansas, grocer David Barnes over a card game at the Junction Saloon on May 10, 1885.

Dryden, Texas
Ben Kilpatrick, the Tall Texan and former member of Butch Cassidy's Wild Bunch, was killed with his partner Ole Beck attempting to rob a train here on March 12, 1912.

Eastham, Texas
Clyde Barrow and Floyd Hamilton mortally wounded Major (given name) Joseph Crowson during a prison farm break on January 16, 1934.

El Paso, Texas
Dallas Stoudenmire came to the aid of Constable Gus Krempkau, who had been mortally wounded by John Hale on the street between the Globe Restaurant and Coliseum Saloon. Stoudenmire shot and killed Hale as Hale peered from behind a pillar after shooting Krempkau on April 14, 1881. Stoudenmire himself was killed in an El Paso gunfight the next year.

John Selman, Sr., assassinated John Wesley Hardin at the Acme Saloon on August 19, 1895. The next year (April 5, 1896) Selman

himself was killed by lawman George Scarborough near the
Wigwam Saloon before Selman could even draw his weapon.

The Coliseum Saloon and the Gem Saloon were on El Paso Street,
while the Wigwam stood nearby on San Antonio Street. The site of
the Coliseum Saloon was more recently occupied by the Camino
Real Hotel.

Fort Concho, Texas
Birthplace of noted Indian Territory gang leader Crawford Goldsby,
better known as Cherokee Bill.

Fort Griffin, Texas
John Selman, Sr., and Sheriff John Larn killed a half-deaf suspect
who walked away from them after being ordered to halt in early
March 1877.

Fort Worth, Texas
Sam Bass robbed the Weatherford and Fort Worth stage of $400 near
here on January 26, 1878.

Butch Cassidy, the Sundance Kid, and three associates unwittingly
informed authorities of their whereabouts by posing for a photograph at the Swartz Studio, 705 South Main, in 1900. An observant
Wells Fargo agent noticed the picture and picked up their trail.

Longhair Jim Courtright and others were ambushed by railroad
strikers on December 20, 1876, at Buttermilk Switch, about two
miles south of the Fort Worth depot. His fatal gunfight with Luke
Short occurred near the White Elephant Saloon, then located at 306-
310 Main Street, on a site later occupied by the S. H. Kress
Building. After 1896, the White Elephant Saloon was located at
606-608 Main Street, while the affiliated Turf Exchange gambling
facility was nearby at 610 South Main.

Grand Saline, Texas
Hometown of Wiley Post, renowned aviator and perhaps the only
former bandit in America for whom a state building was named.

Grapevine, Texas
Henry Methvin killed State Highway Patrolmen E. B. Wheeler and H. D. Murphy near the intersection of Highway 114 and Dove Road, on April 1, 1934.

Haskell, Texas
Legendary lawman George Scarborough killed a man whom he had recently arrested for cattle rustling. The QT Saloon grew noisy as Scarborough and his brother resolved the dispute permanently on October 15, 1877.

Houston, Texas
Former Texas residents Harry and Jennings Young perpetrated the largest massacre of lawmen in United States history on January 2, 1932, near Springfield, Missouri, then fled to Houston. The brothers were trapped at 4710 Walker Avenue and committed suicide there three days later.

Houston Press reporter Harry McCormick interviewed Barrow gang members Ralph Fults and Ray Hamilton near the intersection of Hempstead Road and Satsuma on March 18, 1935.

Former Barrow gang member W. D. Jones meddled in a domestic dispute at 10616 Woody Lane and was shot to death on August 20, 1974.

Hutchins, Texas
Texas Express messenger Heck Thomas prevented the Bass gang from stealing about $4,000 during a train robbery by simply hiding the money before the train trip even started on March 18, 1878. Heck's brother, also a Texas Express employee, had been the victim of an earlier train robbery.

Joplin, Missouri
The address of 3347½ 34th Street was the site of a June 13, 1933, shootout between the Barrow gang and local police, two of whom were killed.

Kaufman, Texas
Bonnie Parker, Clyde Barrow, and associate Ralph Fults were forced

to flee from an attempted hardware store robbery in a humiliating mule-back escape after their car stalled in mud. The burro-powered bandits fled to nearby Kemp, where Parker and Fults were captured on April 18, 1932.

Lampasas, Texas
Epicenter of the Horrell-Higgins feud, which began in 1873.

Las Cruces, New Mexico
About four miles outside town, former lawman Pat Garrett was assassinated on February 29, 1908.

Lubbock, Texas
"Deacon" Jim Miller assassinated defense attorney James Jarrott near town after Jarrott successfully defended small ranchers derisively called "Nesters" by larger ranching interests (1904).

Marshall, Texas
Railroad detective James Currie shot Maurice Barrymore, remote kinsman of actor Drew Barrymore, and killed performer Benjamin C. Porter during a late-night restaurant argument on March 19, 1879.

McKinney, Texas
A posse surrounded the John T. Morris house near McKinney on May 23, 1874, hoping to capture Jim Reed, an outlaw. Reed avoided the trap, but Morris became a specially appointed deputy U.S. marshal and killed Reed himself about three months later near Paris, Texas.

Medicine Lodge, Kansas
Henry Brown, a former Oldham County, Texas, deputy sheriff and New Mexico associate of Billy the Kid, was killed by irate citizens on April 30, 1884, after taking time off from his position as city marshal in nearby Caldwell, Kansas, to rob a bank.

Mobeetie, Texas
Bat Masterson killed Sergeant King of the Fourth United States Cavalry here on January 24, 1876, in a quarrel over the affections of young

Molly Brennan, who was accidentally killed by King in the melee.

Near Mundy Springs, Franklin Mountains, Texas
About eight miles north of El Paso, Texas Ranger Charles Fusselman was fatally ambushed on April, 17, 1890, in the canyon which now bears his name.

Oakland, California
Former Texas lawman John Coffee Hays and others founded Oakland in 1850. Gunman Frank Leslie walked away from a pool hall in Oakland in 1927 and was never heard from again.

Oklahoma City, Oklahoma
Barrow gang stalwart Joe Palmer learned about the death of Bonnie and Clyde while lounging in the lobby of the Hutchins Hotel, at 16-26 North Broadway, on May 23, 1934.

Paris, Texas
Seat of the federal district court for the Eastern District of Texas. In March 1892, Deputy U.S. Marshal Tom Smith recruited about twenty law officers here for the Johnson County War. The outlaw Jim Reed, first husband of Belle Starr, was killed sixteen miles northwest of Paris on August 6, 1874.

Pecos, Texas
Gunman Barney Riggs killed "Deacon" Jim Miller associates John Denson and Bill Earhart here on March 3, 1896. Riggs himself was killed in a family feud four years later.

Platte City, Missouri
A gunfight between the Barrow gang and local authorities erupted on July 18, 1933, at the Red Crown Tourist Court, then at the intersection of highways 59 and 71, about six miles south of Platte City,

Price, Utah
Former Texas Ranger Jack Watson was assassinated here in 1890,

five years before Texas gunman Joe Walker shot the place up for no reason at all.

Round Rock, Texas
Suspicious lawmen confronted Bass gang associates inside the building at the southeast corner of Georgetown Avenue and May Street, then occupied by Koppel's General Merchandise Store, triggering a shoot-out in which Deputy Sheriff Ellis Grimes and bandit Seaborn Barnes were killed. Sam Bass was mortally wounded while escaping. He was captured and returned to Round Rock, where he died two days later on his twenty-seventh birthday, July 21, 1878.

Rowena, Texas
Hometown of the notorious Bonnie Parker. Train robber Wylie "Doc" Newton capped his career by robbing a bank here at age seventy-seven.

San Antonio, Texas
The northwest corner of Soledad and Main Plaza was occupied on July 11, 1882, by the Harris Vaudeville Theater and Saloon owned by Jack Harris. Ben Thompson killed Harris at the theater that day, then met death there himself about two years later with his friend John King Fisher.

Scyene, Texas
Belle Starr, Jim Reed, and the Younger brothers lived in and near Scyene after the Civil War.

Shafter, Texas
Texas Rangers John R. Hughes and Ira Aten and undercover informant Ernest St. Leon, a former Ranger, intercepted and killed three mining thieves here in 1889.

Sherman, Texas
Jesse James undoubtedly visited his younger sister, a Sherman schoolteacher and wife of former guerilla Allen Parmer, here before his death in 1882.

Clyde Barrow murdered the elderly manager of the Little Food Store, at the intersection of Vanda and Wells Avenue, on October 11, 1932, during a robbery.

Spokogee, Creek Nation, Indian Territory
Cooke County, Texas, transplants Willis Brooks, Jr., and Clifton Brooks were killed in a gunfight on September 2, 1902, in present-day Dustin, Oklahoma. The deaths resulted from a longstanding feud with the McFarland family. The sole surviving Brooks patriarch, one Peg Leg, removed to the ancestral home in Alabama after serving six years for horse theft. Alabama authorities killed him in 1920 during a gunfight.

Tascosa Texas, near Amarillo
Billy the Kid sold his prized but stolen sorrel horse to Dr. Henry F. Hoyt here on October 24, 1878. Legend has it Billy bested Temple Houston and Bat Masterson in a shooting match on the same trip.

Temple, Texas
Clyde Barrow and W. D. Jones killed Doyle Johnson in cold blood when he resisted their theft of his automobile at 606 South Thirteenth Street on Christmas Day 1932. Legendary Texas Ranger James Gillett died in Temple five years later.

Tombstone, Arizona
Texas gunman Luke Short killed Charles Storms in a gambling argument at the Oriental Saloon on February 25, 1881.

Upper Calaveritas, Caleveras County, California
Texan Longhair Sam Brown and others killed three miners in a gambling dispute, on July 8, 1855, then retreated to a nearby cabin where he calmly surrendered to Sheriff Ben K. Thorn. Sam served two years in San Quentin for manslaughter, then was killed by a hotelkeeper in 1861.

Uvalde, Texas
Birthplace of Thomas O'Folliard, a protégé of Billy the Kid. Young

Tom was killed at Fort Sumner, New Mexico, on December 19, 1880.

White Sands, New Mexico

Former Texas state senator, New Mexico politico, and one-time gunfighter Albert Fountain disappeared in the desert on April 1, 1896, with his young son Henry. The suspects in his disappearance are legion.

Yorktown, Texas

Residence of Sutton stalwart Joseph "Captain Joe" Tomlinson during the Sutton-Taylor feud, in which Captain Joe was nearly killed in a June 1873 DeWitt County ambush.

Texas Outlaws and Lawmen

These profiles are intended to highlight many of the significant or otherwise notable outlaws, gangsters, and lawmen connected to present-day Texas. Regrettably and of necessity, a good many other colorful and compelling figures have been set aside for another time.

Aliases, nicknames, and epithets have been inserted in parentheses after the names. In some entries, locations have been inserted to distinguish similar names. Where possible, approximate life dates have also been inserted in parentheses. All references are abbreviations of resources that can be found in the bibliography.

Allison, Robert A. Clay (Clay) (1840-87)
A native of Waynesboro, Tennessee, Allison was a Civil War veteran and a notorious gunman. In spite of a deformed foot, he joined the Confederate Army, but was eventually discharged for physical disabilities and mental "derangement," yet served later as a scout for Gen. Nathan Bedford Forrest, it is said. Following release from Union captivity he struck out for Texas with three brothers, his sister, and a brother-in-law. The gateway to the Lone Star State was a ferry on the Red River, where Clay introduced himself by pummeling ferry owner Zachary Colbert, whose nephew Allison would kill some five years later in New Mexico. In 1866, he was employed by cattlemen Charles Goodnight and Oliver Loving, all but certainly serving in the crew of eighteen that established the Goodnight-Loving trail through Texas, New Mexico, and Colorado.

In 1875 or the next year, Allison apparently further injured his already deformed foot during an attempted theft of army mules either by shooting himself or by being kicked by one of the four-legged victims. Later, he partnered with his brother-in-law Lewis Coleman and Isaac W. Lacy to establish a Colfax County ranching operation. His violent nature then became apparent in a series of lynchings, gunfights, and other difficulties. In 1878 he became a cattle broker in Hays, Kansas, but moved on to Hemphill, Texas, about two years later. There he married and established a new ranch in Lincoln County, New Mexico, by 1886.

Perhaps his most famous adventure occurred that year on a trail drive to Rock Creek, Wyoming. Nearby, Allison took revenge on an inept Cheyenne dentist by using the good doctor's own mouth to demonstrate how a decayed tooth should be pulled, or so the story goes. Death finally found Allison on July 1, 1887, in Pecos City, Texas, where he had purchased supplies. There, a wagon Allison was driving for a friend struck a hole in the road, causing him to be pitched from the driver's seat. Clay struck his head against a wagon wheel and died of a fractured skull.

Selected Gunfights and Other Notable Incidents
Waynesboro, Tennessee, March 1862

Home on medical release, Allison killed a looter from the Third Illinois Cavalry for breaking one of his mother's favorite pitchers, or so the story goes.

Elizabethtown, near Cimarron, New Mexico, October 1870

Allison led a mob which lynched Charles Kennedy, whose wife reported that Kennedy had killed and robbed travelers for years, and recently had killed their own infant daughter. Following a slaughterhouse hanging, Allison severed Kennedy's head, then placed it on a pike for display in the Henri Lambert Saloon.

Clifton House, Colfax County, New Mexico, January 7, 1874

After competing in a horse race, Clay Allison and reputed killer Chuck Colbert ordered lunch at the Clifton House, accompanied by Colbert's friend Charles Cooper. Colbert asked Allison to pour coffee, but the etiquette-challenged killer declined, perhaps noticing the six-shooter pointed toward him. Colbert proceeded to pour the coffee himself, while at the same time clumsily firing into the table instead of Allison, who promptly blew Colbert's brains out. Within a few days, Charles Cooper mysteriously disappeared, prompting murder charges against Allison two years later. Eventually the allegations concerning Cooper were dropped for lack of sufficient evidence.

Cimarron, New Mexico, November 1, 1875

Reputed gunman Pancho Griego and young Luis Vega met Clay Allison the evening of November 1 in front of the St. James Hotel to discuss the demise of Cruz Vega, a murder suspect in the death of a popular Methodist preacher. Vega, the father of young Luis and business partner of Griego had recently been lynched at the insistence of Allison. The trio went inside Lambert's Saloon for a quiet discussion. Griego and Allison soon retreated to a corner. After a few minutes, dialogue became gunplay, leaving Griego mortally ventilated by three pistol shots. Apparently, Allison was never charged with either killing.

Cimarron, New Mexico, January 19, 1876

Clay Allison resolved editorial differences with the *Cimarron News and Press* by dumping the firm's printing press into the Cimarron River. He further emphasized his concerns with editorial comments about Allison by distributing partially printed copies of the paper around town, with the hand-printed headline, "Clay Allison's edition."

Las Animas, Colorado, December 21, 1876

Holiday cheer enjoyed that evening by Clay Allison, his brother John, and a pair of local beauties at the Olympic Dance Hall was interrupted by Charles Faber, then unfortunate enough to be on duty as a local constable and deputy sheriff. Shortly after the boys declined to comply with the local ordinance against carrying weapons, patrons began to whine that the Brothers Allison seemingly could not avoid stepping on the feet of other dance floor revelers. After appointing two special deputies, Faber approached the Allisons again, this time with a double-barreled shotgun, which he fired at Allison, narrowly missing the shootist. Allison fired four times in response, finding Faber's chest with one bullet. While dropping to the floor, Faber stumbled and fired his second charge into John's leg. The special deputies were chased away by Allison. Charges against John and Clay were eventually dropped.

Dodge City, Kansas, September 1878

Allison was recruited by local political enemies of Assistant City Marshal Wyatt Earp to avenge the recent killing of Texas cowboy George Hoy. According to most reports, Allison left town after a brief conversation with Earp, then returned some ten days later with Earp's permission.

O'Neal, *Encyclopedia*, 19-22; Metz, *Encyclopedia*, 4-5; Tefertiller, 59-60, 62-63.

Allison, William Davis (Dave Allison) (1861-1923)

Allison served under John R. Hughes in the Texas Rangers, but left on April 27, 1903, to work in Arizona for one hundred ten dollars per month. He was noted there for bravery and level-headedness, demonstrated in the arrest of an armed murderer hiding in an old house. When a gambling problem cost him his Arizona commission, Allison found work in the employ of the Canenea Consolidated Copper Company, a mining company owned in the United States but operated in Sonora, Mexico.

Riots broke out on June 1, 1906, when management soaked angry protesters with high-pressure hoses. Three hundred volunteers from the United States arrived to break up the mob, and found Allison and some companions alive but low on ammunition. Allison led the posse that killed Pascual Orozco and four other Mexican political firebrands, and the lawmen were charged with the murder of these men. They were aquitted in October 1915. Allison was murdered with Horace Roberson on April 1, 1923, at Seminole, Texas. Roberson's wife Martha angrily chased the fleeing felons with her dead husband's .25-caliber revolver, and managed to wound both of them. The outlaws were captured a few miles outside of town when their escape car ran out of gas. Allison and Roberson had been scheduled to testify against their murderers, Hill Loftis and Milt Good, in a case involving stolen cattle.

Metz, *Encyclopedia,* 4; Alexander, *Fearless Dave Allison,* 9-23, 29-65, 87-113, 159, 240-71.

Anderson, David L. (Billy Wilson) (1862-1918)

Usually known as Billy Wilson, this south Texas resident was born about 1862 in Trumball County, Ohio. Following a brief cowboy stint, he removed to White Oaks, New Mexico, where he established a livery stable and passed counterfeit money. Charged with the crime, he joined Billy the Kid and was captured with him at Stinking Springs. Anderson was convicted, but escaped to Texas, where he died as the sheriff of Terrell County. Anderson had received a pardon with the assistance of his old enemies, Pat Garrett and Jimmy Dolan.

Gunfights

Jim Greathouse Ranch, Lincoln County, New Mexico, November 27, 1880
Dave Rudabaugh, Billy Wilson, and the Kid were discovered by Deputy Sheriff James Carlyle and posse at the Greathouse Ranch. Carlyle volunteered to exchange himself for Greathouse and was either killed by the gang or perhaps killed mistakenly by the posse. Wilson, Rudabaugh, and the Kid escaped in the confusion.

Near White Oaks, New Mexico, November 29, 1880
Wilson and the Kid were spotted by a posse, which gave chase, killing their horses and forcing the pair to flee on foot.

Fort Sumner, New Mexico, December 19, 1880
Wilson, Billy the Kid, and others were ambushed by Pat Garrett, who mortally wounded Billy's protégé Tom O'Folliard. Rudabaugh escaped only by sharing Wilson's horse.

Sanderson, Texas, June 14, 1918
Owner of the Old Cottage Bar, and popular enough to be elected county sheriff in 1916, Anderson was mortally wounded by besotted cowboy Ed Valentine, an acquaintance Anderson attempted to arrest for disturbing the peace. Valentine was lynched for his transgressions.

Nolan, 213, 223, 225, 227-28; O'Neal, *Encyclopedia,* 24; Metz, *Encyclopedia,* 265; Nash, 6.

Anderson, Hugh (d. 1873)

A Texas cowboy, Anderson was a one-time associate of John Wesley Hardin, who triggered one of the most violent episodes in the Old West at Newton, Kansas, on August 20, 1871. Shortly beforehand, Anderson had arrived at the cow town with cattle driven from Salado, Texas. Soon he discovered that fellow Texan William Bailey (perhaps Baylor) had been killed by city employee Mike McCluskie in a dispute over Bailey's management of an August 11 bond election. Anderson surprised and shot McCluskie several days later, setting off a bloody melee that resulted in his own death some two years later at the hands of McCluskie's brother.

Gunfights

Sumner, Sumner County, Kansas, July 6, 1871

A posse consisting of Hugh Anderson, John Wesley Hardin, Jim Rogers, and John Cohron found one Bideno in the town. Bideno, a cowboy, had killed their friend, twenty-two-year-old trail boss William "Billy" Cohron. Hardin entered a restaurant within a saloon and shot Bideno, who had "resisted arrest."

Newton, Kansas, August 20, 1871

About nine days after the death of William Bailey, Anderson surprised McCluskie at the Tuttle Saloon about 1:00 A.M. McCluskie was mortally wounded, and three of his friends and a Texas cowboy named Jim Martin joined him in death during the ensuing bloodbath.

Medicine Lodge, Kansas, June 1873

McCluskie's brother tracked Anderson down, challenged him, then met him in a gunfight. The dispute was concluded when the pair knifed each other to death in an empty city lot.

One minor mystery remains. Was McCluskie Arthur Delaney of St. Louis, as he claimed near death? If so, why would the brother who revenged his death some two years later bear the same McCluskie name?

Metz, *John Wesley Hardin,* 59-66; O'Neal, *Encyclopedia,* 24, 205; Metz, *Encyclopedia,* 102; Nash, 7.

Anderson, William C. (Bloody Bill) (1837-64)

Bill Anderson, the principal lieutenant of William Quantrill, was born in Jefferson County, Missouri, on February 2, 1837. His preexisting homicidal tendencies were accentuated when his sister Josephine Anderson was among the five women crushed to death in an 1863 accident erroneously presumed by many secessionists to be an intentional act of murder. The women had been arrested as Confederate sympathizers. Federal authorities in Kansas City had converted the first floor of a dilapidated Kansas City building owned by renowned artist George Caleb Bingham into a makeshift jail which collapsed under the weight of supplies carelessly stored on the second floor.

Anderson, other Quantrill irregulars, and many temporary volunteers took revenge against Unionist Lawrence, Kansas, on August 21, 1863, killing some 150 to 180 men and boys supposed to be over the age of twelve, leaving only the women and young boys alive. This out-and-out massacre was followed by an equally lethal yet numerically less significant atrocity on October 6, 1863, at Baxter Springs, Kansas, on the Indian Territory border, where, during an ambush of Federal forces, even musicians and a young drummer boy were added to the body count.

Just before Christmas, Anderson led a boisterous raid on Sherman, in which the fun-loving guerillas carefully destroyed every door lock on the main thoroughfare, as well as the town clock. Later, certain Quantrill irregulars somehow were left off the invitation list for a holiday dance at the Jim Chiles residence in Sherman. Undeterred, the rejects attended anyway, breaking up the festivities.

This busy calendar did not deter Anderson from romancing a dance hall princess named Bush Smith. One source states that they married on March 3, 1864, though evidence of later nuptial bliss is rather sparse.

That spring, Missouri Confederate general Sterling Price promoted Quantrill and directed him to reorganize his company, deploying some troops to service with the regular Confederate Army.

Jealousy or other factors led Anderson to turn informant. He informed Gen. Henry McCulloch, then encamped at Bonham, Texas, that Quantrill was responsible for certain North Texas robberies and murders. Tension between Anderson and his commander came to a boiling point when Quantrill ordered the execution of a guerilla accused of inflicting robbery and murder on the Texas citizenry.

Anderson separated from Quantrill, taking some twenty men with him, while charges of robbery and murder against unnamed Missourians in the McKinney area continued unabated. Naturally, Quantrill and Anderson blamed each other for these problems, but General Henry McCullough attempted to resolve the matter by arresting Quantrill, who was loosely guarded and promptly escaped. Back at the Mineral Springs camp, the separate commands of Quantrill and Anderson actually fired upon one another before Quantrill began the journey back to Missouri on March 10, 1864.

Anderson and his command of some twenty men, first headquartered at Bonham, then returned to Missouri, where his murderous ways continued, culminating in atrocities committed at Centralia on September 26, 1864. There he terrorized the citizenry before ordering the massacre of some twenty unarmed, furloughed Federal soldiers on the train station platform. Union pursuit of Anderson then began in earnest, led by dedicated but naive Maj. A. V. E. Anderson, who was ambushed, yet lived long enough to see his entire command destroyed before Jesse James killed him.

Federal efforts only intensified, leading to the demise of Anderson near Orrick, Missouri, exactly one month following the Centralia massacre. The guerilla chieftain was killed in October 1864 leading a charge against Union militia, having killed some fifty men himself. Anderson's head was displayed for all to see at Richmond, Missouri.

Metz, *Encyclopedia,* 6; Peterson, 38, 40, 342-43, 345-46, 349-50, 352; Boswell, 22, 84, 102, 163.

Armstrong, John Barclay (Barkley, McNelly's Bulldog) (1850-1913)

Joining the Texas Rangers in 1875 Armstrong served in the posses that captured John King Fisher in 1874 and John Wesley Hardin in 1877. A native of McMinnville, Tennessee, Armstrong was a protégé of Texas Ranger captain Leander McNelly. Born in January

John Barclay Armstrong (seated center), famed Texas Ranger and pioneer rancher, poses with acquaintances. The others are identified as: standing, left to right: James B. Gillett, J. H. Rogers, unidentified man; seated, John B. Jones (far left) and W. J. "Bill" McDonald (far right). (Courtesy of the Nina Stewart Haley Memorial Library, Midland, Texas, J. Evetts Haley Collection)

1850 to a doctor, he explored Arkansas and Missouri before arriving at Austin prior to 1871. Early exploits included border conflicts with Mexican authorities and eventually the capture of John Wesley Hardin. In later years, Armstrong operated a fifty-thousand-acre ranch in Willacy County. He died there on May 31, 1913.

Gunfights
Near Carrizo, Texas, October 1, 1876

Armstrong and other Rangers pursued members of the John King Fisher gang to Espantosa Lake, arriving in the early morning hours shortly after midnight. Along the trail, they arrested gang member Noley Key, a Fisher associate, and forced him to lead the way.

After arriving near the camp, Armstrong left Key under guard and proceeded into the camp itself, where rustlers George H. Mullen, Jim Roberts, and John Martin were killed resisting arrest. Meanwhile Key attempted to escape and was killed as well.

Wilson County, Texas, December 7, 1876

John Lewis Mayfield was convicted of murdering Robert Montgomery in Parker County, then escaped from jail while waiting to be hanged. Texas Rangers John Armstrong and T. W. Deggs confronted Mayfield at his home in Graytown, then killed the murderer when he resisted arrest. While word of the killing spread throughout the Graytown community, Deggs and Armstrong retreated, in time to avoid a confrontation with Mayfield's revenge-seeking friends and relatives.

Pensacola, Florida, August 23, 1877

Undeterred by a recent accidentally self-inflicted gunshot wound or the untidy lack of extradition papers, Armstrong limped into a passenger coach occupied by John Wesley Hardin and young Jim Mann. Hardin reacted to impending arrest by attempting to draw a weapon, but clumsily hung up the six-gun in his expensive, stylish suspenders. Mann drilled Armstrong's hat but did not live to brag about it. John mortally wounded the young gunman, then returned Hardin to Texas after a robust pistol-whipping.

Parsons and Little, 270, 289-90; Gillett, 85-87; O'Neal, *Encyclopedia*, 26; Metz, *Encyclopedia*, 91; Nash, 325; Parsons, 1-2, 24, 27-29, 31-34, 40, 47-61.

Arrington, George W. (John C. Orrick, Jr.) (1844-1923)

Arrington was an Alabaman who killed a man after the Civil War then fled to Texas. Serving as a Texas Ranger in 1875, he assisted in the capture of sixteen murder suspects from the Texas Panhandle and twenty other felons in 1878. A Confederate veteran, Arrington changed his name after murdering a Greensboro businessman. Joining the Frontier Battalion, Texas Rangers, about 1875, he quickly rose through the ranks to become captain of Company C in 1877. After dealing with vigilantes near Fort Griffin, he was assigned the wild Panhandle region, which included notoriously raw Tascosa and Mobeetie. Retired from the Rangers by 1882, he died of a heart attack on March 31, 1923.

Gunfight
Wheeler County, November 1887
County sheriff Arrington killed accused cattle rustler John Leverton and was acquitted of murder.

Sinise, 2-39, 50-60; Metz, *Encyclopedia,* 9; Nash, 13; Wilkins, *The Law Comes to Texas,* 124.

Aten, Ira (1862-1953)

Aten was born on September 3, 1862, to a Methodist minister descended from early New York Dutch colonists in Cairo, Illinois, but moved with his family at age fourteen to Round Rock, Texas. On July 28, 1878, Aten, his brother Frank, and their father were present in Round Rock when the mortally wounded Sam Bass was returned from a thwarted escape and questioned. Aten was so impressed by Maj. John B. Armstrong that he resolved to join the Texas Rangers himself. Aten was assigned to Texas Rangers Company D, camped near Uvalde under the command of Capt. Lamar P. Seiker. Aten was promoted soon after he and fellow Ranger John R. Hughes tracked notorious outlaw Judd Roberts to the Texas Panhandle in 1887 and killed him. Aten organized a police force in Dimmitt, Texas, in 1893 and moved on to California about 1904. Nineteen years later Aten served as a member of the Imperial Valley District Board in California. His memoirs were published in 1945, and Aten died of pneumonia on August 5, 1953, eulogized as the last of the old-time Rangers.

Selected Gunfight
Texas Panhandle, July 1887

Murder suspect Judd Roberts escaped from the San Antonio jail to pursue a new career in the Texas Panhandle. Rangers John Hughes and Ira Aten tracked Roberts to a ranch where he was employed. Roberts resisted arrest, exchanged gunfire with the Rangers, then died in the arms of the rancher's daughter, or so the story goes.

Preece, 1-248; Webb, *The Texas Rangers,* 428-37; Metz, *Encyclopedia,* 10; Adams, *More Burs Under the Saddle,* 141; Thrapp, *Encyclopedia,* IV, 19; Miller, *Sam Bass and Gang,* 261, 380 n. 100.

Bailey, Harvey (1887-1979)

Occasional Texas bank robber and resident felled by kidney failure on March 1, 1979, at Joplin, Missouri, after a dangerous life of crime, Bailey was born on August 23, 1887, to a Union veteran and his wife in West Virginia. The family moved to Green City, Missouri, in about 1900.

Bailey's criminal life began in earnest in about 1918, when he began to run whiskey. During the Roaring Twenties, his partners reportedly included Oklahomans Frank "Jelly" Nash and Al Spencer. Other suspected Oklahoma associates included Fred Barker, Alvin Karpis, and George Barnes (Machine Gun Kelly). Most of his bank robberies occurred in Minnesota, Iowa, Ohio, and Indiana. On April 3, 1932, Bailey, Frank Nash, George Barnes, and others robbed the Central State Bank of Sherman, Texas.

His body of work included the theft of about $500,000 ($5,175,703 today) in bills from the Denver Mint in 1922 and a one million-dollar heist at the Lincoln National Bank, in Lincoln, Nebraska. Captured on August 12, 1933, near Paradise, Texas, while sleeping on a cot in the yard of George Barnes's in-laws, Boss and Ora Shannon, Bailey was carrying $680 in ransom money Barnes had extorted from the Urschel family. Harvey then became the first in a series of criminals to escape the Dallas County Jail on September 3, 1933, with help from a guard. Released from prison in 1964, he returned to his father's occupation, cabinetry.

Kohn, 19; Maccabee, 65-66, 79.

Baker, Columbus Winfield (Sam) (1859-1911)

Texan Sam Baker was born near Frankfort, Alabama, on January 24, 1859, and saw action on both sides of the badge. His first experience was during a Reconstruction feud in which his father-in-law Willis Brooks, Sr., was killed. Eventually Baker and his Brooks in-laws moved to the Cross Timbers area of Cooke County, Texas, then to Collins, now Collinsville, in the Cherokee Nation, north of Tulsa. He finally settled about 1894 near Bonds Switch, present-day Onapa, Oklahoma.

Sam had been suspected but not charged in a train robbery at Gordon, Texas, on October 19, 1894. Eventually he became involved, according to some, with Al Jennings, Dynamite Dick Clifton, Little Dick West, and other Oklahoma outlaw luminaries. Eventually, Deputy U.S. Marshal Bud Ledbetter convinced Baker and his brother-in-law Willis Brooks to make a career move and assist in the apprehension of Clifton and West. Clifton was killed on November 7, 1897, and West shortly thereafter on April 8, 1898.

After serving as a deputy city marshal and a deputy sheriff of McIntosh County and engaging in various gunfights, Baker was killed in a dispute with two merchants at Checotah on October 7, 1911. The merchants were initially charged but not prosecuted.

Butler, *Oklahoma Renegades,* 24, 31-41.

Baker, Cullen Montgomery (1835-69)

A Tennessee-born bully, Baker was killed for revenge while dozing. Born on June 22, 1835, in Weakly County, Tennessee, he was taken to Texas as a child and grew up in Cass County.

Baker was a crack shot who did not hide his skills under a basket. He had killed two men by 1856, the last one in a knife fight, prompting a rapid trip to Arkansas just before the Civil War. Apparently, Baker was attracted to the soldier's life or more likely, the enlistment bonus, because he joined the Confederate Army, and promptly deserted, then served the Union Army as a civilian employee, and again deserted, and finally became a Confederate irregular (guerilla). More bully than robber, he was killed by vigilantes in January 1869 after killing three men in quarrels.

Selected Robbery
Near Linden, Cass County, Texas, October 6, 1867
Baker robbed a supply wagon about two miles south of the Sulphur River, killing the driver and forcing the four escort guards to flee.

O'Neal, *Encyclopedia,* 5, 31-32, 192; Crouch and Brice, 4, 18-55, 60-64, 75-78, 97, 114, 131-61.

Ballew, Bud (1877-1922)

A Carter County deputy sheriff, Ballew was born in Fannin County, Texas, in 1877, with a penchant for gunplay, which began soon after his 1912 appointment. Among other altercations, he killed the Wirt city marshal after defeating him in an election, then promptly killed his rival, Deputy U.S. Marshal Dow Braziel, in a gunfight at the California Cafe in Ardmore, Oklahoma. Ballew was killed on May 5, 1922, in Wichita Falls, Texas, by two police officers quelling a disturbance in which Ballew was involved.

Selected Oklahoma Gunfights
Wirt, West of Ardmore, Oklahoma, August 19, 1915
Advised of a robbery, Ballew entered a saloon and confronted three masked gunmen, killing Robert Pete Bynum. Ballew was wounded, and a patron in the next room was killed.
Carter County Oklahoma, April 13, 1919
Ballew rescued Sheriff Buck Garrett, a Texas veteran of Wyoming's Johnson County War, in a gunfight, killing robber Arthur "Dusty" Miller in the process.
Carter County Oklahoma, February 20, 1922
Ballew's mentor, Sheriff Buck Garrett, was ousted from office on February 17, 1922. Ballew and other deputies resigned. Three days later, a fistfight between the resigned deputies and new staff evolved into a gunfight, which Ballew and all participants survived.

Owens, *Oklahoma Heroes,* 43; O'Neal, *Johnson County War,* 228-29.

Barkley, Clinton

A Texas native and brother-in-law to Merritt Horrell, upon finding himself wanted on a murder charge, Barkley accepted Horrell protection, arriving at Lampasas in 1873. Following a gunfight with local authorities, Barkely joined the Horrells in a feud with Higgins family rivals, eventually riding off to obscurity.

Selected Gunfights
Lampasas, Texas, March 14, 1873

Barkley and three brothers, Martin, John, and Sam Horrell, opened fire on Capt. Thomas Williams and three officers at the Matador Saloon, killing all but one. Several days later, Barkley and others freed Martin Horrell from the Georgetown jail, ignoring incoming fire from an enraged citizenry.

Lampasas, Texas, June 7, 1877

Barkley and other Horrell partisans exchanged gunfire with Higgins associates Frank Mitchell, who was killed, Bill Wren, who was wounded, and several others.

Lampasas County, Texas, July 1877

Higgins and hired gunmen attacked the Horrell ranch, withdrawing after a two-day siege.

Sonnichsen, *I'll Die Before I Run,* 98, 104; Gillett, 74-80; O'Neal, *Encyclopedia,* 32.

Barnes, George (Machine Gun Kelly) (1900-1954)

The nation focused on Paradise, Texas, in the summer of 1933, thanks to the efforts of George "Machine Gun" Kelly and his wife, Kathryn. A Paradise, Texas, resident, Barnes was born in Chicago in 1900; his family moved to Memphis, Tennessee, where his father was an insurance executive. Barnes attended Mississippi A&M, married a wealthy debutante, and tried a number of legitimate businesses, including goat farming, before turning to a life of crime. In the 1920s he was involved in bootlegging operations in Oklahoma and other states, drawing a 1927 liquor arrest in New Mexico and a vagrancy arrest in Tulsa. Arrested for liquor sales in the Osage Nation, Barnes was sentenced to three years at Leavenworth, where he met Frank "Jelly" Nash, of Kansas City Massacre fame.

His associates included Harvey Bailey and Wilbur Underhill, who escaped on May 30, 1933, from the Kansas State Prison at Lansing and regrouped in the Cookson Hills of Oklahoma. They allegedly conducted several bank robberies. Barnes masterminded the first nationally prominent kidnapping since the Lindbergh tragedy, the July 22, 1933, abduction of oil magnate Charles F. Urschel in Oklahoma City. His ambitious wife, the Paradise, Texas, vamp Cleo Mae Brooks, who adopted the more stylish name Kathryn, married three times before crossing paths with George Barnes in a Fort Worth nightclub. Kathyrn pushed relentlessly toward greater and greater criminal triumphs and a lifetime of regret.

The once famous plea "Don't shoot, G-men" was attributed to Barnes (or his wife). Barnes died of a heart attack in prison in 1954, and his wife, who worked in an Oklahoma hospital, died in 1985. The federal judge in the Urschel kidnapping trial paid for the college education of Kelly's stepdaughter and was reimbursed by the kidnapping victim.

Selected Robberies

Willmar, Minnesota, July 15, 1930
Barnes combined efforts with Tommy Holden, Harvey Bailey, and others, taking $70,000 from the Bank of Willmar. Three minor gang members were killed, possibly by the others.

Sherman, Texas, April 3, 1931
Barnes, Harvey Bailey, Frank Nash, and others relieved the Central State Bank of $40,000.

Denton, Texas, February 6, 1932
Barnes and Albert Bates robbed the Pilot National Bank of an undetermined amount.

Tupelo, Mississippi, November 30, 1932
Eddie Doll and Barnes took about $38,000 from the Citizens National Bank.

Hamilton, 68-179; Burrough, 545; Maccabee, 24, 136, 184-85; Helmer and Mattix, 164, 168, 173, 178.

Barrow, Blanche Caldwell (1911-88)

Born on January 1, 1911, at Garvin, Oklahoma, to Matthew and Lillian Fountain, Blanche married Marvin Ivan "Buck" Barrow in 1931 at America, Oklahoma, and died on December 24, 1988, at

Tyler, Texas. Her biography, published in 2004, states that she and Buck met Bonnie and Clyde "in Oklahoma" on March 29, 1933. However, her active life of crime with the Barrows was apparently founded on April 13, 1933. Blanche calmly strolled out onto the street, looking for her pet dog Snowball, undeterred by the gunfire around her, in a Joplin, Missouri, shoot-out in which two law officers were killed. She also claimed that in June 1933 the Barrows and Bonnie traveled to the Floyd farm near Sallisaw, Oklahoma, in a futile effort to team up with Charles Arthur Floyd. During her last illness, Blanche refused to see her ninety-three-year-old mother, who attended the funeral anyway.

Barrow, 33-34, 40, 73, 195, 214, 261; Ramsey, 11, 41, 100, 105, 138, 184, 222.

Barrow, Clyde Chestnut (1909-34)

Born on March 24, 1909, Clyde was first arrested for turkey rustling in Dallas at Christmastime. Big brother Buck helpfully claimed Clyde "didn't know the turkeys were stolen." Clyde Barrow, Bonnie Parker, and native Oklahoman Raymond Hamilton were involved in the shooting of two officers at Stringtown, Oklahoma, on August 5, 1932; Deputy E. C. Moore was killed when officers challenged gang members for drinking moonshine at an open-air dance. About October 12 of that year, the gang again crossed the Red River to engage in a series of Oklahoma robberies. They reportedly stole a physician's bag and car at Enid, on July 24, 1933, returning two days later to rob an armory then located at what would become Phillips University.

Their work required frequent commutes through Oklahoma. On April 6, 1934, they engaged in a gunfight with authorities at Commerce, resulting in the death of Constable Cal Campbell. Five days later, Clyde, or someone using his name, mailed an endorsement of the Ford V-8, his favorite car, to Henry Ford from the Tulsa post office. On May 23, 1934, Bonnie and Clyde were killed by lawmen in Louisiana.

Texas Robberies and Gunfights
Palestine, Texas, July 16, 1932

Clyde Barrow and Ray Hamilton robbed the Palestine Ice Company of $989, according to bookkeeper Roy Evans, who was kidnapped.

Near Carlsbad, New Mexico, August 14, 1932

Bonnie and Clyde and Raymond Hamilton kidnapped Deputy Sheriff Joe Johns, then released him at San Antonio. Johns had noticed the out-of-state tags on their car, confirmed that it was stolen, and attempted to arrest the trio.

Near Wharton, Texas, August 15, 1932

Hamilton, Bonnie, and Clyde escaped a police trap at Wharton, Texas.

Sherman, Texas, October 11, 1932, 6:20 P.M.

Clyde Barrow murdered Howard Hall, an elderly food store manager at the Little Food Store, Vanda and Wells Avenue, for nothing more than rebuking Barrow for robbing the store.

Cedar Hill, Texas, November 25, 1932

Raymond Hamilton, Gene O'Hare, and Les Stewart robbed the State Bank of $1,800. All three were captured and convicted.

Temple, Texas, December 25, 1932

W. D. Jones and Clyde Barrow killed Doyle Johnson while stealing his car from his residence at 606 South Thirteenth Street.

Grapevine, Texas, December 29, 1932

Bonnie and Clyde associates Odell Chambless and Les Stewart robbed the Home Bank of $2,800.

West Dallas, Texas, January 6, 1933

Bonnie and Clyde escaped a police trap at the home of Lillie McBride, Hamilton's sister, killing Deputy Sheriff Malcom "Lon" Davis.

Eastham Prison Farm, January 16, 1934

During a prison break arranged by Clyde Barrow and Floyd Hamilton, Major Joseph Crowson was mortally wounded and died eleven days later.

Near Grapevine, Texas, Easter Sunday, April 1, 1934, about 3:30 P.M.

Methvin killed highway motorcycle patrolmen H. D. Murphy and E. B. Wheeler.

Near Commerce, Oklahoma, April 6, 1934

Clyde and Henry Methvin killed Constable Cal Campbell and kidnapped Commerce police chief Perry Boyd, then dropped him near Fort Scott, Kansas.

Milner, 60-160; Helmer and Mattix, 178-79, 211; Knight, 53, 57; Milner, 127-28.

Barrow, Marvin Ivan (Buck) (1903-33)

Born on March 14, 1903, at Jones Prairie, Texas, Buck married Margaret Heneger and was eventually convicted of theft and sentenced to a five-year prison term. He later walked away from a work detail to freedom. He then married Blanche Caldwell on July 3, 1931, at America, Oklahoma. She soon convinced him to surrender. When he was paroled in 1933, Buck, Blanche, Bonnie, and Clyde rented an apartment at 3347½ 34th Street in Joplin, Missouri, soon drawing the suspicion of local authorities. A shoot-out at the residence on April 13 left two law officers dead.

Following forays into Enid, Oklahoma, on June 24 and Oklahoma City on June 26, gangly and alcoholic Buck and the others arrived at the less-than-luxurious Red Crown Tourist Court in Platte City, Missouri, on July 18, drawing local authorities like moths to a flame. The ensuing shoot-out left Buck mortally wounded. He died on July 29, 1933, in a Perry, Iowa, hospital.

Selected Robberies and Gunfights

Denton, Texas, November 29, 1929

Buck Barrow and Sydney Moore burglarized a Denton garage, drawing the attention of local police, who wounded Buck in the course of an arrest. Efforts to eliminate the evidence went awry when jewelry thrown out of the second-story courthouse jail landed at the feet of the arresting officer.

Fort Dodge, Iowa, July 18, 1933

While Bonnie recovered from injuries suffered in an automobile accident the previous month, Clyde systematically robbed Fort Dodge service stations.

Platte City, Missouri, July 18, 1933, 10:00 P.M.

A gunfight erupted between the Barrow brothers, W. D. Jones, and local authorities at the Red Crown Tourist Court.

Dexfield Park, Iowa, July 24, 1933

W. D. Jones and the Barrows were surrounded at Dexfield Park, near Dexter, Iowa. Bonnie, Clyde, and Jones were wounded, but shot their way out.

Steele and Scoma, 29, 33, 46, 104, 108, 114; Helmer and Mattix, 187, 189; Knight, 22, 100, 105, 110.

Bass, Samuel (Sam) (1851-78)

Bass was an Indiana-born thief who died on his twenty-seventh birthday of wounds suffered in his last robbery attempt. Born in Mitchell, Indiana, and soon orphaned, he moved to Denton, Texas, by 1870 and became a roustabout and teamster. There, he was employed by Sheriff W. F. Eagan as a blacksmith and handyman, but success at horse racing allowed him to pursue new ventures. His initial winnings included a horse "won" from an Indian near Fort Sill, Indian Territory, which he took under questionable circumstances.

Bass met bartender Joel Collins in San Antonio, where they ran a crooked horse racing operation. Although neither was a cowboy, Collins arranged for the pair to make a trail drive to Kansas in the late summer of 1876 with cattle he had purchased as well as livestock belonging to Texas cattlemen. After the cattle were driven to Kansas and sold, Collins and Bass spent all the proceeds on gambling, drinking, and romantic pursuits.

Financially embarrassed, Collins and Bass began stagecoach robbery as a means of supporting themselves in and near Deadwood, South Dakota. Soon, they turned to train robbery at Big Springs, Nebraska, where Collins and five others including Bass took $60,000. Regrettably for the gang, twenty of the sixty thousand dollars was recovered by authorities when gang leader Joel Collins and Bill Heffridge were killed at Buffalo Station, Kansas. Vital intelligence about the gang's whereabouts was obtained from gang member Jim Berry, who was mortally wounded at a friend's house in Mexico, Missouri.

Meanwhile, Bass had reorganized in Texas, where he led at least two stagecoach robberies and four train holdups, before being mortally wounded the day before a planned bank robbery at Round Rock, near Austin. Members of the Collins-Bass gang on the whole fared very badly. Arkansas Johnson was killed at Salt Creek, prompting Henry Underwood to leave the gang and disappear. Jim Berry was mortally wounded at his hometown of Mexico, Missouri, while Joel Collins and Bill Heffridge were killed at Buffalo Station, Kansas, all within a week of the Big Springs robbery. Tom Nixon escaped, it is said to Canada, while Jack Davis supposedly escaped to South America.

Selected Gunfights and Robberies
Near Deadwood, South Dakota, March 25, 1877

Collins gang member Robert "Reddy" McKemmie killed driver Johnny Slaughter during a stagecoach robbery and was banished from the gang, which included Joel Collins, Sam Bass, Jack Davis, and Tom Nixon.

Big Springs, Nebraska, September 18, 1877

The Collins gang, six in all, forced the station agent to stop the Union Pacific eastbound No. 4 train. Initially the engineer refused to stop and threw coal at the gang, but he was soon persuaded by six-shooters to halt. The gang members, who included Sam Bass, Jim Berry, Bill Heffridge, Jack Davis, and Tom Nixon, found three wooden express boxes each containing $20,000 in gold, then robbed some of the passengers as well.

Near Fort Griffin, Texas, December 22, 1877

Sam Bass, Henry Underwood, and Francis M. Jackson robbed the Concho stage, but Underwood was soon captured. Bass gallantly gave breakfast money to each victim.

Near Fort Griffin, Texas, January 26, 1878

Bass and Jackson robbed the Weatherford and Fort Worth stage. Somehow, the gang overlooked about $400 that a passenger hid in a pair of gloves he held over his head at the command "hands up!"

Allen, Texas, February 22, 1878

Joined by Seaborn Barnes and Tom Spotswood, who sported a glass eye, Bass and Jackson robbed the Houston and Texas Central Railroad, taking about $1,400

Hutchins, Texas, March 18, 1878

The gang attempted to rob a train, but most of the $4,000 in express company money had been hidden earlier by a young guard and future lawman, Henry "Heck" Thomas.

Eagle Ford, Texas, April 4, 1878

The Bass gang struck the Texas and Pacific, taking a few hundred dollars at midnight.

Mesquite, Texas, April 10, 1878

Train passengers, convict guards, and nearly everyone but the dining car cook greeted the Bass gang with gunfire, thwarting a successful robbery, netting the thieves only $150, despite the efforts of new members Albert G. Herndon and Samuel J. Pipes.

Salt Creek, Wise County, Texas, June 13, 1878

Bass was reunited with his first Texas employer, Sheriff W. F. Eagan, in less than amicable circumstances, when a posse including Texas Ranger captain Junius Peak and Wise County sheriff George N. Stevens attacked. The posse killed Bass associate Arkansas Johnson and all the horses, looped together as they were, making for a tricky escape by the surviving gang members.

Round Rock, Texas, July 19, 1878

All of the gang except Jim Murphy went to new Round Rock on a Friday, the day before a planned robbery. Murphy lingered in old Round Rock, on the pretext of buying corn for his horse, having alerted local authorities to the bank robbery plans. Law officers in Koppel's General Merchandise store did not recognize the gang, but did recognize the bulges under their clothing indicating weapons banned by a town ordinance. When challenged, the gang opened fire, killing Deputy Sheriff Ellis Grimes, while Seaborn Barnes was killed in return fire. Bass himself was mortally wounded making an escape, but was rescued by Frank W. Jackson, who dropped the outlaw outside the town at the direction of Bass. Jackson escaped entirely, dying years later, it is said, in Arizona as Bill Downing. Bass died two days after the gunfight.

Miller, *Sam Bass and Gang,* 27-32, 50, 63-72, 115, 121-23, 125-30, 133, 149, 248, 345; O'Neal, *Encyclopedia,* 35; Metz, *Encyclopedia,* 16; Adams, *Burs Under the Saddle,* 71, 79, 105-6, 253, 256, 431, 494; Adams, *More Burs Under the Saddle,* 4, 150.

Bean, Roy (c. 1823-1903)

Bean was a Kentuckian who found his calling late in life as a justice of the peace in Langtry, Texas. Born in Mason County, Kentucky, on the Ohio River, he ventured into Mexico, New Mexico, and California before stepping off a Southern Pacific train at a desolate dusty hellhole he supposedly named for world-renowned singer Lily Langtry, known as "the Jersey Lilly"—or so the story goes. His previous adventures, if his stories are to be believed, included a stint with the California Rangers, the kidnapping of a Spanish maiden, and leadership of Confederate guerilla aspirants whimsically named the Free Rovers.

Although long forgotten, his brothers were significantly more accomplished. Josh Bean became the first mayor of San Diego only to be murdered in 1852. Sam Bean became the first sheriff of Dona Ana County, New Mexico. Roy Bean, on the other hand is remembered for the peculiar judicial forum he created on the frontier's edge, unrestrained by appellate courts. Bean was a legal entrepreneur of sorts, with a fixed price list for divorces and inquests. Less well known is his long feud with local land baron, competing saloonkeeper, and sometime justice of the peace Jesus P. Torres, who actually owned most of the land on which Langtry was situated. Torres apparently stood helplessly by as Bean named the town for the then famous songbird Lily Langtry rather than for Torres.

Bean helped make ends meet by suggesting at the beginning of each court session that all present should purchase a snort in his adjoining saloon. Once, he is said to have fined a corpse the forty dollars he found in a pocket for carrying a concealed weapon.

Perhaps Bean is best known for his unrequited love for Lily, one of the most famous performers of her time. All visitors to his courtroom were strongly encouraged to toast her before legal proceedings began. Although an early marriage to child-bride Virginia Chavez had foundered in spite of producing two daughters and two sons, the self-styled jurist remained an incurable romantic, transferring his affections to Langtry. In 1888, the normally verbose Bean supposedly watched Lily's San Antonio performance from an expensive front row seat, but was too tongue-tied to visit her backstage.

Sadly, Lily learned of his shy affection some six months after his death on March 16, 1903, then visited Langtry long enough to carry away his revolver and dancing bear, or so the story goes. The pistol remained on her mantle for the rest of her life.

Nash, 30-32; Sonnichsen, *Roy Bean,* 3-12, 27-39, 47-65, 84-111.

Bell, James W. (Jim Long) (1853-81)

An excellent marksman noted mainly for the manner of his death, Bell once traveled to Austin to acquire Model 1873 Winchesters on behalf of Company D of the Texas Rangers. Bell retired from the Rangers in the spring of 1879 to join O. W.

Williams in search of Colorado gold, but when success eluded them the men returned to Texas. After a second attempt to find mineral wealth in White Oaks, New Mexico, Bell began working as a deputy sheriff and deputy U.S. marshal.

During that time he served in a posse headed by Jim Carlyle in pursuit of Billy the Kid and several of his associates. When the lawmen successfully tracked the gang to the Whiskey Jim Greathouse Ranch, the outlaws, in response to a note asking for a peaceful surrender, requested that Carlyle be sent in to negotiate terms. Carlyle agreed, but only on the condition that Greathouse take his place and become a hostage.

Soon, the posse feared for Carlyle's safety, and threatened to execute Whiskey Jim Greathouse if he was not released. A shot was accidently discharged by J. P. Eaker, and Carlyle, assuming Greathouse had been killed, jumped through the window and was shot dead. The facts were unclear regarding who actually shot Carlyle; it could have been the outlaws or possibly his own nervous men. The posse eventually tracked down Billy the Kid and his associates in Stinking Springs, New Mexico, after which Billy was sentenced, in Mesilla, to die for the murder of Sheriff William Brady in Lincoln. He was returned to Lincoln on April 21, 1881, to await his execution on the second floor of a courthouse, formerly the Murphy-Dolan general store. On April 28, 1881, the Kid, chained and guarded by Bell and Bob Olinger, somehow managed to acquire Bell's six-shooter, and murdered him on an interior staircase in the courthouse. The Kid then killed Olinger with his own shotgun. James Bell was buried at White Oaks.

Nolan, 233-34, 252, 269, 271, 273, 275, 323 nn. 4, 19; Metz, *Encyclopedia,* 20; Thrapp, *Encyclopedia,* I, 91.

Bender, Kate (ca 1849)

A mass-murderer who according to some fled to Texas, voluptuous twenty-something Kate spread handbills across southeastern Kansas, offering to cure blindness, fits, and other maladies at Benders Inn, some twenty-two miles north of the Cherokee Nation, near Independence. The inn offered meals described as mediocre at best, with the dessert being peeks at Kate's figure as she leaned over to serve one-course meals, or so the story goes. The unadvertised special, however, was murder. While locals and groups could safely leave the inn with nothing more than indigestion, the lone traveler was often placed with his back to a curiously soiled burlap sheet strung as a divider midway across the interior of the small "inn." Pa Bender or his "son" John, neither of which have ever been positively identified, would then conk the victim in the head with one of three hammers, slit his throat, and temporarily store the body in the basement after removing all clothing and valuables.

Realizing they were suspected by relatives of a recent victim, the group, consisting of Kate, Pa (John, Sr.), John, and "Mrs. Bender," true names unknown, disappeared in April 1873. Later, excavations adjoining the inn revealed eight bodies, including that of a little girl of indeterminate age murdered with her father. The fate and true identity of the Bender family is one of the most perplexing mysteries of the West. The trail led first to nearby Thayer, where they left a wagon and their faithful dog behind. An observant St. Louis station agent remembered the older Benders checking their luggage through to Vinita, Indian Territory. There the trail grows dim, with unverified stories of the Benders departing for an "outlaw colony" on the Texas-Mexico border.

Another version also has the Benders departing from Thayer, but for points north. In 1889, two females somewhat resembling Kate and "Ma" Bender were arrested in Michigan and extradited to Kansas. Mrs. Almira Griffith and her daughter Mary were bound over for trial on murder at Parsons, but released in February 1890, when Mrs. Griffith produced documents indicating she had been in Michigan in 1872, when at least some of the murders had taken place. The authenticity of the documents was quickly presumed, perhaps, some say, because the extradition and trial were costing the county a small fortune.

According to one elderly Michigan citizen, someone resembling "John Bender Sr." committed suicide at Benton Harbor in 1889. Rumors of extra-judicial killings also persist, fed by the reminiscences of elderly citizens.

The fate of "John Bender Jr." is simply unknown.

Still, the question remains, did the Benders flee north to Michigan, south to the mysterious Texas "outlaw colony," or simply get off the train at Vinita and disappear into the vast loosely governed expanses of Indian Territory?

Wood, 5-15, 74, 78, 85, 90; Garza, 113, 140, 161-72, 186, 192, 205.

Borger, Asa Phillip (Ace) (1888-1934)

A promoter who developed oil towns across Oklahoma and Texas, Borger was born on April 12, 1888, to Phillip and Minnie Ann (West) Borger near Carthage, Missouri. He married Elizabeth Willoughby in 1907. After selling real estate in Picher, a new northeastern Oklahoma community, he began a town-building business with fabled Oklahoma wildcatter Tom Slick and Lester A. Borger, a younger brother. The trio laid out Slick, Oklahoma, which became a thriving oil town near Bristow, however briefly.

In 1922, Ace moved on to Cromwell, where he refined his promotion skills, then founded Borger, Texas, maintaining homes in both places. Chamber of Commerce glad-handing was not an essential part of his modus operandi. He contracted with tough but apparently nearsighted Two-Gun Herwig for law enforcement. Dixon Street (now Tenth Street) in Borger became a quintessential vice row featuring speakeasies, gambling dens, and dance halls, which many supposed were controlled by another Borger crony from Oklahoma, Mayor John Miller. Herwig was assumed by many to be a close associate of W. J. "Shine" Popejoy, aspiring "King of the Texas Bootleggers." Such rumors eventually drew the unwelcome attention of Texas governor Daniel J. Moody.

Texas Ranger captains Frank Hamer and Thomas R. Hickman reduced but did not eliminate the violence and corruption that culminated in the assassination of District Attorney John A. Holmes on September 18, 1929, at the hands of persons unknown. The initial Borger boom busted in the early thirties, leaving Ace Borger time to quarrel with his nemesis, County Treasurer Arthur Huey. Borger had allowed a bank he owned to fail in 1930, drawing Huey's criticism.

Later, in 1934, Huey was convicted of embezzlement. Huey asked Borger for help with his financial difficulties and was refused. Huey then caught Borger by surprise at the town post office on August 31, 1934, where he shot him five times, then finished off the town father with his own pistol. Somehow Huey avoided conviction in the subsequent trial by claiming that Borger intended to kill him. Perhaps the jury missed the fact that Huey had also mortally wounded an innocent bystander.

Sterling, 97-114; Tyler, *New Handbook of Texas,* vol. 1, 649.

Briant, Elijah S. (Lige) (1854-1932)

Briant was a druggist and sheriff who killed notorious desperadoes Will Carver and George Kilpatrick on April 2, 1901, at Sonora, Texas. Alerted that two suspicious strangers were in town, Briant and four deputies confronted the pair and and shot them to pieces. Carver was an occasional member of Butch Cassidy's Wild Bunch and the Black Jack Ketchum gang. One authority theorizes that George Kilpatrick was a brother to the Tall Texan, Ben Kilpatrick. Briant later became a county judge and died in 1932.

Pointer, 254; Metz, *Encyclopedia,* 39; Nash, 50.

Broadwell, Richard L. (Texas Jack) (d. 1892)

A Dalton gang member of uncertain Texas associations, Broadwell was also known as John Moore and "Jack of Diamonds" for continuously singing that tune. Broadwell's forebearers were reportedly associated with Abraham Lincoln in some fashion. Reputedly robbed and dumped by his betrothed in Houston, Texas, he turned to robbery as a consequence. He was killed by citizens in the Coffeyville, Kansas, raid on October 5, 1892. Charles Colcord, himself a deputy U.S. marshal in the early days of Oklahoma Territory, was shocked to learn of Broadwell's banditry. Broadwell had attended school with Colcord's wife.

Smith, *Daltons,* 50; Samuelson: "Bill Power and Dick Broadwell"; Colcord, 173.

Brooks Brothers

Lacking the sartorial splendor of their namesakes, the famous eastern clothiers, Texans Willis Brooks, Jr., Clifton Brooks, and various relatives nevertheless made their mark the hard way in eastern Oklahoma. Their father, Willis Brooks, Sr., of Lawrence County, Alabama, had been killed in a Civil War-related feud, which embroiled his son-in-law Sam Baker and his brother Henry "Peg Leg" Brooks.

Willis Junior and other clan members migrated first to Cooke County, Texas, and eventually to the Dogtown area of the Creek Nation, some twenty-five miles west of Eufaula, in 1894, only to become embroiled in yet another dispute, this time with the McFarlands in 1896. The feud culminated in a gunfight on September 22, 1902, at Spokogee (now Dustin) in the Creek Nation in which McFarland ally George Riddle, Willis Brooks, Jr., and Clifton Brooks were all killed. The surviving patriarch, Peg Leg, then removed to Alabama after serving six years for horse theft. He was killed in a gunfight with authorities on January 11, 1920.

Butler, *Oklahoma Renegades,* 43-52.

Brown, Henry Newton (1857-84)

Brown was an Oldham County deputy sheriff whose curriculum vitae included riding in New Mexico with Billy the Kid and other Regulators in the Lincoln County War. After leaving Oldham County, he moved on to present-day Woods County, Oklahoma, then to Caldwell, Kansas, where as city marshal he defended townspeople from assorted villains. Brown decided to establish a side business in bank robbery and apparently started at nearby Medicine Lodge, Kansas, with his deputy, Ben Wheeler (Ben Robertson), William Smith, and John Wesley, two experienced outlaws.

After killing the bank president and chief cashier, the crew was trapped by irate depositors in a box canyon. Brown was killed attempting to escape, and the others were lynched. Brown explained his motives in a letter to his wife shortly before the jailbreak, saying that "It was all for you." Among the posse that captured Brown was Barney O'Connor, his former Oklahoma employer.

Nolan, 92; O'Neal, *Encyclopedia,* 48; Nash, 54.

Brown, Sam (Longhair Sam) (1830-61)

A two-hundred-pound, redheaded Texas native, Brown was active in Calaveras County, California, during the 1850s, as co-leader with

Jess Miller of the Miller-Brown gang. On July 8, 1855, while dealing monte in Upper Calaveritas, Longhair Sam was confronted by one "Lorenzo," a Chilean miner who insisted on grabbing and gambling with someone else's money. Such misconduct prompted a gun and knife melee in which three Chileans were killed, while Brown and his associate Bunty Owens fled to a cabin on a nearby creek.

Ben K. Thorn, renowned sheriff of Calaveras County, avoided a bloody shoot-out simply by surrounding the cabin, lowering his weapon and asking the astounded Longhair Sam to come out.

During a preliminary hearing at a nearby sawmill, some one hundred Chilean miners surrounded the place to express their displeasure, but somehow a lynching was avoided that day. Sam served two years for manslaughter at San Quentin, only to be shotgunned to death on July 7, 1861, by a meek hotelkeeper. Ben Thorn, on the other hand, continued as a sheriff and manhunter well into his seventies, dying as an old man in San Francisco, on November 15, 1905.

Boessenecker, 61-65, 84; Thrapp, *Encyclopedia,* I, 179.

Bryant, Charles (Black Face Charlie) (d. 1891)

A Wise County, Texas, native, Bryant was a pockmarked victim of an opponent's muzzle blast. Charlie reputedly participated in several Dalton gang raids. Following the "Battle of Twin Mounds," he checked into the Rock Island Hotel at Hennessey, Oklahoma Territory, where Deputy U.S. Marshal Ed Short arrested him. Subsequently the two men shot and killed each other on August 23, 1891, in a stereotypically classic gun battle on a passenger train near Hennessey.

Smith, *Daltons,* 32, 49, 51, 53, 56-57, 62; O'Neal, *Encyclopedia,* 53.

Bullion, Laura (Della Rose) (1876-1961)

A Kentucky native who moved to Texas as a child, Bullion reportedly became a San Antonio prostitute. Her supposed outlaw love interests included Wild Bunchers Will "News" Carver, who had been married to her aunt, Viana Byler Carver before Viana's death on July 22, 1892, and Ben Kilpatrick, the Tall Texan. Although the trail is dim, she became the companion of Ben Kilpatrick after

Carver was killed. The couple often used the names J. W. and Della Rose. In any event, she was arrested for forgery, while in the company of Ben Kilpatrick, on November 6, 1901. Upon her own release from prison on September 19, 1905, she waited for Kilpatrick and upon his death became Mrs. Fredia Lincoln of Memphis, Tennessee. She died on December 2, 1961, at Memphis.

Selected Robbey
Tipton, Wyoming, August 29, 1900
   Bullion participated in the robbery of Union Pacific Train No. 3, in which the Wild Bunch encountered express car messenger Woodcock, a recent acquaintance, according to one source (Nash). Earlier, on June 2, 1899, at Wilcox, Wyoming, Woodcock was nearly killed when he refused to open the express car for the same gang and was dynamited out. This time Woodcock was more cooperative, opening the express car door for the bandits, who blew the safe and extracted $50,000.

Pointer, 255; Metz, *Encyclopedia,* 39, 141-42; Nash, 58, 69, 70, 201, 358; Ernst, *Women of the Wild Bunch,* 15-31.

Burrow, Reuben Houston (Rube) (Charles Davis) (d. 1890)
   Leader of the most prolific train robbers to follow the James-Younger gang, operating primarily in Texas and Alabama, Burrow was born on December 11, 1854, in Lamar County, Alabama. Reuben moved to Stephenville, Texas, at age eighteen, then married in 1876. He was a respectable citizen until 1886, when crop failure apparently led him to reject respectability and follow the owlhoot trail, capitalizing on his expert marksmanship. Reuben, his brother Jim, Nep Thornton, and the Brock brothers operated between 1886 and 1889, before coming to predictably violent ends. Rube himself was killed either in Tennessee in late 1889 or in Linden, Alabama, on October 7, 1890.

Selected Train Robberies and Gunfights
Bellevue, Clay County, Texas, December 1, 1886
   Rube Burrow, Jim Burrow, and Nep Thornton launched a new

career robbing the Fort Worth and Denver train of a few hundred dollars, also taking a considerable amount of ammunition from soldiers riding as passengers.

Near Benbrook, Texas, June 1887

The gang took $3,000 from the Texas and Pacific, then repeated the feat in September, taking approximately the same amount.

Near Genoa Station, Arkansas, December 9, 1887

The Burrows netted $3,500 from the mail car of a St. Louis, Arkansas and Texas train, barely eluding a large posse.

Lamar County, Alabama, early January 1888

Jim Burrow was nearly captured by Pinkerton detectives at the family farm, escaping out the back door. Several weeks later, Jim was captured in a train passenger car while Rube escaped. Jim died of consumption on October 5, 1888.

Montgomery, Alabama, January 23, 1888

After several more train robberies brought the attention of the Pinkerton detectives and prompted nationally distributed wanted posters, the Burrows were recognized by a vigilant conductor who wired ahead to Montgomery. Journalist Neil Bray also recognized the pair and was shot for his trouble as he attempted to alert police.

Near Buckatuna, Alabama, September 29, 1888

Burrow and his new partner, Joe Jackson, robbed a Mobile and Ohio train of $11,000. Several months later, Rube's cousin Rube Smith was mistaken for the bandit and killed.

Duck Hill, Mississippi, December 15, 1888

Rube and others robbed an Illinois Central train, killing passenger Chester Hughes where he sat for complaining about the inconvenience.

Linden, Alabama, October 7, 1890

According to one source, Rube Burrow was killed in a gunfight with storekeeper C. Carter, who recognized Burrow from reward posters. Detectives later heaved the remains off a train at Sullivent Station, Alabama, or so the story goes. Another source states that Burrow's death occurred the previous year in Tennessee.

O'Neal, *Encyclopedia*, 53; Nash, 59, 358.

Canton, Frank (Joe Horner) (1849-1927)

The outlaw born as Joe Horner took the name Frank Canton after escaping from a Texas prison to start a new life as lawman, gunman, detective, and National Guard adjutant general. Horner was born on September 15, 1849, in Henry County, Indiana, a son of Confederate surgeon John W. Horner. Joe became a Union soldier in the waning days of the Civil War, in spite of his many relatives who fought for the South. Late in 1866, Horner moved with his family to the Ozark, Missouri, environs, then on to Texas, where he became acquainted with Samuel Burk Burnett, a renowned Texas rancher. Burnett became his friend and mentor for a lifetime.

Horner became a member of the Jack County, Texas, "minutemen," charged with tending cattle and thwarting Cheyenne, Kiowa, and Comanche raids on the livestock. Although many of his fellow minutemen later joined the Frontier Battalion of the Texas Rangers, Horner followed another trail, establishing a ranch in about 1872 some eighteen miles north of Jacksboro, the county seat of Jack County which adjoined Fort Richardson. There, Horner partnered with William W. Cotnam and somehow acquired a large herd in that same year, but then became a habitué of Jacksboro saloon shacks with pretentious names such as Union Headquarters and the Emerald.

Soon the partnership became known as the Horner-Cotnam gang, justly or otherwise. Charter members included Baldy Johnson, a subsequent member of the John Kinney organization. Another associate, Horace Jeffries, a southwest Missouri native who worked under the moniker Henry Jones, supposedly killed the sheriff of Greene County, Missouri. Less is known about the final gang member, William Z. Redding, known as Reddy.

Jeffries was killed during an early 1874 robbery in Jacksboro, while resisting the efforts of posseman Henry W. Strong to arrest him on suspicion of burglary. Horner was arrested that year for aggravated assault and battery, then indicted for two counts of cattle theft. He found additional trouble in October, when two buffalo soldiers from Fort Richardson accosted him, soliciting free drinks in a saloon. Horner responded by shooting one bar denizen, then later set off a long-distance rifle duel with other soldiers, resulting in the injury of his hired hand, lifetime friend, and associate Frank Lake.

Cotnam was reportedly killed in the aftermath of the incident.

Meanwhile, Horner's legal problems mounted. He faced two assault charges and four cattle theft indictments by February 1875. Joe was jailed, but escaped on September 11 and apparently organized a bank robbery with his brother George and William Redding at Comanche, Texas, the next January, taking about $5,500 from the H. R. Martin Bank. While enjoying recuperative down time in San Antonio with his brother George, Horner was captured on February 2, 1876, and sent to a dark and dreary hoosegow in the Bexar County judicial complex which inmates called "the bat cave."

Undeterred, Horner-Cotnam gang alumnus William Redding operated in northern Texas until April 1876 when Reddy was launched into the great beyond with recruits Joe Watson and Larapie Dan on Stinking Creek in Shackelford County. The carefully arranged funeral was conducted by "Dr. Lynch" (as such "necktie parties" were called in those days) under the direction of Sheriff John M. Larn, whose real name may have been Bill Redden.

Impatient with the judicial process, Horner escaped the bat cave and made his debut in stagecoach robbery, only to have his career path thwarted again by arrest on April 19, 1877. This time, lodgings following conviction were found at Huntsville Prison, whose privatized and profit-oriented management imprudently assigned Horner to an outside contract work detail, facilitating his escape on August 4, 1879.

Horner soon reinvented himself as Frank Canton. Eminent scholar C. L. Sonnichsen theorized that perhaps Joe simply reversed the given names of his friend M. Frank Lake and adopted the Texas town of Canton as his surname. Shielded from his past by the name change and perhaps by the "ask no questions" ways of the West, he was hired in August 1881 as a Wyoming Stock Growers Association inspector, after several months of cattle work in Montana, Wyoming, and Colorado.

A good work record yielded appointment as deputy sheriff of Johnson County, Wyoming, and election as sheriff on November 4, 1884. Among other accomplishments, he captured and jailed James-Younger gang member Jim Cummins in February 1885. Cummins had reformed, to all appearances, and was working as a Buffalo, Wyoming, shoemaker. The Clay County, Missouri, authorities declined extradition for reasons that remain unclear.

Canton became a detective of the Wyoming Stock Growers

Association in January 1887, and by June 1889 had developed a case against certain small ranchers, deemed "rustlers" by the Wyoming cattle barons. Prominent on his suspect list were a number of Texans, including Jack Flagg, Martin Tisdale, L. A. Webb, William Diamond, Tom Gardner, and William "Black Billy" Hill. Among the small ranchers who were "suppressed" during this period was Texan John A. Tisdale, who was ambushed and killed on December 1, 1891. The shadow of guilt fell upon Canton. Although he was acquitted by a "camp court" in Buffalo, Wyoming, a criminal information was later filed against him, but was never successfully prosecuted.

The year 1892 heralded the best known, most visible phase of the Johnson County War, in which Wyoming cattle barons followed a course of action conducted by Montana ranchers some seven years earlier. Frank Canton or someone with whom he worked closely compiled a thirty-four-name death list that included Texans Nate Champion, Jack Flagg, Nick Ray, and Edward "One-Eyed Tex" Cherpolloid.

Fighting fire with fire, the cattle barons employed a private army of "Regulators," which included some twenty Texans, notably including Canton, Tom Smith, William Armstrong, Buck Garrett, and David E. Booker. In early April 1892 this "Texas Army," which included the cattle barons themselves and two newspaper reporters, assembled in Cheyenne and boarded a train for Casper, Wyoming. The contingent was nominally led by Frank E. Wolcott of New York, who had been a major in the Union Army. After Wolcott and Canton quarreled regarding logistics in a baggage car, Wolcott in effect resigned as expedition leader, ceding de facto command to Canton.

April 8, 1892, found the Regulators moving through a winter gale to a cabin on the KC Ranch, then occupied by Nate Champion and Nick Ray, two leaders of the small ranchers (labeled "rustlers" by the Regulators). The next morning, Ray was mortally wounded by sniper fire at the front door of the cabin. During the next few hours, Champion exchanged gunfire with the Regulators and cared for Ray until Ray died at about 9:00 A.M. Remarkably, during the rest of the siege, Champion penned a journal, until he was himself killed by twenty-eight bullets that afternoon in a futile escape attempt after a burning wagon was pushed against the cabin. Champion's journal was found near his body.

In July 1894, with a good prospect of law enforcement employment in Oklahoma Territory, Canton applied for a full pardon from Texas governor James S. Hogg, an accomplished politician and dead-ringer for the future silent movie star Fatty Arbuckle. Responding favorably to the request, Hogg noted Canton's exemplary life since his escape from the Huntsville prison and the futility of future confinement.

Later, while Canton was serving as a deputy sheriff in Pawnee County, Oklahoma Territory, he killed gunfighter-turned-bounty-hunter William B. "Bill" Dunn on November 6, 1896, at Pawnee in a gunfight witnessed by Deputy U.S. Marshal Charles Colcord. Dunn apparently took exception to remarks Canton made regarding how the Dunns had killed Doolin gang stalwarts Bitter Creek Newcomb and Charlie Pierce for reward money on May 1, 1895. The Dunns claimed that the outlaws died game in a fair gunfight. Bullet holes in the feet of the corpses suggested a more nocturnal scenario to Canton, who was impolite enough to say so.

Canton served as a deputy U.S. marshal in Oklahoma Territory and Alaska Territory and eventually became adjutant general of the Oklahoma National Guard in 1907.

The West was changing, and Canton became an instrument of reform, canceling prizefights in Oklahoma City, Sapulpa, and Tulsa, often with little or no assistance from local authorities. In February 1913, with moral indignation and the assistance of heavily armed National Guardsmen, he climbed into a boxing ring and confronted an Oklahoma City crowd replete with state legislators and local politicos to announce that the scheduled prizefight would not be held. Canton had done so before, spoiling a scheduled match between Jack Johnson and another contender for the title of heavyweight champion near Tulsa on July 4, 1911.

Similar raids in Sapulpa, Tulsa, and elsewhere culminated in a dramatic confrontation between Canton and Tulsa horse racing impresario R. J. Allison, who had scheduled an open horse race with open gambling on July 4, 1914, with the assistance of the Tulsa Fair Association. The county attorney reportedly left town, leaving Adjutant General Canton to enforce an injunction that Governor Lee Cruce had obtained from Tulsa judge L. M. Poe. Local racing touts did not take Canton seriously and smirked at him for the cameras. Nevertheless, the injunction was enforced with the assistance of

National Guardsmen carefully selected from outside Tulsa. Canton was vindicated, despite subsequent litigious efforts of the crestfallen Tulsa gambling community.

Canton died peacefully in 1927, one of the most respected and regarded lawmen of his time. Among his many notable friends was Owen Wister, author of the once famous novel, *The Virginian*. In the flexible, easygoing Oklahoma of the 1920s few noted that years earlier, Canton had quietly obtained a full pardon from the crimes of his youth.

Selected Gunfights
Checotah, Indian Territory, January 1895

Canton and a posse including prominent Tulsan Dr. John C. W. Bland and Deputy U.S. Marshal Dean Hogan tracked "Q" County outlaws Bill Shelly, John Shelly, Bill's wife, and a Newfoundland dog to a cabin near Checotah, Indian Territory. After an all-day gunfight, the Shellys were forced outside when the posse pushed a blazing wagon to the cabin.

Pawnee, Oklahoma Territory, 1895

While arresting Kansas murder suspect Oscar Radar at the Lone Star Livery stable owned by Alonzo "Lon" McCool, Canton thwarted death by shooting McCool in the forehead with a small pistol. Canton threw the pistol away in disgust when McCool survived.

Osage Nation, Indian Territory, August 1895

Canton, Deputy U.S. Marshal Steve Burke, and others trailed horse thief Ben Cravens to a remote cabin, where Canton killed Cravens's horse, then arrested Cravens without further incident.

DeArment, *Alias Frank Canton*, 7-21, 49-120, 147-201; O'Neil, *Encyclopedia*, 94-95; Metz, *Encyclopedia*, 37.

Carver, William (News) (d. 1901)

A Texan and a news junkie and clippings collector, Carver became a member of the Ketchum gang, later joining Butch Cassidy and the Sundance Kid. Carver continued alone on the outlaw trail after law enforcement wiped out the gangs. On April 2, 1901, accompanied by George Kilpatrick, a possible brother of Wild Bunch associate

Ben Kilpatrick, Carver entered Sonora, Texas, to case a possible bank robbery. Sheriff E. S. Briant and four deputies intercepted Carver and Kilpatrick at a grain store and attempted to arrest them. Carver was wanted for the death of Oliver C. Thornton, who was killed several days earlier at Paint Rock, Texas. Carver and Kilpatrick resisted arrest, and a gunfight ensued. Kilpatrick survived in spite of fourteen wounds, but Carver died on March 27, 1901, shortly after muttering, "Die game, boys." His grieving widow was courtesan Callie May (Lillie Davis).

Pointer, 254; Kelly, 260, 262, 266, 277-81; Metz, *Encyclopedia,* 141; Nash, 66; O'Neal, *Encyclopedia,* 190.

Chambers, Lon (prom. 1880s)

A Texas lawman turned train robber, during the 1870s, Chambers was a Texas Panhandle law officer recruited by Pat Garrett. Chambers moved to New Mexico, then participated in the ambush of Tom O'Folliard at Fort Sumner on December 19, 1880. Within a year he switched sides and was captured following an unsuccessful train robbery. He was released for lack of evidence and disappeared.

Selected Robberies
Texas Panhandle, November 16, 1880
Lon Chambers, Jim East, and others led by Charles Siringo were directed by "Outlaw Bill" Moore to pursue cattle rustlers, presumably including Billy the Kid. On November 16, the Siringo posse encountered and joined a posse led by Pat Garrett and Barney Mason. About a month later, the combined posse ambushed and killed Billy the Kid stalwart Tom O'Folliard.
Coolidge, Kansas, September 29, 1883
A gang, presumably led by Chambers, stopped a night train, killed engineer John Hilton, and wounded the fireman. The gang fled, only to be captured by Dave Mather. The suspects were tried, but set free for lack of evidence.

Nolan, 240-42, 244, 321 n. 5; O'Neal, *Encyclopedia,* 54; Nash, 71.

Champion, Nathan D. (1857-92)

Nate and his twin brother Dudley were born near Round Rock, Texas, and became the target of Wyoming Regulators during the Johnson County War. The Champions had arrived in Wyoming on an 1881 cattle drive and liked what they saw. Soon, the brothers took the part of small ranchers and homesteaders against the wealthy, large-scale cattlemen who were harassing them.

Nate became known as "King of the Cattle Rustlers." Whether the sobriquet was accurate or not, he found himself facing forces led by skilled manhunter Frank Canton (Joe Horner) in 1891. Within a year Nate was shot to pieces and became a martyr of sorts to the small ranchers of Wyoming.

Gunfights

Powder River, Wyoming, November 1, 1891

Champion and Ross Gilbertson were surprised while resting in a line cabin by Frank Canton, Tom Smith, and two other Regulators, who opened fire, but were eventually driven off, leaving their horses and a Winchester. Gilbertson preferred charges but then prudently disappeared, and the matter was dropped.

KC Ranch, Wyoming, April 9, 1892

Nate Champion and Nick Ray, Champion's partner in a ranch lease, were cornered at dawn by Canton and a posse which included journalist Sam Glover of the *Chicago Herald.* During the ensuing gunfight, Ray was mortally wounded before Champion ended it all attempting to shoot his way to a nearby ravine. Thus deprived of an interview, Glover published a detailed journal found near Champion's body. Dudley Champion was killed the next year by range detective Mike Shonsey.

O'Neal, *Johnson County War,* 114-25; DeArment, *Alias Frank Canton,* 49-120; O'Neal, *Encyclopedia,* 55; Metz, *Encyclopedia,* 122, 135; Nash, 71.

Cherrington, Patricia (1903-49)

Born Patricia Long on September 26, 1903, to an Arkansas farming family that migrated to Dallas, Texas, then Chickasha,

Oklahoma, she moved on to Tulsa. There she married in 1920, deserted her husband, and moved to Chicago with a daughter in 1922. Following a dancing career, which may have been exotic, she became associated with the Dillinger gang through Dillinger's love interest Evelyn "Billy" Frechette. Cherrington was present during the Little Bohemia Lodge gun battle and was eventually convicted of harboring fugitives. She was released from prison and died on May 3, 1949, in Chicago.

Poulsen, 8, 75, 405.

Christian, William T. (Black Jack) (1871-97)

Christian was born near Fort Griffin, Texas, but raised near Sacred Heart Mission in present Pottawattomie County, Oklahoma, where he was accused of stealing merchandise from one John F. Brown of the Seminole Nation. He also killed Deputy Sheriff Will Turner near the whiskey town of Violet Springs, Oklahoma Territory, on April 27, 1895. During a jailbreak in which he and his brother Bob escaped with Jim Casey, they shot and killed Oklahoma City police chief Milton Jones, but Casey was killed. On April 28, 1897, Bill was ambushed and killed near Clifton, Arizona, while Bob disappeared following a Chihuahua, Mexico, jailbreak.

Selected Gunfights
Nogales, Arizona, August 6, 1896
Texans Will Christian, Bob Christian, Code Young, Bob Hayes, and George Musgrave, known as the "High Fives," arrived at the International Bank at Nogales, flush that day with $10,000 (some say $30,000) in cash ready for an area rancher to close a cattle purchase. Citizens herded into a back room seized an opportunity to escape and did so when bank president John Dessert distracted the bandits as he attempted to flee through the front door. During the confusion, cashier Frank Herrera grabbed a hidden pistol, then fired at Bob Hayes and George Musgrave, wounding the latter. The gang fled toward Mexico, but left most of the loot behind.
Skeleton Canyon, Arizona, August 1896
Several days after the Nogales fiasco, a Tucson posse led by Sheriff

Bob Leatherwood was ambushed by Code Young, Bob Hughes, and Bob Christian. Deputy Sheriff Frank Robson was killed in the first volley, and the trio escaped.

Rio Puerco Trestle, New Mexico, October 2, 1896

About thirty-five miles south of Albuquerque, an eastbound Atlantic and Pacific train stopped for an impromptu inspection of a faulty piston rod, making a planned robbery by the High Fives so much the easier, at least until Deputy U.S. Marshal Will Loomis emerged from a passenger car and killed Code Young with his shotgun. The rest of the gang scattered to the winds, without so much as a dollar from the train.

Cole Creek Canyon, Graham County, Arizona, April 28, 1897

About twelve miles east of Clifton, the Christian brothers, George Musgrave, his brother, Calvin Van Musgrave, and Sid Moore were hiding out in a desolate canyon. A posse led by Deputy U.S. Marshal Fred Higgins of Roswell, New Mexico, spotted Will Christian and mortally wounded him. Christian died without revealing his name, but the place he died is still known as Black Jack Canyon, in present-day Greenlee County, Arizona. The rest of the gang escaped.

Smith,"The Bad Christian Brothers"; Shirley, *West of Hell's Fringe,* 286-90, 294, 297, 299-301, 322; O'Neal, *Encyclopedia,* 56; Metz, *Encyclopedia,* 44.

Clark, James Nolan (1902-74)

When he died on June 9, 1974, this former bank robber was operating a Muskogee bank parking lot, hardly a predictable end for a man who had terrorized banks in Oklahoma and elsewhere during the Great Depression. A member in bad standing of the Bailey Underhill gang, Clark was born in Mountainsburg, Arkansas, on February 26, 1902, and did his first time at the Granite, Oklahoma, reformatory, then became a Texas farmer and field hand, before robbing a Midland, Texas, bank in 1927. He allegedly participated with Big Bob Brady in the October 1933 robbery of the Frederick, Oklahoma, bank, where the robbers took $5,000, but reportedly missed $15,000 in the tellers' cages and $65,000 (today $880,510) in the vault. In less than a week Clark found himself arrested in Tulsa and returned to his prior domicile, the Kansas State Prison. At the time of his 1933 Memorial Day escape from the Kansas State Prison, he had already served three terms in Oklahoma for attempted robbery and cattle rustling.

Oklahoma Bank Robberies
Black Rock Bank, June 16, 1933
Partnered with Ed Davis, Jess Littrell, Bob Brady, and George "Dewey" Shipley, Clark robbed the Black Rock Bank of $29,000.
Peoples National Bank, Kingfisher, Oklahoma, August 9, 1933
Persons unknown, but assumed to include Clark, robbed the Kingfisher bank of $6,000.
Bank of Geary, Oklahoma, September 6, 1933
Teamed with Bob Brady and possibly Walter Philpott, Clark robbed the Geary Bank of $5,000, a tidy sum by Depression standards.
Ultimately convicted in January 1935 of the Kingfisher robbery, he served time at both Leavenworth and Alcatraz. However, when he died in 1974, two of his pallbearers were reportedly bankers.

Morgan, 156, 184, 330.

Clements, Emmanuel Senior (Mannen or Mannie) (d. 1887)
Hot-tempered Mannen Clements apparently spent his early life in Gonzalez County. In February 1871 John Wesley Hardin, a cousin of Clements, visited the Clements ranch, then participated in a cattle drive north with Mannen's brother Jim Clements. During one such cattle drive to Kansas railheads, Mannen killed brothers Adolph and Joseph Shadden, who disputed his authority just as the herd crossed the Red River into Indian Territory. In about 1874, Mannen and some fifty other Texans confronted lawman Wyatt Earp in Wichita, but the conflict was quickly defused by Earp's steadfast resolution.

Mannen broke his cousin John Wesley Hardin out of jail in October 1872 after Hardin was charged in various shootings. In the years that followed, his brothers Joe, Jim, and John Gibson "Gip" Clements reportedly participated in the Taylor-Sutton Feud. Mannen Clements accompanied their cousin Hardin to a pivotal meeting with Sutton faction partisan Jack Helm on April 16, 1873, to discuss the possibility of Hardin fighting for the Suttons. When Helm told Hardin that the death of Mannen Clements and Clements brother-in-law George Tennelle was a non-negotiable precondition, Hardin declined the offer. Subsequently, in 1877, Clements found himself in an Austin jail cell with a host of outlaw luminaries, including Hardin, Bill Taylor, John Ringo, and several associates of the Sam Bass gang.

Clements ranched successively in San Saba, McCulloch, and Runnels Counties.

While running for sheriff of newly created Runnels County, he was shot and killed by City Marshal Joe Townsend in the Senate Saloon at Ballenger, Texas, on March 29, 1887. Noted assassin Jim Miller, who had worked for Mannen during the fall and spring roundups of 1886-87 in McCulloch County, married Mannen's daughter in the fall of 1891.

O'Neal, *Encyclopedia,* 64; Shirley, *Shotgun for Hire,* 11-13, 28, 64-65; Sonnichsen, *Pass of the North,* 341-44; Sonnichsen, *I'll Die Before I Run,* 48; Metz, *John Wesley Hardin,* 34, 36, 63-66, 69, 87; Tefertiller, 11.

Collier, Thomas B. (1859-91)

Collier was a Young County deputy sheriff who engaged alleged horse thief and murderer Boone Marlow in a mealtime gunfight on December 17, 1888, near Vernon, Texas. He was born on January 20, 1859, in Randolph County, Alabama, and died on February 12, 1891, at Fort Worth. Collier and Sheriff Marion Wallace had attempted to serve an arrest warrant on Marlow for the murder of James Holdson. In an irrational and besotted moment, Holdson had made his last mistake, challenging Boone to a gunfight. During the arrest attempt, Sheriff Wallace was mortally wounded and died about a week later.

Tise, 557; O'Neal, *Encyclopedia,* 215; Shirley, *The Fighting Marlows,* 41-50; DeArment, *Life of the Marlows,* 63-67, 98-100, 104, 124, 134, 143; Holub, Records of Young County (Texas) Historical Commission.

Coe, Philip Houston (1839-71)

A native of Conzalez County, Texas, and the last known gunfight victim of Wild Bill Hickock, Coe preferred gambling to ranching pursuits. Coe became acquainted with Ben Thompson in Austin. The pair opened the Bulls' Head Saloon at bustling Abilene, Kansas, which had become an important railhead the previous year.

Abilene city marshal Bill Hickock responded to a citizen's request for assistance on October 5, 1871, when Coe and about thirty associates created a disturbance, a feat in itself during those rowdy cowboy days, simply by shooting a stray dog. First, Hickock mistakenly killed Novelty Theater detective Mike Williams, who had approached the crowd to assist him. Wild Bill then shot Coe, who died three days later. Coe and Hickock had quarreled earlier over matters now uncertain, but believed to be a dispute over a woman or the graphic nature of the Bull's Head signage, which the city council had ordered removed.

Barra, 40-41; O'Neal, *Encyclopedia,* 138; Metz, *Encyclopedia,* 47; Nash, 81; Adams, *Burs Under the Saddle,* 250.

Colbert, Chuck (Chunk) (d. 1874)

"He who hesitates is lost," as Colbert learned on January 7, 1874, at the Clifton House, Colfax County, New Mexico. He had developed a reputation as a gunfighter in Texas, New Mexico, and Colorado. Colbert supposedly killed seven men, including Charles Morris, who was apparently too attentive to Colbert's wife.

That January day found Colbert and a companion quarreling with Clay Allison about a horse race. Colbert tried to get the drop on Allison by asking him to pour coffee, while Colbert drew his weapon. However, Colbert shot the table instead of Allison, who simply declined to pour coffee then shot Colbert in the forehead, concluding the matter. Later, he famously stated that he shared coffee and a meal with Colbert before shooting him, because he didn't want to send the man to hell on an empty stomach, or so the story goes. Colbert's companion that day simply disappeared some twelve days later, perhaps a victim of foul play.

O'Neal, *Encyclopedia,* 21; Nash, 81.

Colcord, Charles Francis (1859-1934)

Colcord, a Corpus Christi area resident, enjoyed a varied and colorful life, even by frontier standards, as a cowboy, policeman, county sheriff, deputy U.S. marshal, oilman, and large-scale real estate investor. Although an honest lawman, his early occupations in Kansas and Oklahoma gave him a personal familiarity with notorious outlaws.

He was born on August 18, 1859, near Paris, Kentucky, the son of a man who had raised a Confederate battalion. He moved at an early age to a range some twenty-seven miles west of Corpus Christi, near Banquete, Texas, and later to Kansas in about 1877. While there and associated with the huge Comanche Pool ranching operation, he observed and later met Pat Garrett, Henry McCarty (Billy the Kid), McCarty associates Jim French, John Middleton, and others. Although not entirely free from doubt, an early draft of Colcord's memoirs still in existence strongly indicates that his sister, Maria "Birdie" Colcord was briefly married to the outlaw John Middleton after the Lincoln County War.

Colcord joined the 1889 Oklahoma land run, and became a policeman under the provisional Oklahoma City government that year. After arresting notorious bad man Clyde Mattox, who had murdered the city marshal of South Oklahoma City, and J. C. Adams, who had mortally wounded popular Mayor William L. Couch, Colcord was appointed a deputy U.S. marshal. He then served as the first territorial sheriff of Oklahoma County from 1890 until 1893. Appointed by U.S. Marshal E. D. Nix as deputy in charge of the Fourth District, he supervised Frank N. Canton, Bill Tilghman, Wiley G. Haines, and other deputy U.S. marshals. Colcord worked with Bill Tilghman to maintain order in the notoriously dangerous Hell's Acre section of Wharton (now Perry), Oklahoma Territory.

Although never involved in a recorded gunfight, during his law enforcement career Colcord pursued Little Bill Raidler, Red Buck Weightman, Charley Pierce, and Bitter Creek Newcomb, all of whom he knew personally. Present on May 3, 1895, when the bodies of Bitter Creek Newcomb and Charley Pierce were brought in by the notorious Dunn brothers for reward money, Colcord observed what others perhaps chose to ignore: bullet holes in the soles of the bandits' feet suggesting that they had been shot while asleep and denied the chance to "die game." He also observed the shoot-out in which Frank Canton killed Bee Dunn on November 6, 1896.

Hardly missing a beat, Colcord became one of the most successful oilmen in Oklahoma at the closing of the frontier. Among other ventures, he participated in the fabled Glenn Pool near Tulsa and other oil exploration. Colcord died in December 1934.

Colcord, 1, 146, 156, 170, 196, 198, 202, 225.

Conner, Bill (d. 1887)

A Sabine County outlaw leader, Conner was killed on March 31, 1887, by Rangers of Company F under the command of Capt. William Scott. Connor had planned an ambush of the rangers in heavy Sabine brush, sparking a brief firefight so intense that Captain Scott was shot through the lungs, Rangers Brooks and Rogers and Bill Connor's brother were seriously wounded, while four dogs and a packhorse were killed outright. Surviving members of Connor's gang escaped, but dispersed to the four winds.

Wilkins, *The Law Comes to Texas*, 261-62.

Cook, William Tuttle (1873-1900)

A notorious Oklahoma outlaw, Cook was captured by Borden County Texas sheriff Thomas D. Love on January 11, 1895, near Fort Sumner, New Mexico. Cook had taken refuge in West Texas and was spotted by a rancher, who notified Sgt. W. J. L. Sullivan at Amarillo, and the hunt was on.

Smith, "The Cook Gang"; Shirley, *Marauders*, 1-103.

Cooley, William Scott (1855-76)

Cooley, a gunman and sometime lawman, killed former deputy sheriff John Worley (Johann Anton Wohrle) during the 1875 Mason County War, avenging his friend, employer, and mentor Tim Williamson, a participant. Fundamentally, the Mason County War pitted Anglo Texans and their allies against German immigrants, their descendants, and others largely associated with the forces of Reconstruction. Cooley was an interloper without any personal interest in the feud, other than revenge for the killing of

Williamson. After participating in at least two more revenge shootings, Cooley died in mysterious circumstances near Fredericksburg, during the early morning hours of June 10, 1876.

The Cooley family had moved from Missouri to Jack County, Texas, while Scott was an infant, arriving there by 1856. Jack County residents were periodically attacked by Comanche warriors before and after the Civil War. Contemporary newspaper accounts reported that the Cooleys responded to one attack by killing all members of the Comanche raiding party.

Although traditional stories relate that Cooley's parents were killed by Comanches, recent scholarship has revealed that his father was killed by Joseph Horton on May 26, 1870, following a cattle dispute. Horton himself was killed by Scott's brother Jim the next day.

A former Texas Ranger, Cooley was employed by rancher Tim Williamson, for whom he drove cattle to Kansas on several occasions. Shortly after Williamson's wife nursed Cooley back to health after an attack of typhoid fever, Williamson was murdered by an allegedly "German" mob on May 13, 1875, while in the custody of Deputy Sheriff John Worley. Cooley returned from nearby Menard seeking revenge, with his own committee of gunmen.

After several gunfights, Cooley and his associate John Ringo were jailed and transferred to Austin. With the Mason County hostilities concluded, Cooley reportedly moved on to nearby Blanco County. He reportedly died with symptoms indicating metallic poisoning, but then labeled "brain fever," about twelve miles from Fredericksburg in the early morning hours of June 10, 1876. Contemporary reports indicate that a bottle of whiskey Cooley purchased the previous day was the suspected source of the poison. His recruit John Ringo left Mason County to gain notoriety in Tombstone, Arizona.

Selected Gunfights
Mason County, Texas, August 10, 1875

Cooley found handyman and former deputy sheriff Worley working on a water well with Charles "Doc" Harcourt and "the little Yankee." After some initial seemingly friendly conversation, Cooley asked Worley why he had killed Tim Williamson. When Worley responded, "Because I had to," Cooley shot Worley in the back of the head. After scalping Worley, Cooley rode off, leaving Harcourt stranded at the bottom of the well.

Llano County, Texas, August 19, 1875

Scott Cooley killed German faction adherent Carl "Charley" Bader in a farm field or a road nearby. Cooley deemed Bader complicit in the death of his mentor, Tim Williamson.

Mason, Texas, September 29, 1875

Scott Cooley, George Gladden, and John Baird waited in the Gamel Saloon for an opportunity to ambush Sheriff John E. Clark, a German faction associate. Clark did not appear, but former feudist Dan Hoerster was ambushed, shotgunned to death, and, according to one source, scalped. Twenty-seven days earlier, "German" feudist, Joseph Miller was killed, perhaps by Cooley.

O'Neal, *Encyclopedia,* 732; Metz, *Encyclopedia,* 207; Nash, 85, 330; Johnson, 77, 80-81, 91-113, 128, 145.

Cornett, Brackett (1859-88)

A Goliad County, Texas, native, Cornett was an associate of the Bill Whitley gang (Cornett-Whitley gang) which extracted $45,000 from a bank and committed two train robberies, all within the span of a few days. Gang members included brothers Kep and Victor Queen, who were both killed in Indian Territory. Cornett was an astute planner who often cased prospective robberies and meticulously planned escape routes, an attribute that paradoxically led to his death. After an 1888 train robbery near Pearsall, Texas, a rancher remembered a group of men apparently practicing a horseback escape. The tip enabled law officers to track down and kill the hapless bandit.

Robberies

McNeil, Texas, February 1888

The Cornett-Whitley gang robbed a Missouri Pacific train of $20,000 but was driven away from a Southern Pacific train at Harwood by a sheriff's posse. The gang robbed another train at Flatonia, Texas, shortly thereafter.

Frio, Texas, February 12, 1888

Cornett left the gang and was killed by Alfred Allee. Allee himself was knifed to death in a Laredo barroom brawl on August 19, 1896.

Cisco, Texas, February 15, 1888

After a brief respite in Indian Territory, the gang robbed the bank at Cisco, collecting some $25,000.

Floresville, Wilson County, Texas, September 25, 1888

Remaining gang members were trapped by deputy U.S. marshals on September 25, 1888, and attempted to shoot their way out, resulting in the death of Whitley.

Metz, *Encyclopedia,* 201; Nash, 85; Kohn, 92.

Courtright, Timothy Isaiah (Longhair Jim) (ca. 1847-87)

Courtright was an enigmatic figure often portrayed as a gunfighter even though he lost his only gunfight with a significant opponent. Available evidence suggests his birth about 1847, probably in Sangamon County, Illinois. His family eventually relocated to Grundy County, Iowa. In spite of stories suggesting that he was mentored through his early career by Union general John "Black Jack" Logan, there is scant evidence that Courtright served at all in the Civil War much less served as Logan's scout as widely reported.

Courtright was living in the vicinity of Fort Worth by 1875 and was active in an early fire brigade, then an activity of social importance hard to imagine in the twenty-first century. He became a deputy city marshal and jailer that year, then engaged in his first gunfight of sorts on Thursday, December 16, in an alley near the Club Room Saloon. There, the gunfighter was shot and nearly killed by Richard Alexander "Bingham" Feild (*sic*), scion of a then important local family. Courtright was saved from a seemingly mortal wound through the skillful ministrations of Feild's brother. The talented physician had also saved an earlier victim shot by his brother.

Jim would leave and return to Fort Worth three times in his career. In 1883, Courtright participated in New Mexico's American Valley War, serving in an army accumulated on behalf of Logan, then a United States senator, and his partners, ambitious Irishmen John P. Casey and W. C. "Outlaw Bill" Moore. While in this mercenary capacity, Courtright participated in the fatal shooting of young ranchers Alexis Grossetete and Robert Elsinger, whose small but proximate spread was coveted by Logan and his partners. Reduced in the end to running a protection racket in the guise of a detective agency, he was killed at Fort Worth by Luke Short.

Selected Gunfights
Fort Worth, December 20, 1876

Hell's Half Acre denizen N. H. Wilson placed an advertisement in the *Fort Worth Democrat* chastising the mayor and Jim Courtright for corruption. Later, when Courtright and his deputy William A. "Tip" Clower attempted to search Wilson and the unhappy citizen resisted, Courtright shot him in the leg, at least according to Wilson.

Near Lake Valley, New Mexico, May 6, 1883

Jim Courtright, Jim McIntire, Outlaw Bill Moore, and three others including Texan Mueller W. Scott intercepted Alexis Grossetete, a Kansan of French descent, and Robert Elsinger, both twenty-four years old. Moore shot Grossetete in the head without any discussion. Elsinger was shot by Jim Courtright, Jim McIntire, and two others as he galloped away. Seeking to deflect responsibility, Courtright and others arrested suspected cattle rustlers D. L. Gilmore and John W. Sullivan as well as some Casey spread cowboys. Eventually, all were released, but participant Daniel H. McAllister, a church deacon apparently troubled by his involvement in the affair, turned state's evidence. In spite of McAllister's efforts, within three years all of the accused escaped punishment by judicial dismissals, flight from New Mexico, or hung juries.

Buttermilk Switch, near Fort Worth, April 3, 1886

About two miles south of the Fort Worth depot, Courtright and ten others hired as armed guards were ambushed by strikers who had stopped an inbound train, then commenced firing at the railroaders with Winchesters. Courtright associate Dick Townsend was mortally wounded while Courtright himself and two others were injured. One of the ambushers was convicted and sentenced to life in prison.

Fort Worth, February 8, 1887

Courtright was killed by Luke Short while attempting to enforce a protection scheme.

Contemporary reports indicated that Short and Courtright met in front of a shooting gallery next to the White Elephant. Short had owned an interest in the White Elephant, but sold out, retaining the right to run the second-floor gambling operation. Short claimed that Courtright went for his pistol, but Short drew first, shooting Courtright five times. Longhair Jim died in the street, after mumbling to an acquaintance that ". . . they finally got me."

DeArment, *Jim Courtright of Fort Worth,* 7-8, 14-15, 19, 33, 38-39, 68, 84, 94, 130, 132-33, 136, 141, 191, 196.

Crockett, David (1853-76)

Named for his famous grandfather, the Tennessee-born, Texas-raised shootist eventually moved to Cimarron, New Mexico, to ranch with Peter Burleson. Crockett supposedly joined Clay Allison in the lynching and decapitation of serial killer Charles Kennedy.

It is known with more certainty that Crockett killed three black soldiers in a drunken rage at Cimarron's St. James Hotel on March 24, 1876. Eventually, he was handed a small fine and a firearms conviction.

Crockett was less than endearing to the Cimarron citizenry, who suffered through his occasional antics, such as purchasing a new suit of clothes and sending the bill to Sheriff Isaiah Rinehart, whom Crockett later forced into a drinking bout.

Such insults explain the small posse raised by Rinehart on September 30, 1876, to apprehend Crockett and an associate named Heffron. Crockett escaped the posse, only to be peppered with gunfire as his steed ran out of town. Crockett was found dead in the saddle, while Heffron was captured and escaped to perpetual obscurity.

Metz, *Encyclopedia,* 54.

Currie, James

Currie (or Curry) was an inebriated Texas and Pacific Railroad detective who found fifteen minutes of fame by assaulting three New York actors including a kinsman of actor Drew Barrymore, about midnight on March 19, 1879, at Marshall, Texas. Currie insulted "Miss Nellie" Cummins, whose dinner companions, Maurice Barrymore of the still notable acting family and Benjamin C. Porter, took offense and said so. While Barrymore, a former boxing champion removed his coat, Currie drew two revolvers and shot both men, mortally wounding Porter. Barrymore recovered, only to be later committed to an asylum at Amityville, New York. Currie escaped punishment by pleading temporary insanity, only to kill again in a Lincoln County, New Mexico, brawl with a roommate. He served six years in prison, then was pardoned, and disappeared into obscurity.

Metz, *Encyclopedia,* 56.

Dalton, William Marion (Bill) (1866-94)

Bill, the last criminally active Dalton, was killed on June 8, 1894, at the Houston Wallace farm some twenty-five miles from Ardmore, Indian Territory, while attempting to escape from authorities after robbing a Longview, Texas, bank. He lived in California during much of the time that the Dalton gang terrorized the Indian and Oklahoma Territories. Sometimes he was confused with a California state senator with the same name. About $1,700 from a Longview, Texas, bank robbery was reputedly found in the house where Bill had been staying; he was carrying $285 and change when killed. Members of his "new" gang formed in May 1894 included Jim Wallace (alias George Bennett), Asa Knight, and Jim Knight (Nite). In 1920, a Tulsa paper reported that Bill Dalton associate Jim Nite had been shot by the proprietor of a Tulsa drugstore in the commission of a robbery.

Selected Robberies and Gunfights

Alila, California, February 6, 1891

Someone robbed Southern Pacific Train No. 17 near Alila, Tulare County, California. Bill, Grat, Bob, and Emmett Dalton were charged, perhaps mistakenly.

Caney, Kansas, October 13, 1892

Bill Dalton, Bitter Creek Newcomb, and Oliver "Ol" Yantis robbed a Missouri Pacific train, bagging only about $100 to feed the horses.

Ingalls, Oklahoma Territory, September 1, 1893

Bill Dalton and other Doolin gang members were surprised by authorities but shot their way out, killing three lawmen.

Sacred Heart Mission, April 1, 1894

Bill Dalton and Bitter Creek Newcomb were thwarted in an attempt to rob former deputy U.S. marshal W. H. Carr.

Longview, Texas, May 23, 1894

Four men robbed the First National Bank at about 3:00 P.M., taking $2,600, which included $450 in unsigned bank notes. During the robbery an outlaw tentatively identified as Jim Bennett and citizen George Buckingham were killed, while citizen C. S. Learned was mortally wounded. Although not entirely free from doubt, most modern scholars attribute this crime to Bill Dalton and Jim Nite while the true identify of the other participants is simply unknown. The dead bank robber has often been identified as Jim Wallace (alias George Bennett), while the fourth man, variously identified as Tom Littleton or Charles White, is simply unknown.

Elk, near Ardmore, Indian Territory, June 8, 1894

Bill Dalton was tracked to the Houston Wallace farm and shot in the heart after he climbed through a house window. Legend has it that Dalton died with a smile on his face because his pursuers did not recognize him, fearing that they had killed the wrong man. The exact date of death has been disputed by some authors, such as Ramon Adams, who placed the date as June 14.

Smith, *Daltons,* 168; Shirley, *Guardian of the Law,* 238; Samuelson, *The Dalton Gang Story,* 148; McCullough, 101; Samuelson, "Who Really Robbed the Longview Bank?" 8-14.

Dart, Isham (Ned Huddleston) (1855-1900)

A black Texas native, Dart migrated to Colorado in the 1870s and became a member of the Tip Gault gang. A posse wiped out the entire gang in 1875, leaving Dart as the sole survivor. Dart was reportedly killed by Tom Horn on October 3, 1900, in Brown's Hole, Colorado. Horn had personally signed a complaint against Dart on September 26, 1900, for horse theft. Earlier, Dart's supposed rustling partner, Texan Matt Rash, was killed by persons unknown near Rock Springs, Wyoming, on July 8, 1900. Tom Horn was suspected.

Carlson, 120-21; O'Neal, *Encyclopedia,* 150.

Davis Gang (prom. 1860s)

Operating under aliases, the gang terrorized the Fort Griffin area in 1880. It was comprised of George Davis and his brothers and associates Jesse Evans and John Gunter. In July, George Davis and Ranger G. T. Bingham were killed, but the rest of the gang was captured by Texas Ranger sergeant E. A. Sieker, R. R. Russell, and D. T. Carson, in the Davis mountains.

Wilkins, *The Law Comes to Texas,* 201-3; Thrapp, *Encyclopedia,* I, 379-80.

Dow, Leslie (d. 1896)

A Texas-born operator of a hotel and saloon, Dow killed Zachary Light, then became a Chaves County, New Mexico, deputy sheriff. Later he became sheriff of Eddy County, New Mexico, and a deputy U.S. marshal. While heading a posse near San Simon, Arizona, in 1896 Dow encountered Black Jack Christian and killed his horse, and also killing Bob Hays while the other gang members escaped. The next year, Dow was mortally wounded at Carlsbad, New Mexico, on February 19, 1897, by his enemy, Dave Kemp, while reading mail at the post office.

Nash, 105; O'Neal, *Encyclopedia,* 93, 174.

The Dublin Brothers (prom. 1870s)

The Dublin boys were thieves and supposed associates of the German Faction in the Mason County War.

Nothing is known of their mother, but the notorious Dublin brothers were sired by James "Jimmie" Dublin, whose entire brood was supposedly devoted to cattle rustling and other criminal pursuits. Richard "Dick" Dublin began his misspent career with the killing of two victims at Lankford's Cove in Coryell County. This double murder prompted an escape with his accomplice Ace Lankford into Kimble County, then a nearly impenetrable tangle of woods and waters. Apparently enticed by this outlaw refuge, Jimmie eventually moved the entire clan to Kimble County.

Not to be outdone by his brother Dick, Dell Dublin (b. March 17, 1857) killed neighbor Jim Williams on September 11, 1876, shortly after the clan arrived in Kimble County, drawing the stern attention of Capt. N. O. Reynolds and the Texas Rangers. Williams himself had been arrested earlier on charges of assault and attempted murder then released from the Burnet Jail. He was killed in a cow camp near Cat Mountain in Llano County, about nine miles from Llano, while his associate Ed Cavin escaped. Williams was a brother-in-law of Mason County feudist William Z. "Bill" Redding.

Years later, a series of stagecoach robberies at the Peg Leg station, which had perplexed Kimble County law officers for years, were solved. Each crime was marked by an extremely small footprint attributed to one of the robbers. Embittered Dublin brothers accomplice Bill Allison, a son-in-law of Jimmie Dublin, revealed that James Rolan Dublin (b. April 7, 1856), known as Roll or Role, Dell Dublin, Mack Potter, and Rube Boyce were responsible. The Jimmie Dublin ranch some sixty miles from the station on the South Llano River had served as outlaw headquarters. The Dublin brothers and small-footed Mack Potter were sentenced to fifteen-year prison sentences, while Rube Boyce considered his options, then escaped from the Travis County jail, only to be captured years later at Socorro, New Mexico, then acquitted.

Dick Dublin was not so easy to catch. He recognized three of the Rangers, namely the Bannister boys and James B. Gillett, whom Dublin had known years earlier as young cowhands, and swore vengeance against them. Instead, in January 1878, Gillett and five Ranger privates were tasked to pursue and capture Dublin, and did so, killing him at the Potter ranch as Dick attempted to escape.

Gillett, 87-104; Metz, *Encyclopedia,* 67, 94-95.

Dunn, Morris (d. 1888)

The deputy sheriff of Fannin County, Texas, Dunn was killed on the evening of May 26, 1888, in Indian Territory while attempting to arrest members of the Dyer gang. Although Jim, Joe, and Dick Dyer and "Williams" escaped, the entire crew except Dick Dyer surrendered at Caddo, Indian Territory, the next day. The Fannin County sheriff and another deputy were reportedly killed by Sam and Eli Dyer previously. Records reflect that Sheriff Thomas A. T. Ragsdale was killed on May 11, 1885.

Owens, *Oklahoma Heroes,* 232; Tise, 180.

Early, John (prom. 1860s)

Early was the instigator of the Early-Hasley feud in Bell County, an affair with many twists and turns.

During the Civil War, John Early was an ardent secessionist leader who used his influence to target and have elderly Drew Hasley mistreated, father though he was of Confederate Sam Hasley. Young Sam formed his own crew, which included brother-in-law Jim McRae. Eventually, Early sought to expand his power by befriending local Unionists after the war ended, then charged Drew Hasley with lynching three Confederate deserters. Thus charged, old Mr. Hasley suffered immensely in a drafty jail hellhole in the middle of winter, affecting his health permanently.

Such insults prompted Sam Hasley and Jim McRae to plan the eradication of the Early party and their Unionist allies, including Dr. Calvin Clark and Chief Justice Hiram Christian, then serving as a judge on the Reconstruction-era Military Commissions Court. Each targeted Early feudist was tracked down and killed in Arkansas and Missouri, but at a price. Before Sam Hasley exacted his revenge, Jim McCrae himself was assassinated by John Early.

Sonnichsen, *I'll Die Before I Run*, 6.

East, James Henry (1853-1930)

A Kaskaskia, Illinois, native, East reached Texas as early as 1868, working as a cowboy for such notable ranches as the King Ranch in South Texas, as well as the LX and LIT in the Texas Panhandle. In 1880, he volunteered for a posse led by Charles Siringo, a cowboy who later became a noted detective and author. The posse, which included Lee Hall, Lon Chambers, Tom Emory, and Louis "The Animal" Bousman, was assigned to recover cattle stolen by Henry McCarty (Billy the Kid).

Shortly after arriving in New Mexico Territory, the Texas cohort encountered a posse led by Pat Garrett. Texans East, Hall, Chambers, Emory, Bob Williams, and Bousman were assigned to join Garrett and track Billy the Kid to Fort Sumner.

December 19, 1880, found the combined posse in Fort Sumner, where they mortally wounded Kid protégé Tom O'Folliard in a fog-impaired exchange of gunfire with Dave Rudabaugh, Tom Pickett, Billy the Kid, and Charlie Bowdre.

East nursed O'Folliard through his last thirty minutes, which the remorseless bandit spent cursing Pat Garrett. East also saved the Kid one week later at Stinking Springs, where after a lengthy siege that claimed the life of Charlie Bowdre, Jim East and Lee Hall prevented Barney Mason from blasting the Kid into the next world. The Kid showed his gratitude by giving his prize Winchester to East.

Jim returned to the greater Tascosa area and became the sheriff of Oldham County in 1882. Following the "Great Tascosa Shootout" of March 21, 1886, East conducted an investigation that resulted in four arrests for the murder of four participants. All were acquitted. East killed gambler Tom Clark in an 1889 shoot-out, then ran an Amarillo detective agency before relocating to Douglas, Arizona, where he accepted the position of town marshal. East died there on June 30, 1930.

Metz, *Encyclopedia,* 74-75; Nolan, 240, 242, 244, 247-49, 252, 254-55, 321, n. 5.

Evans, Jesse (b. 1853)

Born in Missouri in 1853, by 1872 Evans was working as a cowboy for the John Chisum ranch in Lampasas County, New Mexico. A few years later he was engaged in cattle rustling among such future outlaw luminaries as Henry McCarty, known as Billy the Kid. Evans participated in the assassination of John Tunstall in February 1878, the event generally accepted as the beginning of the Lincoln County War in which he rode for the Murphy-Dolan faction against Billy the Kid and other Regulators. After settling differences with the Kid and others in Lincoln on February 18, 1879, a besotted Evans murdered Huston Chapman for no reason at all, prompting a retreat to Texas, where he returned to what he was made for: cattle rustling.

In March 1879 he robbed a Fort Davis store, and on July 3, 1880, he killed lawman George Bingham and an innocent bystander. Evans was captured and convicted, but only served two years of a ten-year prison sentence before escaping from a work crew into anonymity.

Selected Gunfights and Robberies
Near Las Cruces, New Mexico, January 1, 1876

During a local dance, Evans and other members of the John Kinney gang, known as "The Boys," engaged several cavalrymen from nearby Fort Selden in a fistfight so brutal that Pvt. Mathew Lynch was mortally wounded. Soon, the Boys returned and poured fire into the dance through doors and windows, mortally wounding another soldier and a civilian reveler. Some nineteen days later, the gang killed Quirino Fletcher, who had killed one Mansfield, a friend of the Boys, then bragged about it.

Grant County, New Mexico, January 1878

Alongside his gang, Evans exchanged shots with the owners of cattle his gang had just stolen. The gang was forced to abandon their ill-gotten gains, but managed to escape despite wounds to Tom Hill and Jesse Evans.

Near Lincoln, New Mexico, February 18, 1878

Jesse Evans, Tom Hill, Frank Baker, and others led by Buck Morton caught merchant, rancher, and Murphy-Dolan faction antagonist John Tunstall alone guarding horses near Lincoln, while John Middleton, Henry McCarty (Billy the Kid), Fred Waite, and others hunted wild turkey nearby. Tunstall was lured to the posse by a promise of safety, then killed by Buck Morton and Tom Hill.

Alamo Springs, New Mexico, March 13, 1878

While pillaging a sheep camp, Jesse Evans and Tom Hill were interrupted by a shepherd, whom they disarmed. After Evans and Hill returned to looting the camp, the man somehow acquired a Winchester and opened fire. His first shots missed, and he took a bullet from one of the outlaws, yet the shepherd garnered enough strength to kill Hill. Evans promptly left, abandoning a rifle and a six-shooter.

About eighteen miles north of Presidio, Texas, along Cibola Creek, July 3, 1880

Evans and three others were attacked by Texas Rangers led by Sgt. E. A. Sieker. The gang surrendered following a long gun battle in which Texas Ranger George Bingham lost his life. A civilian bystander was also killed.

O'Neal, *Encyclopedia,* 105; Metz, *Encyclopedia,* 79; Nolan, 62-68, 79, 81, 83-86, 96-98, 100-102, 104, 106, 108-10.

Ferguson, Lark (Pete Spence) (1852-1914)

Born in Louisiana in 1852, Ferguson seemingly began his career on the right side of the law. He became a Texas Ranger by 1874 and served under (possible relative) Capt. Warren Wallace Ferguson. Spence killed a Mexican cowboy on July 4, 1876. When he killed again under similar circumstances, he left the Rangers, likely dismissed. He robbed the Seeligson Bank on August 24, 1876, less than a month after having charges of horse theivery leveled against him. In order to throw law enforcement off his trail, Ferguson became Pete Spence and moved to Arizona.

He was aquitted of murder charges after an arrest in Pima County in 1878. Spence soon turned to stagecoach robbery in Tombstone, Arizona, with newfound partner Frank Stilwell. The two men joined the Cowboy faction opposed to the Earps and led by the Clantons.

Stilwell and Spence were suspected of wounding Virgil Earp on December 28, 1881, and killing Morgan Earp on March 18, 1882. Spence was taken into protective custody soon after the second shooting, but Stilwell was shot dead by the Earp party in Tucson. Spence then found law enforcement work in Grant County, New Mexico, and beat a man to death a mere week after being hailed as "one of the best peace officers in the West" by a local newspaper. He was sentenced to five years in prison, prompting the *Tempe News* to opine on April 15, 1893, "Pete Spence kills another Mexican in cold blood. THAT MAKES FIVE." (*sic*). He served less than a year and a half of his sentence before being released. He returned to a warm Tombstone reception in 1901, married the widow of Phineas Clanton on April 2, 1910, and died of pneumonia in 1914. Spence is buried in Globe, Arizona.

Metz, *Encyclopedia,* 230; Tefertiller, 103, 107, 143, 156, 229-31, 235.

Fisher, John King (1854-84)

Near legendary Texas rustler and gunmen, among other occupations, Fisher was born in Collin County, Texas. His mother soon died, and the family trooped through a series of ranches with his Confederate-veteran father. Convicted of burglary at sixteen, young John learned the cowboy trade in South Texas, then started the

Pendencia Ranch, near Eagle Pass, Texas. Legend says he posted a sign nearby, warning visitors that "This is King Fisher's Road—Take the Other One."

The 1870s were tumultuous for most Texans, and Fisher was no exception. By 1878 he reportedly admitted the killing of at least seven men, "excluding Mexicans." Legend also says that he once killed four vaqueros in one incident. Public records do confirm an 1875 murder allegation and rustling charges, none of which resulted in convictions. Reasons of his own late that December prompted Fisher to focus on business and avoid legal trouble.

Appointed deputy sheriff of Uvalde County in 1881, his candidacy for sheriff, announced in 1884, was abruptly terminated by his untimely death on March 11 with gunman Ben Thompson at the Vaudeville Theater in San Antonio.

Selected Gunfights
Zavala County, Texas, December 25, 1876
Christmas Day was cheerless for ranch hand William Dunovan, whom Fisher killed for reasons unknown.
Leona River, near Leakey, Texas, 1883
Acting Sheriff Fisher killed alleged stage robber Tom Hannehan at his own ranch, prompting brother Jim Hannehan to give up the loot. Years later, Tom's wife set a brush fire on Fisher's grave on each anniversary of Hannehan's death.
Vaudeville Theater, San Antonio, March 11, 1884
Fisher was killed with Ben Thompson about 10:30 P.M. by friends of deceased proprietor Jack Harris, whom Thompson had killed in the same place, on July 11, 1882. Some say performer Harry Tremaine, gambler "Canada Bill," and a bartender ambushed the pair, even as Fisher loudly told everyone present he wanted no trouble.

O'Neal, *Encyclopedia,* 107; Metz, *Encyclopedia,* 83; DeArment, *Bat Masterson,* 277; Selcer, 96-98, 100-104.

Fountain, Albert Jennings (1838-96)
A Staten Island, New York, adventurer and former Texas state senator, Albert disappeared into the New Mexico desert in February

1896, the presumed victim of foul play. Born on October 23, 1838, as Albert Jennings, he added the surname Fountain for reasons unknown, traveling to California in his twenties. After Civil War service in the California volunteers, he came to New Mexico and took a young bride. During a wide-ranging political and legal career, he was engaged in one gunfight, later killed an escaping prisoner, and was assumed to be himself the victim of gunplay when he and his son disappeared.

Gunfights

El Paso, December 7, 1870

State Senator Albert Jennings Fountain and District Judge Gaylord Judd Clark encountered lawyer B. F. Williams, with whom Fountain had differed during the El Paso Salt War. Fountain, a founder of the "Salt Ring," which had claimed the Salt Beds, had unceremoniously switched sides, drawing the ire of Williams and others. Williams initiated the El Paso melee, but Fountain finished it, dropping Williams with a rifle shot from fifty yards. State Policeman A. H. French then finished the job.

Canutillo, Texas, March 1883

Fountain and his son Albert took custody of Doroteo Saenz and two other fugitives from Texas Rangers for return to Mexico. When Saenz attempted an escape, Fountain brought him down with four shots.

White Sands, New Mexico, April 1, 1896

Fountain and his young son Henry disappeared while returning from Lincoln, New Mexico, to Mesilla, bearing indictments against Oliver Lee and others. Suspects in the disappearance included political rival Albert Fall, James "Killin' Jim" Miller, or perhaps both.

Nolan, 66, 134, 230; Selcer, 129-30; O'Neal, *Encyclopedia,* 111; Metz, *Encyclopedia,* 86.

Fowler, Joe (1849-84)

An Indiana native who moved to Texas in 1875, Fowler was known as a smooth talker with an even demeanor but a bad temper. He fled to Las Vegas, New Mexico, after murdering his wife's love interest, but returned to Texas after committing another murder, establishing a ranch (under an alias) outside of San Antonio. Heavy drinking may have been responsible for his fight with Jim Cale, whom he stabbed to death on October 10, 1883, at the Grand Central Hotel in Socorro, New Mexico, while celebrating the sale of his ranch. Fowler was jailed and sentenced to death, but an angry mob preempted the execution on January 21, 1884.

Selected Gunfights and Robberies
White Oaks, Lincoln County, New Mexico, May 31, 1880
Fowler and other citizens confronted rowdies Virgil Collum and Joe Oaks, who were shooting up the town. When the smoke cleared, Collum had been killed by Fowler.
Socorro County, New Mexico Territory, 1880
Once involved in the ranching business, Fowler enforced a zero-tolerance policy against cattle rustlers. He shotgunned "Whiskey Jim" Greathouse and Forrest Neal, leaving Jim Finley alive long enough for a ranch hand to kill.
Socorro County, New Mexico, 1883
Fowler killed "Butcher Knife Bill" otherwise known as William Childes of Fort Griffin, Texas, then burned his half-brother Pony Neal alive, just to make an impression on moonlight cattlemen of the area.

Metz, *Encyclopedia,* 87; Nash, 131; Thrapp, *Encyclopedia,* I, 515.

Frazer, George A. (Bud) (1864-96)
Born in Fort Stockton, Texas, on April 18, 1864, Frazer probably made his father, a judge, proud when he joined the Texas Rangers in 1880 as a very young man. After spending some time in Pecos County as deputy sheriff, he won election and became sheriff of Reeves County in 1890. While he was serving in this capacity a dispute began with deputy "Deacon" Jim Miller, who had killed an unarmed prisoner. While Miller offered the explanation of an escape attempt, the prisoner was likely killed because of his knowledge of Miller's cattle thievery. Frazer fired Miller and proceeded to charge him with rustling.

Miller was released and made an unsuccessful bid for Frazer's job in 1892. Despite his loss, Miller became city marshal of Pecos. The two rivals had a gunfight in Pecos around 1894. Frazer seemingly retired from law enforcement following his defeat in the November 1894 elections, and settled in New Mexico to run a livery stable. Frazer later returned to Pecos and had another gunfight with Miller. Frazer was charged with attempted murder but acquitted, in May 1896. Miller decapitated Frazier with a shotgun on September 14, 1896, while Frazer was visiting family in Toyah, Texas.

Selected Gunfights and Robberies
Pecos, Texas, April 12, 1894

Frazer tried to gun down Miller in front of the Pecos Hotel, but only wounded him. Miller retaliated, but only injured a pedestrian. Perhaps Miller only had a single shot, because Frazer proceeded to pump multiple bullets into his chest and left him on the ground to die. Miller was apparently wearing a primitive bulletproof vest and survived.

Pecos, Texas, December 26, 1894

Frazer encountered Miller outside of Zimmer's blacksmith shop, and shot him in the right arm and chest. Miller kept fighting, so Frazier turned and ran. He learned, upon his subsequent arrest, that Miller had been wearing a primitive bulletproof vest at each encounter.

Toyah, Texas, September 14, 1896, 9 A.M.

Miller walked into a saloon and blew Frazer's head off with a shotgun, and promised his angry sister the same when she threatened him with a handgun.

O'Neal, *Encyclopedia,* 113; Nash, 131; Shirley, *Shotgun for Hire,* 6-7, 20-22, 25-32, 34-45, 48-49.

Frazier, Charlie (b. 1897)

A habitual criminal and escapist who hailed from Red River County, Texas, Frazier and another convict killed the Angola, Louisiana, State Prison farm manager on September 10, 1933. He participated in the July 22, 1934, attempted breakout from Huntsville Prison in East Texas with Ray Hamilton, Joe Palmer, and Blackie Thompson, aided by the collusion of a guard. Whitey Walker, a former member of the Oklahoma Kimes-Pendleton gang, was shot to death.

Robberies and Gunfights

Hugo, Oklahoma, January 13, 1917

Frazier was captured following an escape from Huntsville prison.

Marion County, Texas, 1926

Under the assumed name R. E. Johnson, Frazier was convicted of robbery and firearms violations, then sent to Huntsville. He escaped with some six other prisoners and killed guard Will Roder in the incident.

Angola State Prison, Louisiana, September 10, 1933

Frazier, imprisoned for robbery and shooting with intent to murder, escaped from the Louisiana prison with eleven other convicts, during a baseball game.

Huntsville Prison, Death Row, July 22, 1934

Raymond Hamilton, Joe Palmer, and Blackie Thompson escaped from Huntsville with the connivance of Charlie Frazier and others. Frazier declined to escape with the other conspirators, but Whitey Walker was shot and killed just as he was about to climb over the wall.

Angola Prison, October 16, 1936

Charlie Frazier attempted to escape from Angola Prison, where he was serving a life sentence for the murder of Warden Singleton. He was shot six times, yet survived to serve the rest of his sentence.

Simmons, 144-49, 153, 169, 171.

Fries, John P. (1848-73)

A deputy U.S. marshal, Fries was killed on October 15, 1873, at Brackettville, Texas, while tracking two fugitives. One McWebber, an army deserter, and one Mansfield were wanted on murder charges. The former had been arrested by Fries one week earlier but had escaped by bribing a guard. Fries was shot through a window at the home of an acquaintance and killed instantly, perhaps by McWebber. The disposition of the murder charges is unknown.

Ernst, *Deadly Affrays,* 97.

Fults, Ralph (1911-93)

A Barrow gang associate, Fults was born on January 23, 1911, in McKinney, Texas, in a family with seven siblings, all honest and law abiding. As a young man, Fults witnessed one of the last public executions in Texas and learned to be a locksmith. He met Clyde Barrow on September 18, 1930, while being transported to Huntsville prison. Fults was later associated with Barrow in the Lake Dallas gang. Captured with Bonnie Parker in 1932, he was convicted and returned to prison, released in 1935, and returned to crime with Ray Hamilton, only to be caught again and imprisoned. He was released from prison in 1944, reformed, and became a counselor at a Dallas area boys home. Fults died on March 17, 1993, in Dallas, having observed that while in prison, he watched Clyde Barrow transform from a schoolboy to a rattlesnake.

Selected Robberies
Mabank, Texas, March 22, 1932
Ralph Fults, Bonnie Parker, and Clyde Barrow stole a car and were pursued by police who captured all but Clyde.
West Dallas, March 25, 1932
Ralph Fults, Ray Hamilton, and Clyde Barrow attempted to rob the Simms Oil Refinery, but the payroll safe was empty.
Mabank, Texas, April 18, 1932
Bonnie, Clyde, and Fults were forced to make a mule-back escape to Kemp, Texas, after a futile hardware store robbery attempt.
Okabena, Minnesota, May 19, 1933
Robbery of the First State Bank, probably by Clyde Barrow, Ray Hamilton, and Ralph Fults, netted $2,400.

Barrow, 193, 238, 253; Knight, 44-47, 187.

Fusselman, Charles (1866-90)
A Greenbush, Wisconsin, native whose parents immigrated to Nueces County, Texas, in about 1870, Fusselman joined Company D of the Texas Rangers at age twenty two. Fusselman worked as a Ranger assigned to Marathon, Texas.

The next year, Fusselman was alerted by former Ranger J. T. Gillespie that gunman Donanciano Beslinga (Beslanga) had shot up a small settlement in the vicinity of Maxan Springs. Fusselman and Gillespie proceeded to the town, then pursued Beslinga, using a railroad handcar, to the vicinity of his home. Beslinga arrived there in a rainstorm and engaged Fusselman in a bloodless but near point-blank gunfight. Fusselman trailed the suspect the next morning and found him about a mile from the Maxan Springs railroad station. In fact Beslinga found him. The gunman rose from a concealed position firing a rifle at close range, but without effect. Fusselman returned fire, hitting Beslinga eight times and mortally wounding him.

In April 1890, Fusselman was alerted to a cattle-rustling operation near Mundy Springs, about eight miles north of El Paso. He gathered a posse consisting of rustling victim John Barnes and police officer George Herold. The initial investigation went smoothly enough, resulting in the arrest of Ysidoro Posas, but as the trio went farther into the Franklin Mountains, trouble erupted. The posse stumbled into the rustlers' camp in what is today known as Fusselman Canyon. There, Fusselman was killed by gang leader Geronimo Parra. The murderer was hanged for the crime in El Paso on January 6, 1900.

Metz, *Encyclopedia,* 89; Hadley, *The Law Comes to Texas,* 282, 285-87, 291-92.

Garrett, Buck (1871-1929)

Born near Paris, Texas, on May 24, 1871, Garrett became a deputy U.S. marshal and participated in the Johnson County War with Frank Canton (Joe Horner), on behalf of Wyoming stockmen against small ranchers. Elected chief of police in Ardmore, Oklahoma Territory, in 1905, he became sheriff of Carter County and with his deputy, Bud Ballew, was involved in fatal shootings of Arch Campbell and Steve Talkington. Defeated through the efforts of the Ku Klux Klan in 1922, he died in Ardmore on May 6, 1929.

Thrapp, *Encyclopedia,* I, 540; Smith, *War on Powder River,* 189; O'Neal, *Johnson County War,* 99-101, 104, 228-29.

Garrett, Patrick Floyd (Pat) (1850-1908)

A Louisiana lawman and Texas Ranger, Garrett is best known as the killer of Billy the Kid. He left his home state at the age of eighteen following the death of his parents, to work as a cowboy in the Texas Panhandle and eventually as a buffalo hunter. He killed his first man in 1876 near Fort Griffin, Texas. Garrett irritated a short but stout Irishman, who charged Garrett with an ax. Garrett fired his rifle, and hit his opponent in the chest, wounding him mortally. Garrett then moved to Fort Sumner, New Mexico, where he tended bar, ran a cafe, then married. His teenaged wife died in childbirth.

Garrett was elected Lincoln County sheriff in 1880, and gathered a posse to pursue the Kid. En route, the men encountered Kid associate Tom O'Folliard. A running gunfight ensued before O'Folliard escaped the posse.

Later Garrett and other lawmen laid a trap for the Kid and his gang at Fort Sumner.

The trap was sprung the evening of December 19, 1880. The Kid, Charlie Bowdre, Dave Rudabaugh, Billy Wilson, and Tom Pickett approached the old fort hospital in a column led by Tom O'Folliard and were ordered to halt. When they refused, O'Folliard was shot in the chest by either Garrett or Chambers, who fired at the same time. O'Folliard tried to flee with the other outlaws, but realized his wounds were mortal and surrendered to the lawmen.

Garrett then led a posse to Stinking Springs, New Mexico, on December 23, 1880, and found the Kid, Charlie Bowdre, and others holed up in an old structure with an open door. Bowdre was shot twice in the chest as he stepped outside, but managed to scramble back inside. Bowdre wanted to go back out for help, and was told to come out with his hands up. According to some stories, the Kid pushed him outside and screamed at him to kill some lawmen before he died. In any event, Bowdre staggered to the posse and died mumbling "I wish." The outlaws tried to gather their horses at the door, but gave up when the lawmen shot one mount. After intermittent gunplay Garrett ordered his men to start fires and prepare a meal. The outlaws raised a white flag and surrendered on condition that they would be well fed and unharmed. The Kid was arrested and held in Lincoln until he killed two men and escaped on April 28, 1881.

Accompanied by Frank Poe and Tip McKinney, Garrett went to Fort Sumner where the Kid was rumored to be hiding. Legend has it that Garrett and the Kid walked right by each other while simultaneously entering the abandoned fort grounds. That night, Garrett visited local citizen Pete Maxwell, to inquire about the Kid's possible whereabouts. While they talked in a dark bedroom, the door opened and in came the Kid, back first, armed only with a worn old butcher knife. When the Kid asked Maxwell to identify the strangers on the porch, Garrett recognized his voice and reacted instantly with a single shot that found its mark Although Garrett fired a second, panicked shot which ricocheted into the headboard of Maxwell's bed, no more gunplay was required. The Kid fell dead with a single groan and was buried near Tom O'Folliard and Charlie Bowdre.

This episode enhanced Garrett's reputation, but not enough to garner renomination for sheriff. Instead, he worked as a Texas Ranger and managed ranches for others before establishing his own ranch near Roswell, New Mexico, and launching an irrigation business. Both ventures failed. He ran for sheriff in Pecos County in 1890, then started a horse ranch in Uvalde, Texas, where he became friends with future vice president John Nance "Cactus Jack" Garner. Garner's influence helped secure Garrett a county commissioner position. Garrett might have abandoned law enforcement for the rest of his days, but for the unexplained disappearance of Judge Albert J. Fountain and his young son in White Sands, New Mexico. Garrett assumed the job of sheriff in Dona Ana County with orders to track down the killers, but neither he nor anyone else ever solved the disappearances.

Later, while still Dona Ana County sheriff, Garrett led a posse of five men to a ranch about thirty miles south of Alamogordo to arrest murder suspects Oliver Lee and James Gilliland. The Lee ranch was very strongly defended, and Garrett lost a deputy, then was himself wounded in the gunfight. The posse was forced to ride off in defeat, both suspects were acquitted of all charges, and Garrett was soon without a job.

He moved to El Paso, Texas, and became a customs inspector, again with the help of Cactus Jack Garner. He quit in 1904 and once again tried his hand at ranching, this time near Las Cruces. Financial problems eventually forced him to lease his land. Worse still, his lessee, Wayne Brazil (Brazel) turned the cattle ranch into a goat-grazing haven, a violation of custom but not the lease.

This breach of ranching etiquette also was a potential economic disaster, due to the voracious grazing habits of goats. Garrett began discussions with Brazil and two prospective cattle-grazing lessees, Carl Adamson and "Deacon" Jim Miller. The Deacon had taken time from his assassination business to involve himself in the dispute. When Garrett left the men in a buggy and inexplicably turned his back to relieve himself, he was shot twice, and died within a few minutes. Although Brazil confessed the crime without any prompting, many modern scholars attribute the murder to Jim Miller, whom Garrett had suspected in the murder of Judge Albert J. Fountain years earlier.

Nolan, 215, 228-31, 233, 235-36, 240-44, 247-50, 252, 254-55; O'Neal, *Encyclopedia,* 115-19; Shirley, *Shotgun for Hire,* 73-90, 101.

Gibson, Volney (1861-91)

A participant in the Jay-Woodpecker feud, Gibson killed Kyle Terry in a courthouse on August 16, 1899, to avenge the death of L. E. Gibson. During the affray, "Jaybirds" approached the courthouse at Richmond, Texas, to confront "Woodpecker" leaders. Two Woodpeckers and one Jaybird were killed, in spite of Texas Ranger presence.

Thrapp, *Encyclopedia,* II, 1337, Nash, 369; Utley, *Lone Star Justice,* 247.

Gillett, James Buchanan (1856-1937)

A colorful South Texas lawman, Gillett finished his career as a cattle baron. Born on November 4, 1856, in Austin, Gillett became a West Texas cowboy who witnessed his first gunfight at age seventeen. He joined the Texas Rangers in 1875, killed South Llano bandito Dick Dublin, and created an international crisis of sorts by kidnapping a fugitive in Mexico. Invited to seek other opportunities because of his brashness, he eventually became an assistant city marshal of El Paso under Dallas Stoudenmire, succeeding the latter to the top job when Stoudenmire was killed by James Manning. Soon, Gillett emphasized his unhappiness with mayor pro tempore Paul Keating in a financial matter by vigorously pistol-whipping the hapless politico. Eventually, Gillett started a ranch with another former Ranger near Marfa, Texas, gradually building the operation into a 30,000-acre empire. Among other adventures, he transported the notorious John Wesley Hardin from Austin to Comanche County for trial in the murder of lawman Charles Webb. Gillett was also the founder of the Cowboy Camp Meeting movement. He died on June 11, 1937, in Temple, Texas.

Selected Gunfights
Menard County, January 1877

Corporal Gillett and other Rangers tracked outlaw and old acquaintance Dick Dublin to a ranch. There, Gillett chased Dublin into a ravine and killed him.

Mendard County, February 1878

Gillett, Lt. N. O. Reynolds, and other Rangers captured fugitive Starke Reynolds on the Junction City and Mason road, while transporting prisoners to Austin.

Ysleta, Texas, December 24, 1881

According to one source, Gillett pursued Onofrio Baca, suspected murderer of newspaper editor A. M. Conklin, across the Rio Grande for a $500 reward. Gillett and another Ranger reportedly captured Baca, then raced back into Texas pursued by a Mexican posse. The pair delivered Baca to a mob, collected the reward, and departed as the vigilantes introduced Baca to "Dr. Lynch." The unseemly raid cost Gillett his Ranger badge.

Gillett, 1-210; O'Neal, *Encyclopedia,* 119; Metz, *Encyclopedia,* 109.

Gilliland, Fine (d. 1891)

A cowboy fugitive, Gilliland was killed on January 31, 1891, near Marathon, Texas, in a gunfight with a Ranger-led posse that included Thalis Cook. Gilliland was accused of killing fellow ranch hand H. H. Poe (Powe) over possession of a steer. Following the gunfight, his friends supposedly branded the steer with the stark inscription: "Murder, January 31, 1891." The beast wandered Brewster County for years, or so the story goes.

O'Neal, *Encyclopedia,* 72; Metz, *Encyclopedia,* 50; Nash, 137.

Godina (prom. 1870s)

Godina (first name unknown) was an unlucky bandit participant in the 1875 Good Friday Nuecestown (*sic*) raid on the store of Englishman Thomas John Noakes. Shot and wounded by Noakes, Godina was transported to Corpus Christi, then dragged from place to place by a mob in search of appropriate lynching facilities. After a church steeple was rejected as unseemly, Godina was hanged from the crossbeam of a ranch gate.

Parsons and Little, 168-69.

Goldsby, Crawford (Cherokee Bill) (1876-96)

Born at Fort Concho, Texas, on February 8, 1876, Goldsby was the son of a sergeant major in the Tenth United States Cavalry and a mixed-blood Cherokee. Reportedly, Crawford once worked north of Tulsa, in Turley, Indian Territory. He really preferred a life of crime. An inventory of his murder victims includes one "Richards" (first name not reported), a railroad agent at Nowata; his brother-in-law George "Mose" Brown at Nowata, whom Crawford killed in a fight over a pig or pigs; Ernest Melton, a curious housepainter who unluckily observed a robbery in progress at Lenapah; and, finally, turnkey Lawrence Keating, whom Crawford killed in a jailbreak attempted at Fort Smith.

Crawford was executed for the murder of Ernest Melton. Robberies in 1894 attributed to him include the Scales store at Wetumka; a train at Red Fork (which may be falsely attributed, since he is known to have engaged U.S. marshals in a gunfight on 14 Mile Creek near Tahlequah that evening); the Parkinson Store at Okmulgee; an express office at Chouteau; and A. F. Donaldson at an unidentified locale in the Cherokee Nation. Following the killing of Ernest Melton, Lenapah reportedly passed an ordinance forbidding the harassment of Goldsby within town limits. According to lore, he also killed train conductor Sam Collins for requesting train fare.

Selected Indian Territory Robberies and Gunfights
Lenapah, November 9, 1894

Goldsby and Sam McWilliams (the Verdigris Kid) robbed the Shufeldt store and post office of $700 (today $14,368). Fatally curious housepainter Ernest Melton, who observed the heist from the building next door, was shot in the face and killed. Goldsby and McWilliams fled to the vicinity of present-day Leonard and eventually Tulsa.

Nowata, December 24, 1894

At about 7:00 P.M., the Kansas-Arkansas Valley depot was robbed of $190 by four individuals believed to be Goldsby, Jim French, George Sanders, and Sam "Verdigris Kid" McWilliams.

Nowata, December 30, 1894

Goldsby allegedly robbed George Bristow, station agent at Nowata, who had turned in his resignation following the Christmas Eve robbery described above.

Fort Gibson, January 14, 1895

Goldsby and French allegedly robbed the F. N. Nash store and the newspaper editor of cash and merchandise.

Near Nowata, January 29, 1895

Goldsby was enticed to the residence of ex-deputy U.S. marshal Ike Rogers by the allure of Maggie Glass, knocked over the head with a piece of firewood, and arrested.

Talala, December 30, 1895

The Christmas pleasantries over, Goldsby killed his brother-in-law Mose Brown, allegedly in a dispute over a herd of pigs or, according to others, in order to eliminate an informant.

May, "The Most Ferocious of Monsters"; Shirley, *Marauders*, 8-22, 32-73, 137-48.

Good, John (prom. 1870s)

A Texas native who began his ranching and reputed rustling operation near Austin in the hill country, Good was prompted to relocate. In June 1877 he moved on to Blanco City, temporarily becoming a hotel owner before resuming ranching, first at Colorado City, then finally near La Luz, New Mexico. John initially left his wife in Texas while starting the New Mexico operation, but did not lack female companionship. "Bronco Sue" Yonker, no stranger to violence herself, was quite happy to console the Texan. However, she transferred her allegiance to one Charley Dawson when the Good family arrived, at least until Good shot him. About three years later, Good quarreled with Oliver Lee and others, then moved again, this time to Arizona, after the death of his son Walter in mysterious circumstances.

Gunfights
Blanco City, Texas, June 10, 1877
   Confronted by a Mr. Robinson and accused of horse theft, an outraged John Good shot the accuser four times, settling his hash permanently.
Las Cruces, New Mexico, August 1885
   After finding his son Walter dead in the White Sands, Good and five others engaged Oliver Lee and four other enemies in a brief gunfight. Walter had been suspected by some of killing George McDonald, with whom John Good had quarreled. Walter's cousin, Milton Paul Good, carried on the outlaw tradition.
La Luz, New Mexico, December 5, 1885
   Good killed Charley Dawson, presumably to restore his exclusive franchise with Bronco Sue Yonker.

O'Neal, *Encyclopedia,* 122; Nash, 53; Alexander, *Fearless Dave Allison,* 225.

Good, Milton Paul (1889-1960)
   Milton Paul Good was born on March 17, 1889, in Lincoln County, New Mexico, to a family of outlaws. His uncle, John Good, was a well-known murderer, and a Texas Ranger once described his father as a "notorious cow thief." His cousin, Walter Good, was killed by the famous Oliver Lee. Paul worked as a cowboy throughout West Texas, and he eventually managed to become a rancher, but the lack of rain threatened to ruin him.
   He was named "world champion steer roper" in Shreveport, Louisiana, in 1920. Horace Roberson and Dave Allison, inspectors with the Texas and Southwestern Cattle Raisers Association, caught him with more than five hundred head of stolen cattle. Good teamed up with Hillary U. Loftis and killed Roberson and Allison in Seminole, Texas, on April 1, 1923, an Easter Sunday, and the very day before they were to testify before a grand jury. Good and Loftis fled, but later surrendered and were imprisoned in Huntsville, Texas. They managed to escape after serving only two years, and parted ways in Oklahoma after a short crime spree. Good was eventually

recaptured and sent back to the same prison, but was pardoned by the governer. He died on July 3, 1960, in a freak accident. He was found crushed against a gate by his own car.

Selected Gunfights and Robberies
Seminole, Texas, April 1, 1923
Alongside Hillary Loftis, Paul Good murdered Horace Roberson and Dave Allison, employees of the Texas and Southwestern Cattle Raisers Association, riddling the bodies with both shotgun shells and .45-caliber bullets.

Alexander, *Fearless Dave Allison*, 29-65, 87-113, 159, 240-71; Metz, *Encyclopedia*, 98, 156.

Gosling, Harrington Lee (Hal) (1853-85)

A Tennessee native born on June 25, 1853, Gosling attended the U.S. Naval Academy and Lebanon Law School before moving west to Parsons, Kansas, then Castroville, Texas. Journalistic and political acumen brought him an appointment as the U.S. marshal for the Western District of Texas in 1882. Gosling launched his new career by charging one of his deputies with financial irregularities. Death found him during a gunfight with two prisoners and their relatives on February 21, 1885.

Gunfight
Near New Braunfels, February 21, 1885
Gosling and two deputy U.S. marshals and others were transporting newly convicted robbers Charles Yeager and James Pitts from a trial at Austin to San Antonio. Suddenly, Yeager and Pitts drew concealed pistols and commenced firing, joined by two female relatives for whom the fatally congenial Gosling had provided seating. Gosling and Pitts were killed. Yeager was captured, but later pardoned. The surviving women were inexplicably acquitted of conspiracy to murder.

Ernst, *Deadly Affrays*, 120; Nash, 140

Graham, William (Curly Bill Brocius) (d. 1882)

A Texas cowhand, Graham is still at the epicenter of a controversy concerning his supposed death in a legendary shotgun duel with Wyatt Earp on March 24, 1882. Graham was apparently born in Missouri and worked as a cowhand in Texas. Traveling farther westward, he stopped long enough in New Mexico to be named "Curly Bill" by a now forgotten cantina singer, then sought his fortune in Arizona. There, he associated with the Clanton Cowboy faction, in opposition to the Earp faction in Tombstone. Most scholars agree that Curly Bill's forte was cattle rustling, rather than gunplay. Nevertheless, in alcohol-fueled confrontations, he killed Tombstone city marshal Fred White unintentionally, then challenged White stalwart Billy Breakenridge some six months later, receiving a gunshot in the neck for his trouble.

This much of Curly Bill's life is relatively free of controversy. However, scholars debate to this day whether Brocius was killed at Iron Springs, Arizona, by Wyatt Earp on March 24, 1882, while participating in an ambush of the Earp faction. Traditional accounts state that Wyatt, his brother Warren, Doc Holliday, and "Texas Jack" Vermillion traveled to Iron Springs early that Friday morning for money to be delivered by a Tombstone ally. Unfortunately for the Earps, their friend Charlie Smith was detained in Tombstone. Two Cowboy factionists were sent on to the Springs with the cash, accompanied by some seven well-armed Cowboys. Earp sensed something was wrong as he approached the Springs. His presentiment was confirmed when the Cowboy contingent arose from the brush and commenced firing, killing the horse that Texas Jack Vermillion rode in on. When the smoke cleared, however, only Cowboys were in the dust. Brocius was killed outright by Wyatt Earp, traditional accounts relate, while his comrade Johnny Barnes was mortally wounded. Wyatt Earp, his brother Warren, Doc Holliday, and even Johnny Barnes related in contemporary newspaper interviews that Curly Bill had been killed. Some cowboys related later that Curly Bill was buried in a secret location nearby. A few Cowboys related that Brocius was not killed at all.

Some serious scholars contend that Brocius returned to Texas. Certainly, stories of Curly Bill's adventures after 1882 abound in Western literature, however reminiscent of Elvis Presley sightings in modern times. Nevertheless, no fully credible, verifiable account of Curly Bill's supposed survival beyond the Iron Springs incident has been discovered to this day.

Gunfights

Tombstone, Arizona, October 28, 1880

Newly appointed city marshal Fred White, assisted by Virgil and Wyatt Earp, attempted to corral Graham and other well-lubricated cowboys, only to be unintentionally, but fatally shot while wrestling Graham. White's last words were that the shooting was accidental, setting the stage for a subsequent acquittal.

Galeville, Arizona, May 25, 1881

Curly Bill and his associate Jim Wallace, a Lincoln County War veteran, drunkenly accosted Deputy Sheriff Billy Breakenridge of Tombstone, a colleague of Fred White. Breakenridge shot and seriously wounded Curly Bill, who decided to hang his hat in another state after a long convalescence.

Teferteller, 238-40; O'Neal, *Encyclopedia,* 122-23; Tanner, *Doc Holliday,* 179; Barra, 260-65; Alexander, *John H. Behan,* 192, 200, n. 85.

Griffin, Frank (d. 1872)

A deputy U.S. marshal, Griffin was killed during a gunfight against brothers James and Thomas Flyanne, suspects in a series of Texas post office robberies. On October 6, 1872, Griffin accompanied U.S. Marshal Thomas Purnell to the Flyanne residence about two miles north of Galveston. While searching from room to room for the suspects, Griffin was mortally wounded by a shotgun blast, prompting the other lawmen to retreat. A third attempt to set the house afire finally forced the brothers from their home. Both were sentenced to prison.

Ernst, *Deadly Affrays,* 129.

Grimes, A. W. (Caige) (d. July 19, 1878)

A Williamson County deputy and former Texas Ranger, Grimes was with Richard Ware and John Coffee Hays and others who slipped into Round Rock, Texas, to look for notorious Sam Bass and his gang. When Grimes and Deputy Morris (Maurice) B. Moore followed three of Bass's men into a store and asked whether they were carrying weapons, the outlaws let loose a fusillade of lead at the officers. Grimes was killed instantly. Moore was wounded and hit the floor, but not before he managed to shoot two fingers off of Bass's right hand.

Selected Gunfights
Round Rock, Texas, July 19, 1878
Grimes was killed and Deputy Moore wounded engaging Bass and his gang inside the Koppel store at Round Rock, Texas.

Miller, *Sam Bass and Gang,* 1-27, 55-97, 169-204, 241-63; Thrapp, *Encyclopedia,* II, 590; O'Neal, *Encyclopedia,* 34-35; Utley, *Lone Star Justice,* 185-86; Metz, *Encyclopedia,* 258.

Grounds, William A. (Billy the Kid, Arthur Boucher) (d. 1882)
A Texas native, Grounds moved to New Mexico Territory following a violent episode with one Sam Good. Grounds found himself in the town of Shakespeare, New Mexico, then in Tombstone, Arizona. There his associates included Cowboy faction notables Curly Bill Brocius, Johnny Ringo, the Clantons, and others. Grounds wrote home to Dripping Springs, Texas, that all was well, but neglected to mention that he and his associates were once reduced by poverty to pilfering a church. Bad company brought "Billy" to his death at the hands of a posse led by Deputy Sheriff Billy Breakenridge on March 29, 1882.

Gunfights and Robberies
Charleston, Arizona, March 25, 1882
Engineer M. R. Peel was found dead at the Tombstone Mill and Mining Company, an apparent robbery victim. Zwing Hunt and Billy Grounds were soon at the top of the suspect list, drawing the unwelcome attention of Deputy Sheriff Billy Breakenridge at the behest of Sheriff E. A. Harley.
Near Tombstone, John Chandler Ranch, March 29, 1882
Information led Breakenridge and posse to the Chandler ranch just outside Tombstone, where a gunfight ensued. Grounds was mortally wounded while posseman John Gillespie was killed outright. Badly wounded Zwing Hunt was taken to a Tombstone hospital and promptly escaped.

Tefertiller, 96, 242; Metz, *Encyclopedia,* 101.

Hall, Jesse Lee (Red) (1849-1911)
The son of a Civil War surgeon, and a widely experienced

adventurer, Hall was born on October 9, 1849, in Lexington, North Carolina, then moved to Grayson County, Texas. Jesse taught school before beginning his law enforcement career as city marshal of Sherman, Texas. Opportunities as a deputy sheriff and a Texas Ranger lieutenant serving with Capt. L. H. McNelly placed him near the center of the Sutton-Taylor Feud, a Reconstruction affair in DeWitt County pitting former Confederates who supported Reconstruction against those who didn't. He participated in the elimination of Sam Bass, on July 21, 1878, at Round Rock, Turning to ranching in 1880, he unknowingly provided a wealth of future stories to a young boarder named Will Porter, who later became the once famous writer O. Henry. Apparently, restlessness led him to accept a position as Indian agent at Anadarko, Indian Territory, in 1885. After successfully refuting corruption charges, he joined the army, fought in the Philippines, then turned to oil and gas speculation before dying peacefully in San Antonio on March 17, 1911.

Gunfights
Indian Territory, 1873
   Undeterred by lack of a valid warrant, Hall accepted a challenge to fight an outlaw in the Territory, shot him out of the saddle, and then killed him. Seriously wounded himself, Hall was rescued by two passing cowboys.
Indian Territory, June 1874
   Hall wounded the outlaw Mike Gormly about twenty miles from the Red River, but the bandit and his gang escaped.
Wolf City, Atascosa County, Texas, November 1879
   Acting on a tip, Hall and other Texas Rangers surprised four store robbers, killing two and capturing one, while the fourth escaped.
Las Islas Crossing, Rio Grande, February 9, 1885
   Jesse Hall and LaSalle County sheriff Charlie McKinney joined three Mexicans to discuss border problems. All participants were armed. Hall and the other Americans were invited to a fiesta across the border, but sensing trouble turned around and galloped into Texas with their hosts in hot pursuit.

Miller, *Sam Bass and Gang,* 245; Webb, *Texas Rangers,* 292-94; O'Neal, *Encyclopedia,* 125.

Hamer, Frank (1884-1955)

Frank Hamer was a Texas lawman who bridged the horseback and modern eras of the Texas Rangers and ambushed the notorious Bonnie and Clyde. Hamer was born on March 17, 1884, at the Welch Ranch, San Saba County, Texas, the son of a blacksmith and cavalryman stationed at Fort Clark, Texas. By 1901, Hamer was a wrangler for Barry Ketchum, brother to outlaws Tom and Sam Ketchum, near Sheffield, Texas. Hamer made his first arrest, as an ordinary citizen, in 1905 at a ranch near Sheffield, providing assistance to Sheriff D. L. Barlar, who one year later recommended him for service in Company C of the Texas Rangers. In 1920, two years after his son Frank Hamer, Jr., became a Texas Ranger, Frank, Sr., resigned to join the U.S. Prohibition Service, in reaction to the efforts of Governor Jim Ferguson to politicize the Rangers. Some seventeen months later, he returned, accepting command of Company C, stationed at Del Rio, and promptly fired the entire company, then rehired the few in whom he had confidence.

His appointment as captain of the Austin headquarters company in 1922 essentially marked the end of the horseback Rangers. Between befriending Hollywood luminaries such as famous silent star Tom Mix and the cowboy-actor Will Rogers, Hamer took on a variety of duties. 1927 was a busy year for Hamer, who took over a corrupt county government at Borger during that period. He also sought a pardon for old-time outlaw Frank Jackson, a seventy-eight-year-old retiree from the Sam Bass gang hiding in New Mexico some forty-nine years after the Bass gang demise at Round Rock, Texas. Regrettably, Jackson died before the effort came to fruition.

The next year a serious law enforcement crisis developed. The well-meaning Texas Bankers Association initiated a "Dead Bank Robbers" Reward Program, offering $5,000 for each deceased evildoer, with no questions asked. While bank robbery was reduced, the program became, in the words of Frank Hamer a "killing machine," which motivated Hamer to ask questions and allege that a few unscrupulous officers lured vagabonds and Mexican nationals into robberies with fatal surprise endings. Hamer blew the whistle on such scams and prosecuted ringleaders for two unjust killings at

Stanton, Texas, prompting the bankers to be more selective in reward payments.

Undoubtedly, his most famous assignment was the ambush of Bonnie Parker and Clyde Barrow near Gibsland, Louisiana, on May 23, 1934, at the behest of Huntsville Prison warden Lee Simmons. Hamer was on leave from duties as a special investigator for a Houston oil company at the time of the ambush. He died on July 10, 1955.

Selected Gunfights

Near Del Rio, Texas, early December 1906

Hamer shot Ed Putnam (Ed Sibley), who was accused of murdering J. W. Ralston near Box Springs.

Sweetwater, Texas, October 1, 1917

At about 1:30 P.M., former sheriff and Texas Ranger Gee McMeans attempted to kill Hamer, who thwarted death by grabbing the barrel of a pistol McMeans had already fired. Hamer's wife returned fire with a pistol, preventing a second gunman, H. E. Phillips, from attacking Hamer and killing McMeans.

Tomate Bend, Rio Grande River, October 4, 1918

Hamer, Sheriff W. T. Vann, and Sgt. Delbert Timberlake intercepted Mexican nationals smuggling liquor across the Rio Grande. A notorious bootlegger called "Delgado" was killed by Hamer, while Sergeant Timberlake was mortally wounded, as he himself had predicted earlier than morning.

Brownsville, Texas, 1922

Hamer and a Ranger contingent ambushed and killed Ralph "Red" Lopez and nine members of his outlaw gang. Hamer himself received a minor wound.

Mexia, Texas, January 7, 1922

Hamer and other Rangers were dispatched to Mexia, which had become a notoriously corrupt and wild oil boomtown about seventy miles southeast of Dallas. Hamer promptly raided the Winter Garden, popularly known as the Chicken Shack, for reasons which leave little to the imagination. The Shack, which was built on land previously owned by a deputy sheriff, became Hamer's headquarters, from which he led raids leading to more than six hundred

arrests and the destruction of some nine thousand quarts of whiskey.
Near Gibsland, Louisiana, May 23, 1934

Frank Hamer, Bob Alcorn, Ted Hinton, and a host of lawmen
ambushed the notorious Bonnie and Clyde with the assistance of
Henry Methvin and the Methvin family. Keenly aware of the fate
suffered by law officers who gave Barrow a chance to surrender, the
posse gave the murderous couple no chance at all.

Frost and Jenkins, 1-98; Simmons, 126-36, 143-44, 163-68;
Burrough, 279; Milner, 60-160.

Hamilton, Raymond (Ray) (1913-35)

A Dallas bootlegger and car thief, Hamilton was born in a tent on
the Deep Fork River near Schulter, Oklahoma, on May 21, 1913.
Ray was a childhood friend who became an associate of Bonnie
Parker and Clyde Barrow. Hamilton apparently participated in the
wounding of Sheriff C. G. Maxwell and the killing of Under Sheriff
Eugene C. Moore near Atoka at Stringtown, on August 5, 1932. He
was captured at Bay City, Michigan, four months later. He was executed on May 10, 1935, for the murder of a prison guard.

Selected Gunfights, Robberies, and Kidnapping
Hillsboro, Texas, April 30, 1932

Arrogant, razor-thin Hamilton cased a service station and gift
shop for robbery, then returned about 10:30 P.M. and accidentally
killed the proprietor while robbing him.
Oak Cliff Neighborhood, Dallas, August 1, 1932

Clyde Barrow, Ray Hamilton, and Everett Milligan robbed the
Neuhoff Packing Company of a payroll, then successfully eluded
Dallas Police Department officers A. F. Deere and Roy Richberg in
a car chase. Four days later, Barrow and Hamilton wounded Sheriff
C. G. Maxwell and killed Under Sheriff Eugene C. Moore at
Stringtown, near Atoka, Oklahoma.
Eastham Prison Farm, Eastham, Texas, January 16, 1934

Hamilton escaped prison with the assistance of Clyde Barrow, his
brother Floyd Hamilton, and others, mortally wounding Major
Joseph Crowson.

Lancaster, Texas, February 27, 1934
Clyde Barrow and Roy Hamilton robbed the R. P. Henry Bank of about $4,000.
Grand Prairie, Texas, March 19, 1934
Raymond and Floyd Hamilton robbed the State Bank of $1,500.
West, Texas, March 31, 1934
Ray Hamilton and his new paramour, Mary O'Dare, robbed the local bank of $1,862. Mary was the wife of Hamilton associate Gene O'Dare, then a prison resident.
Lewisville, Texas, April 25, 1934
Ray Hamilton and Ted Brooks robbed the First National Bank of between $1,000 and $2,300, but were later captured at Howe, Texas.
Huntsville Prison, Huntsville, Texas, July 22, 1934
Ray Hamilton escaped prison again, this time with Joe Palmer and Blackie Thompson.
Handley, Texas, January 19, 1935
Two gunmen robbed the First National Bank of $500. Ray Hamilton was identified as one of the suspects.
Carthage, Texas, February 4, 1935
Ray and Floyd Hamilton robbed a local bank of about $1,000. Thirteen days later, Ray Hamilton and Ralph Fults stole eight Browning automatic rifles from a Beaumont, Texas, armory.
Houston, Texas, March 19, 1935
According to Harry McCormick, then a reporter for the *Houston Press* and prison reform advocate, he was contacted by an intermediary and driven to a meeting with Ray Hamilton and Ralph Fults. The fugitives gave him a brief interview and $2,000 for Joe Palmer's defense fund. McCormick was bound and gagged as if he had been kidnapped, providing a means of writing a story about the interview. Hamilton was captured in Fort Worth the next month and executed at Huntsville, on May 10, 1935, after coaxing his accomplice Joe Palmer to go first.

Kohn, 161; Knight, 200-201; Milner, 101-6, 159; Helmer and Mattix, 175-76, 200, 210-12, 217, 227-28; Phillips, 254-58, 310.

Hardin, John Wesley (Wes, Little Arkansas) (1853-95)
John Wesley Hardin lived up to many standards of his circuit-riding Methodist-preacher father, when he wasn't killing people.

John Wesley Hardin, Reconstruction-era Robin Hood or cold-blooded killer, depending on where one stood on the issue. (Courtesy of the El Paso Public Library, Southwest Collection)

Contrary to numerous stories, he was not the scion of the Hardin clan that produced numerous Texas patriots and a signer of the Texas Declaration of Independence. Instead, Hardin was born on May 26, 1853, at Bonham, Texas, and supposedly developed his gunfighting skills shooting at makeshift effigies of Abraham Lincoln, perhaps setting the tone for his Reconstruction-era killings.

Eleven-year-old Wes had "issues," as it were, which manifested in his stabbing a fellow schoolboy and mortally wounding a former slave with whom he had quarreled some four years later. Three Federal soldiers who attempted to arrest him were the next to die. Former Confederates hid the bodies, enabling his murderous career to continue.

He compiled a death count of twenty to fifty individuals, leaving some time for romantic pursuits and a late second career as a lawyer.

Hardin is perhaps best known for shooting Charles Cougar in Abeline, Kansas, in August 1871, supposedly for snoring. One newspaper of the time merely reported that Cougar was shot in his hotel room, sitting in bed reading a newspaper. However, Hardin's capture and imprisonment stemmed from the May 26, 1874, killing of Brown County deputy sheriff Charles Webb in a saloon fight. An enraged mob missed Wes, but lynched his brother Joe and brothers Bud and Tom Dixon. Hardin fled to Florida, where he was arrested in the death of lawman Charles Webb, then returned to Texas, where he served fifteen years and eight months at Huntsville, studying law in his spare time.

Mixing the practice of law with romance proved to be his undoing, hardly an uncommon occurrence in the legal profession. Hardin was colorful in affairs of the heart as well as affairs of "honor." Jane Bowen, whom he married in 1872, gave him two daughters and a son before her death some twenty years later. The forty-one-year-old gunfighter soon married fifteen-year-old Callie Lewis, then returned her home at her request after a brief honeymoon. His final love interest, Beulah Morose (Mrose), retained the newly minted El Paso attorney on behalf of her cattle-rustling husband Martin Morose, then exiled in Mexico. Morose somehow learned that his wife had retained Hardin with more than money when she did not promptly return to Juarez, so he threatened extrajudicial action against Hardin. Three or perhaps four Texas lawmen supposedly arranged for Morose to be lured across the river with the hope of a reconciliation with Beulah. Instead he was ambushed and apparently robbed, setting the stage for Beulah to edit Hardin's biography when the couple was not quarreling or otherwise occupied.

This blissful domesticity was complicated by a feud with the Selmans, a father and son law enforcement team that had become a force in El Paso. John, Jr., arrested the lovely Beulah for drunk and disorderly conduct, drawing Hardin's ire and the protective interest of John Selman the Elder. Although the reasons and circumstances are not entirely clear, the senior John Selman assassinated Hardin with no warning or fanfare at the Acme Saloon on August 19, 1895.

Selected Gunfights

Near Moscow, Texas, November 1868
   Hardin wrestled for fun with a former slave named Mage, who became angry and threatened him. The next day, Mage blocked Hardin's path and was mortally wounded for his last mistake.

Near Sumpter, Texas, November 1868
   On the run, Hardin ambushed and killed three Federal soldiers sent to arrest him.

Towash, Texas, December 25, 1869
   Christmas Day found Hardin sporting a string of winning hands in a card game with a sore loser named Bradly (*sic*). Later, Bradly took his last target practice against Hardin, drawing bullets in the chest and head.

Horn Hill, Texas, January 1870
   Few nineteenth-century Westerners could resist a circus, and Wes was no exception. Less than impressed by the performance, Wes joined local citizenry in a feud with the performers and capped his evening by killing one. Soon thereafter, a young boy-girl bandit team attempted to rob Wes, who sternly disciplined the young man with a fatal bullet in the face.

Near Marshall, Texas, January 1871
   In custody, if only temporarily, Wes seized an escape opportunity presented when one of the two guards went to a nearby farmhouse for horse feed. Drawing a hidden pistol, Hardin shot the remaining guard and escaped.

Gonzalez County, Texas, February 1871
   Under the protective eye of his Clements cousins, Hardin stopped in a Mexican cow camp for a friendly game of monte. Soon the event became distinctly unfriendly when Wes quarreled with the dealer, then shot two other players.

Indian Territory, May 1871

Wes killed an Indian during an ambush, then buried him to avoid retribution.

Bluff City, Kansas, July 7, 1871

Hardin capped the murder of the Indian shooting by killing Juan Bideno, a fugitive wanted for murdering Hardin's friend Bill Cohron.

Abilene, Kansas, August 1871

Hardin killed Charles Cougar for reasons that are still unclear. The long-told story that Cougar was killed for snoring is unsupported by contemporary newspapers and is an apparent myth.

Smiley, Texas, October 1871

Hardin encountered two black state policemen who were pursuing him, killing Green Paramore and wounding John Lackey.

Hemphill, Texas, June 1872

An appropriately surnamed state policeman named Spites was wounded by Hardin in a frank discussion of a pending court case.

Trinity City, Texas, August 1872

Hardin wounded a Mr. Sublett in a bowling dispute and was himself wounded.

Angelina County, Texas, August 1872

Hardin was ambushed and wounded in the thigh by two state policemen while recovering from his bowling accident.

Cuero, Texas, April 1873

Deputy J. B. Morgan picked the wrong opponent for a saloon fight and paid with his life.

Albuquerque, Texas, July 1873

Sutton-Taylor Feud participant Jack Helm, a Sutton faction leader, was killed by Hardin with an assist by Jim Taylor.

Comanche, Texas, May 26, 1874

Accompanied by a host of well-wishers, Hardin celebrated his twenty-first birthday by killing Comanche County deputy sheriff Charles Webb in a saloon fight. Enraged citizenry lynched his brother Joe and the Dixon brothers while Hardin escaped.

Pensacola, Florida, August 23, 1877

Texas Ranger John Armstrong captured Hardin after grabbing Hardin's gun and fatally shooting young Hardin loyalist Jim Mann in the chest.

El Paso, Texas, August 19, 1895

John Selman, Sr., shot Hardin in the back of the head, then finished the job with a slug to the chest. Hardin never drew his weapon. Conveniently enough, Selman surrendered to his son and was later acquitted.

Metz, *John Wesley Hardin*, 1-33, 40-67, 88-118, 125-40; O'Neal, *Encyclopedia*, 126; Metz, *Encyclopedia*, 108.

Harris, Jack (ca. 1834-82)

Jack Harris was not a real gunman, but he attempted to play one at his own Vaudeville Theater on the evening of July 11, 1882, with tragic consequences. Born about 1834 in Connecticut, young Jack went to sea at an early age. Nineteen-year-old Harris joined in a force under the command of William Walker that invaded Nicaguara in 1855, in an adventure then known as a "filibuster." Harris became a San Antonio policeman about five years later, then served a Civil War interlude with the Second Texas Cavalry.

Along the way he entered the saloon business, then a common career path for policemen in the West. After a few years on Market Street in San Antonio, in about 1871 he purchased the old Cosmopolitan Saloon on Main Plaza in San Antonio with partners, then reinvented the place as the Harris Vaudeville Saloon and Theater in about 1875. The establishment, which also sported gambling rooms and other amenities, was apparently the first vaudeville theater west of the Mississippi. Harris became a local power in the Democratic Party, and as such a popular personality.

In spite of his local standing, Harris ran afoul of authentic gunman Ben Thompson about 1880 in a gambling dispute the details of which are now uncertain. On the evening of July 11, 1882, Thompson, then serving as marshal of Austin, was back in San Antonio. In spite of the best efforts of friends to keep him confined at the Menger Hotel, Thompson somehow escaped and walked directly to the Harris Vaudeville Saloon and Theater nearby, seeking an interview with Harris. Theater personnel warned Harris, who armed himself with a shotgun and waited behind a flimsy, transparent Venetian blind in the front of the theater. Soon Thompson approached in the dark outside and saw Harris and his shotgun conveniently silhouetted by theater lighting. "What are you doing with that shotgun?" Thompson inquired. When Jack suggested that Thompson should show some affection to the Harris posterior. Ben declined to do so, but instead quickly pumped two neat shots into Harris's chest, mortally wounding him.

Harris was soon buried at City Cemetery No. 1 with the full panoply of funeral honorifics available on the frontier, including a wailing bevy of floozies, accompanied by the howling of his favorite dog "Skeezicks."

Thompson was indicted, acquitted, and soon reassumed his position in Austin, but quickly turned to heavy drinking, burdened, some say, by the Harris killing. The Vaudeville Theater closed its doors about two years later, but not before Thompson himself and his friend John King Fisher were killed there on March 11, 1884, even as the hapless Fisher protested that he wanted no trouble. These deaths and a prior 1850's incident nearby, in which Dr. J. M. Devine killed political rival J. H. McDonald, caused the intersection of Soledad and Main Plaza in San Antonio to be known as "The Fatal Corner."

Selcer, 53, 57-58, 91-94; O'Neal, *Encyclopedia,* 319-21.

Hays, John Coffee (Jack) (1817-83)

Near present-day Fredericksburg, at a place called Enchanted Rock, Texas Ranger Jack Hays reportedly held off a large number of Comanche warriors in the early 1840s, until rescued by other Rangers. The incident is considered fanciful by some, but remains a significant part of Texas lore. Hays was born near Nashville, Tennessee, on January 28, 1817. His father was a relative of President Andrew Jackson's wife and named young Jack for a Jackson protégé. The death of the elder Hays in 1832 prompted Jack to seek new opportunities in the Texas Republic. He participated in the Plum Creek battle against Comanche warriors on August 12, 1840, and came to be greatly admired by Sam Houston, who eventually chose him to command a company of Texas Rangers on the frontier, as well as leading troops during the Mexican War. Eventually, Hays moved farther west and became one of the founders of Oakland, California.

Wilkins, *The Legend Begins,* 202; Robinson, *Men Who Wear the Star,* 55-71, 107-8, 125-26, 170, 295 n. 3; Metz, *Encyclopedia,* 113.

Heath, John A. (Heith) (ca. 1854-84)

"Don't mutilate my body or shoot me full of holes" croaked vain, shoeless and shirtless John Heath on March 28, 1884, just before facing eternity in Tombstone. His early origins are still a mystery, but by 1880 he was in Dallas, attracting the unwelcome attention of police suspicious of his possible roles in certain burglaries and horse thefts. Unfazed, he partnered with colorful whore Georgia Morgan to start a bordello. Later, they expanded into saloon operations.

Reasons now unknown prompted John's departure for Bisbee, Arizona, where he founded a dance hall and pursued "other interests," fitting quite well into the young community from all appearances.

Mining was a mainstay of the greater Bisbee area. Since the new town did not have a bank, the Copper Queen Mine payroll was managed by the Goldwater and Castenada Store. On payday, Saturday, December 8, 1883, five young men appeared for the disbursement. Unfortunately, none of them was employed by the Copper Queen. Daniel "Big Dan" Dowd, "Red" Sample, James "Tex" Howard, William Delaney, and Daniel "Yorkie" Kelly were there to steal the payroll, but had arrived before the money did. After treating themselves to $600 in petty cash from the safe, the quintet stepped into the streets and was fired upon by James Krigbaum, a concerned citizen. Responding with suppressing fire, the gang missed Krigbaum, but killed five noncombatants, including Annie Roberts, who was with child.

An enraged posse led by Sheriff Jerome L. Ward and his predecessor John H. Behan included young Mr. Heath among its numbers. Luben Pardu (*sic*), a rancher who operated nearby, claimed he had recently seen the five killers, accompanied by an additional suspect. Then Pardu dropped a bombshell. The apparent gang leader was riding with the posse. John Heath protested his innocence and even asked later for a separate trial. Once captured, his five confederates were convicted of murder and sentenced to be hanged.

Heath himself was convicted of second-degree murder and sentenced to life in prison. The sentence was commuted to "one day in" by a disgruntled Tombstone crowd, which lynched him from a telegraph pole, however badly dressed. The five killers were legally hanged in Tombstone on March 28, 1884.

Alexander, *Dan Tucker,* 128, 139; Metz, *Encyclopedia,* 114; O'Neal, *Encyclopedia,* 22.

Helm, Jack (d. 1873)

Although no Thomas Edison, this Texan found time to patent a cotton worm remover between cold-blooded killings. Usually, Helm acted on behalf of the Sutton faction in the Sutton-Taylor Feud. After an initial Texas appearance as a cowboy for legendary rancher Shanghai Pearce, Helm emerged as a Sutton faction leader. His curriculum vitae included an attack on August 23, 1869, near Creed Taylor's De Witt County ranch, which left Hays Taylor dead and his brother Phillip "Doboy" Taylor slightly wounded.

Assisted by Bill Sutton and others, Helm used his authority as a captain of the Reconstruction-era state police to arrest Taylor's shirttail relatives Henry and William Kelly on the pretext of a complaint for disturbing the peace in Sweet Home, a deceptively named burg near the center of the feud. Helm's true intentions became apparent soon thereafter when the peace of the neighborhood was indeed disturbed by gunshots marking the Kellys' departure from this earthly refuge.

Not to be outdone, the Taylors settled accounts in July 1873, when John Wesley Hardin and Jim Taylor killed Helm at a blacksmith's shop. Undoubtedly, if he saw the attack coming, Helm regretted that he had been unable to recruit Hardin for the Sutton cause.

O'Neal, *Encyclopedia,* 133-34; Sonnichsen, *I'll Die Before I Run,* 47-48.

Higgins, John Calhoun Pinckney (Pink) (1851-1914)

A Macon, Georgia, native, Higgins was born on March 28, 1851, and raised in Austin and on his parents' ranch in Lampasas County, Texas. Higgins spent his early post-Civil War years combining a business career with membership in the local chapter of the Ku Klux Klan. Early Indian fighting and experience on the cattle trails undoubtedly prepared him for an emerging feud with the Horrell brothers. When the Horrells killed Pink's son-in-law and two other peace officers, Higgins took revenge in a series of shootings before signing a peace treaty of sorts at the insistence of the Texas Rangers.

Years later, he moved the Higgins family to a new Kent County, Texas, ranch where the fifty-one-year-old rancher dueled and brought down Bill Standifer, with whom he had quarreled. On Wednesday, October 1, 1902, when Higgins telephoned the sheriff to report the shooting, he was urged to make sure Standifer was dead. Higgins died of a massive heart attack on December 18, 1913.

Selected Gunfights
Lampasas County, Texas, ca. 1874

Horrell hand Zeke Terrell killed a Higgins calf for dinner, only to be stuffed into the carcass himself, after Pink dropped him from ninety yards away, or so the story goes.

Lampasas, Texas, Monday, January 22, 1877

Some two years after one source says Higgins killed Horrell ranch hand Ike Lantier, Higgins found Merritt Horrell in the Matador Saloon and concluded a livestock dispute by putting four rifle slugs into his adversary for cow theft.

Sonnichsen, *I'll Die Before I Run,* 105-6, 108-12, 118; O'Neal, *Encyclopedia,* 139-41; Metz, *Encyclopedia,* 231; O'Neal, *Pink Higgins,* 6-7, 19-20, 34-70, 80, 151.

Holliday, John Henry, D.D.S. (Doc) (1852-87)

Holliday was the son of a Griffin, Georgia, businessman. Educated in dentistry in the early 1870s, he moved to Dallas, Texas, for health reasons and initially practiced his profession with success. A series of difficulties, coupled with his own propensities and his senior partner's disdain for Holliday's gambling habits led him to turn his hobby into an occupation. Still, as the years went by he continued to practice dentistry intermittently.

Holliday established a reputation as a fearless gunfighter, which undoubtedly was an asset in his new occupation. His first gunfight of record in Dallas pitted Holliday against a saloonkeeper in a dispute over card handling. Although shots rang out, neither man suffered any injury. Doc followed the gambling circuit, which then included Texas stops at Denison, Fort Griffin, San Angelo, and Breckenridge. He met and befriended Wyatt Earp at Fort Griffin, Texas. Thereafter, the two men were seen together regularly in towns throughout Texas, Kansas, and Arizona. Wyatt credited Doc with saving him from an ambush in a long-forgotten cattle town gunfight

John Henry "Doc" Holliday. Holliday was a dentist, gambler, gunslinger, and ardent friend and supporter of the Earps. (Courtesy of the Nina Stewart Haley Memorial Library, Midland, Texas, Robert N. Mullin Collection)

and remained a Holliday stalwart for the rest of his life. This loyalty prompted Holliday's participation as a member of the Earp faction in the historic gunfight at the O.K. Corral.

Holliday's only other intimate during adulthood was his paramour

Mary Katherine Harony, a former lady of joy known through most of her life as Big-Nosed Kate. Mary Katherine considered Holliday to be her husband throughout their life together.

In the end, Holliday was no match for the tuberculosis that lingered within. On November 8, 1887, at a hotel in Glenwood Springs, Colorado, Doc's luck ran out. Soon thereafter, all his worldly possessions were shipped to his childhood friend and cousin, Sister Mary Melanie, a Sister of Mercy living in Georgia. Years later, their mutual kinswoman Margaret Mitchell used the good Sister as her model for the impossibly sweet character Melanie in *Gone With the Wind*. Among the few valuable possessions delivered to Sister Melanie was an expensive stickpin, from which the diamond had long since been removed.

Selected Gunfights

Dallas, Texas, January 1, 1875

In his first verifiable gunfight, Holliday and a saloonkeeper named Austin exchanged shots in an argument over a card game. Neither man was injured.

Las Vegas, New Mexico, July 19, 1879

Holliday killed former army scout Mike Gordon with a single round after Gordon shot up a saloon in which Holliday was a partner. Gordon's former paramour had refused to quit her saloon job and join him, prompting the gunplay.

Las Vegas, New Mexico, June 1880

Bartender Charlie White was seriously wounded by Holliday following the continuation of a long-held disagreement between the two. Months earlier, Holliday and White had clashed in Dodge City, forcing White into a rapid exodus. When Holliday heard White was in Las Vegas, he sought him out, and a gunfight quickly erupted. After White crumpled behind the bar, Doc left him for dead. White, however, did not die and made a full recovery.

Tombstone, Arizona, April 1881

Hearing that saloon owner Mike Joyce had accused him of participating in a recent stagecoach robbery, Holliday burst through the saloon doors and commenced firing. Joyce received a gunshot wound to the hand while a bartender nearby caught a stray bullet to the foot.

Tombstone, Arizona, October 26, 1881

The conflicts that caused the famous gunfight at the O.K. Corral were far from simple. Like many frontier towns, Tombstone experienced frequent tensions between town people and cowboys from surrounding ranches. One such Tombstone character was Ike Clanton, a cowboy who had serious problems with Wyatt Earp, Doc Holliday, and nearly everyone associated with them.

Most significantly, however, according to the biographer of Doc Holliday, the Earp-Clanton relationship was complicated by a secret arrangement Wyatt and Ike had worked out concerning a potentially large sum of reward money. On Tuesday, March 15, 1881, at 10:00 P.M. about one mile north of Contention City, four men attempted to rob the Kinnear stage, which was carrying about $80,000 in silver bullion. Although the attempt failed, the gang killed a guard and a passenger. And since the stage carried mail, the robbery attempt was a federal offense. Doc Holliday was suspected due to certain indiscreet statements by his paramour Big-Nosed Kate while she was inebriated.

Wyatt, in his capacity as a Wells-Fargo detective, offered to see that in spite of their mutual animosity, Clanton and others would receive a hefty reward if the identities of the Kinnear stage robbers were disclosed, thus assuring Earp's own success in running for sheriff of Cochise County in coming elections, while also clearing Doc from suspicion of that crime. Clanton wanted the reward, of course, but he did not want other members of the Cowboy faction to know about his secret deal with the Earps. On October 25, 1881, he became agitated upon the suspicion that Doc Holliday and perhaps others knew about his collaboration with Earp.

Against this background, tension between Ike Clanton, his associates, and the Earp faction grew geometrically in the hours before the gunfight. Perhaps this was on Ike's mind as he exchanged insults with Doc over an early morning repast shortly after midnight at the renowned Can Can Lunch and Eating Counter. Ike continued to drink through the wee hours while even night owl Doc Holliday went home to bed.

After telling everyone who would listen that he would kill the Earps, Clanton found himself arrested for carrying concealed weapons. By early afternoon, Ike and his brother Billy, Frank and Tom McLaury, and Billy Claiborne gathered in a vacant lot near Doc's boarding house, perhaps hoping for an ambush opportunity. Instead, they were confronted by Doc Holliday and the three Earps.

Once the firing began, Doc jerked a shotgun from beneath his long coat and trained it on naively unarmed Tom McLaury, who stood behind his horse, probably wishing he had the rifle that was in his saddle scabbard. After being hit by Wyatt, Frank McLaury fired a shot into Doc's side. The wound was not serious enough to put Doc out of action, as Tom McLaury learned when the diminutive dentist pulled the trigger, fired his shotgun again, and killed him instantly. Holliday then switched to his revolver and hastily shot at a fleeing Ike Clanton, but missed. When the hostilities concluded, the McLaurys and Billy Clanton were dead, while Holliday, Morgan Earp, and Virgil Earp were wounded. After provoking the whole thing, Ike Clanton somehow escaped with Billy Claiborne.

Tucson, Arizona, March 20, 1882

Following the ambush killing of Morgan Earp two days earlier, Wyatt gathered a posse to pursue the suspected killers. Frank Stilwell escaped as far as the Tucson train yard where the posse, consisting of brothers Wyatt Earp and Warren Earp, and Doc Holliday, confronted him. Although there were no eyewitnesses, Stilwell's body was found peppered with more than thirty shots.

Tombstone, Arizona, March 22, 1882

On their return from Tucson, the same group located Florentino "Indian Charlie" Cruz, whom they suspected of involvement in the murder of Morgan Earp. Florentino was camping not very far outside Tombstone when discovered and killed execution style.

Leadville, Colorado, August 19, 1884

Holliday's illness and drinking did little to improve his gambling performance in Leadville. He borrowed five dollars from bartender Bill Allen, but was unable to repay the debt as agreed. Allen bragged that if the debt were not repaid soon he would take the debt out of Holliday's hide. When Allen attempted to make good his promise and followed the sickly, much smaller Holliday into a saloon, the dentist merely produced a pistol and fired at Allen, causing the mixologist to retreat, but only after Holliday shot him again although not fatally. Holliday was arrested, but acquitted following a trial.

Metz, *Encyclopedia,* 118; O'Neal, *Encyclopedia,* 144-46; Nash, 162-65; Tanner, *Doc Holliday,* 91-109, 173, 179, 221, 245.

Horn, Tom (1860-1903)

In August 1890, Tom accompanied C. W. "Doc" Shores, then working both as sheriff of Gunnison, Colorado, and as a railroad agent, into Oklahoma Territory on a manhunt. They chased train robber Burt "Red" Curtis through the Texas Panhandle, finding him near Pauls Valley at Washita Station, and later arrested Thomas Eskridge (Peg Leg McCoy). The two fugitives were reputed alumni of Butch Cassidy's Wild Bunch.

Alquist, 16.

Horrell Brothers (prom. 1870s)

The Horrell brothers were the Texas-born sons of Alabamans Samuel and Elizabeth Horrell, who immigrated to Texas in time for some of their sons to serve as Confederate soldiers. The year 1868 found the entire crew near Las Cruces, New Mexico, where the patriarch was killed by Apaches, and brother John (1841-68) was killed in a wage dispute.

After the Horrells' return to Lampasas in 1869, peace apparently prevailed until 1873, when fugitive Clint Barkley (Bill Bowen), brother-in-law of Merritt Horrell (1854-77) sought sanctuary while pursued by authorities on murder charges. Captain Tom Williams led a contingent of the Reconstruction-enforcing Texas State Police into Lampasas. There, the captain and three of his troops were promptly slain for their efforts.

James Martin "Mart" Horrell (1846-78) and four associates were jailed as suspects. After a few months, the Horrells at large freed Mart and associates, prompting a speedy relocation to New Mexico. There the brothers apparently helped start the first Lincoln County War, more often called the Horrell War to avoid confusion with the later conflict involving Billy the Kid and others. That four-year Horrell exile led to the deaths of Benjamin F. Horrell (1851-73) and some ten to twenty other combatants.

The Horrells were chased by stern-faced New Mexican citizenry into Texas in 1874. Acquittals in their trial for the deaths of Captain Williams and others left the Horrells free to quarrel with their neighbors, notably including no-nonsense Pink Higgins who accused the clan of cattle rustling. Higgins emphasized his unhappiness by killing Merritt in the Gem Saloon at Lampasas on January 22, 1877. Still unsatisfied, Higgins ambushed Martin and Tom Horrell (1850-78) on March 26 on Battle Creek near Lampasas. A June 7 fracas in town led to the intervention of Texas Ranger John B. Jones, who negotiated a truce. Again finding themselves with clear calendars, Martin and Tom Horrell were free to seek other illicit opportunities, resulting in the death of storekeeper J. T. Vaughn. An impatient mob shot Mart and Tom to death on December 15, 1878, in Meridian, Texas, while the pair awaited trial. Sam Horrell, the sole surviving brother among this brood, died peacefully in California on August 8, 1936.

Selected Gunfights

Lampasas, Texas, March 19, 1873

The Horrells rode into town with Bill Bowen, where they learned local law enforcement officials intended to arrest them. Brothers Mart and Tom were wounded, and Mart was arrested with associate Jerry Scott and others, but later freed at gunpoint.

Lincoln, New Mexico, December 20, 1873

The Horrells retaliated for the death of brother Ben by opening fire on a wedding party, killing four.

Eagle Creek, Lincoln County, New Mexico, January 1874

County sheriff Alex Mills accompanied by five dozen locals demanded the surrender of the Horrells who refused and exchanged fire with the posse for hours.

Near Lampasas, Texas, March 26, 1877

Accompanied by his brother Tom, Mart proceeded into town for a court appearance. Instead, the two brothers were ambushed just outside town by the Higgins boys, who had accused the Horrells of cattle rustling.

Lampasas County, Texas, June 1877

Tom, along with some of his brothers and ranch hands, ambushed Higgins employees at a line camp, leaving them all dead or dying.

Lampasas, Texas, June 14, 1877

The Horrells and Higgins covered the town square with gunfire for about three hours, resulting in the death of two Higgins partisans,

including Frank Higgins. Finally the locals arranged a truce.
Lampasas County, Texas, July 1877
   Pink Higgins led fourteen men in an assault on the Horrell ranch, leaving after a two-day assault, only because ammunition ran low.
Lampasas County, Texas, July 25, 1877
   The Horrells killed Higgins gunmen Carson Graham, leaving their brand in the dust as a possible clue.

Sonnichsen, *I'll Die Before I Run,* 97-118; O'Neal, *Encyclopedia,* 155; Metz, *Encyclopedia,* 124.

Houston, Temple (1860-1905)

   The son of Sam Houston, the Texas patriot, Temple was born in the Governor's Mansion at Austin on August 12, 1860, and bore a striking resemblance to his father. The younger Houston worked as a Colorado cowboy and clerked both on a Mississippi steamboat and for the United States Senate. Educated at the predecessor to Texas A&M, Temple was admitted to the Texas bar at age twenty-one. He eventually became the district attorney of Oldham County, Texas, then served in the Texas legislature intermittently during a four-year period that began in 1884. Temple Houston gave the dedication speech at the opening of the new Texas state capitol on May 16, 1888.

   Temple moved to the small frontier town of Woodward, Oklahoma Territory, along the Cherokee Strip during the land run of September 16, 1893. There, he established a law practice and sent for his family. His flair for ostentatious dress and jury trial theatrics was legendary. Once, during the trial of a gunman, he shot a gun filled with blanks at the jury to emphasize a point, prompting a mistrial and the eventual freedom of his client following a second trial. Temple settled a legal conflict with real bullets in 1895 at Woodward, when he shot and killed Ed Jennings in a trial-related brawl at a local saloon, supposedly motivating the victim's younger brother to abandon the practice of law and become the inept and comedic train robber Al Jennings.

   Temple Houston became enormously popular and allowed his name to be placed on the list of candidates for Oklahoma's first governor. Poor health overtook him on August 15, 1905, in Woodward, where he died following a brain hemorrhage. His colorful life inspired the character Yancey Cravatt in the once-popular novel *Cimarron,* by Edna Ferber.

Shirley, *Temple Houston,* 8, 14-21, 151, 159, 167, 215-19, 306, 309.

Howard, Charles (d. 1877)

An enthusiastic Missouri entrepreneur, Howard laid claim to disputed salt lakes near El Paso, then mortally shotgunned Louis Cardis, a local organized labor advocate with whom he disagreed over the issue on October 10, 1877, in El Paso. Howard was captured by Texas Rangers who were forced to hand him over to impromptu execution by firing squad at San Elizario on December 12, 1877. Howard himself gave the order to fire.

Sonnichsen, *Pass of the North,* 172, 193-200, 203, 205-9; Metz, *Encyclopedia,* 76.

Hudgins, Bill (d. 1894)

Bill Hudgins was the Texas outlaw leader of a ten-man gang operating in the Chickasaw Nation, Indian Territory, during the 1890s. The gang consisted of Hudgins, a preacher's son named Alex Davis, William Poe, Thom Montgomery, Oscar Smith, Joe Cosh, Walter and Henry Howeth, and full-blood Chickasaw Albert Wolf. The gang conducted at least two store robberies and killed William Carey at Fred, a small community on the Little Washita River, before being captured by Deputy U.S. Marshal Seldon Lindsey in February 1891.

When arrested, mortally wounded Bill Hudgins revealed the location of a hideout twenty-two miles north of Tishomingo, Indian Territory. Investigating officers found stolen goods valued at $5,000, a live captive from Iowa, and the skeleton of an unfortunate whose ransom was evidentially unpaid.

McCullough, 65-72.

Ben and James Hughes (1860-1945, 1858-1949)

The Hughes brothers were born in Missouri but moved to Texas while very young and became train robbers. In Clay County, Texas, they robbed a Fort Worth and Denver train on December 1, 1886, and conducted another robbery on January 29, 1887. This Gorman, Texas, target was a Texas and Pacific train stopped for refueling. Yet another Fort Worth and Denver train was the next target at Benbrook, Texas, on June 3, 1887.

The Hughes were arrested about three months later, and by November had been convicted of train robbery, then sentenced to nearly one hundred years of hard labor. Incredibly, they won their freedom in a subsequent trial, supposedly due to an impassioned speech by James Hughes.

Joining their father in Indian Territory, now Oklahoma, the brothers supposedly shot James Nakedhead, a Cherokee Indian Police deputy, in a shoot-out near Checotah, Oklahoma. The brothers were found not guilty of train robbery soon after. They were subsequently tried in Fort Smith by Judge Isaac Parker, but were acquitted on technicalities relating to warrants, and returned to their ranch in Oklahoma. The brothers were acquitted once again for the lynching of Lute Houston, the brother of Ben's ex-wife, who had spied on the brothers as an undercover special deputy U.S. marshal. Jim served thirty-seven months of a four-year sentence handed down in 1923 for transporting a stolen car across state lines. Ben was caught shoplifting clothes and convicted of grand larceny in 1911. After serving five months of a four-year sentence, Ben moved to Harmon, Oklahoma, where he died at age eighty-four in 1945, and Jim Hughes died four years later at the age of ninety.

Butler, *Oklahoma Renegades,* 127-31, 161-65, 192-200.

Hughes, John Reynolds (Border Boss) (1855-1947)

John Reynolds Hughes was born on February 11, 1855, in Cambridge, Illinois. He moved to Indian Territory at age fourteen. A year later his right arm was badly injured while battling Indians. He then became proficient as a left-handed shooter. Hughes ranched for a time, but his efforts were thwarted by cattle rustlers, although he did kill three and arrest two others while attempting to recover a herd. Hughes then volunteered to assist Texas Ranger Ira Aten in the Texas Panhandle. Although the manhunt was successful, the fugitive died in a short gun battle. Hughes joined the Rangers in 1887 and

Company D, Texas Rangers, Frontier Battalion. Taken in 1894, the company of Rangers includes: standing, left to right: Deputy U.S. Marshal F. M. McMahon, William Schmidt, James V. Latham, Joe Sitter, Edward Palmer, T. T. Cook; seated, left to right: unidentified prisoner, George Tucker, J. W. Saunders, Sgt. Carl Kirchner, Capt. John R. Hughes. (Courtesy of the Nina Stewart Haley Memorial Library, Midland, Texas, Clayton Wheat Williams Collection)

quickly rose through the ranks. He pursued Texas outlaws until his retirement in 1915, when he became president of an Austin bank. Hughes committed suicide on June 3, 1947, at the age of ninety-two, perhaps motivated by ill health.

Selected Gunfights
Choctaw Nation, Indian Territory, 1870
    At age fifteen, while protecting his Indian trader boss, Art Rivers, during a clash with Choctaw Indians over a hog sale, Hughes was almost shot as the rifle bullet passed through his clothing. During the ensuing scuffle, Hughes suffered a permanent injury to his right arm, prompting him to become a "left-handed gun."
Northwestern Texas, April 15, 1887
    Accompanied by Sheriff Frank Swafford and a deputy, Hughes encountered rustlers who were suspected of ambushing Hughes.

Sgt. John R. Hughes of the Texas Rangers, seated far right, in 1890 photograph taken after he and others broke the Shafter Silver Mines embezzlement ring. The other lawmen are: standing, left to right: Bob Speaks and Lon Oden; seated: Jim Putnam (Putman). (Courtesy of the Nina Stewart Haley Memorial Library, Midland, Texas, J. Evetts Haley Collection)

Four rustlers, led by the Renald brothers, resisted Hughes and the lawmen, receiving fatal injuries as a consequence.

Texas Panhandle, July 1887

Accompanying Texas Ranger Ira Aten in the manhunt of escaped killer Judd Roberts, the two jumped the convicted murderer at a ranch where he had been courting the rancher's daughter. Roberts attempted to fight his way to freedom but was shot six times by his two pursuers. Roberts died in the arms of his paramour, or so the story goes.

Shafter, Texas, 1889

As a Texas Ranger, Corporal Hughes went under cover working at a Shafter silver mine to determine who was embezzling substantial quantities of the precious ore. Eventually he discovered that a crooked mine foreman was loading the ore on the backs of burros for transport across the Rio Grande into Mexico. Hughes set a trap near the mine entrance and an hour-long gunfight ensued. Hughes and fellow Ranger Lon Oden, along with informant Ernest "Diamond Dick" St. Leon, killed three outlaws. Hughes arrested the foreman the next day.

Near Vance, Texas, December 25, 1889

Hughes and fellow Texas Rangers Ira Aten and Bass Outlaw along with Deputy Sheriff Will Terry set an ambush for cattle rustlers Will and Alvin Odle in the early morning hours. When the rustlers crossed into Texas from Mexico near Vance, the lawmen ordered their surrender. Instead the Odles chose to fight it out, with fatal consequences. Will was shot from his horse and died instantly, while Alvin died within minutes of being shot.

San Antonio Colony, Texas, 1893

Rangers John Hughes, Lon Oden, and Jim Putnam had already arrested the outlaw Desidario Duran near the village of San Antonio Colony, a Mexican village on the Texas side of the Rio Grande, when they spotted three known fugitives riding through town. Hughes and Oden galloped after the pair, leaving Putnam with Duran. The short chase ended when Oden's horse was killed by Florencio Carrasco, just before Carrasco was shot from his horse and killed.

Bajitas, Texas, March 1896

After effecting the arrest of notorious bandit leader Miguel de la Torre, Hughes and three other Rangers came under fire from Torre's gang. The Rangers dismounted and returned fire from behind their horses, wounding three assailants in the process, while the rest escaped.

Nogalitos Pass, Texas, September 28, 1896
Horse thieves Ease Bixler and Art and Jubel Friar were one step ahead of the Rangers and a posse, but fatally chose to stop and make a stand. Rancher Jake Combs, who had lost horses to the rustlers, quickly killed Jubel with a head shot, prompting brother Art to shout a surrender offer and raise his hands. But as Hughes and Thalis Cook approached, Art produced a pistol and began firing, and then was silenced forever by the Rangers. Only Bixler escaped by mounting one of the stolen horses bareback and galloping into the hinterlands.

O'Neal, *Encyclopedia,* 160-63; Nash, 168; Tyler, *The New Handbook of Texas,* vol. 3, 773; Utley, *Lone Star Justice,* 266-67, 286; Martin, 1-19, 85-100, 102-12, 131-42.

Jackson, Charles W. (d. 1841)

Jackson was born in Kentucky and began his professional career as a steamboat captain on the Mississippi and Red Rivers. Eventually he owned a Shreveport, Louisiana, store, which he abandoned due to legal problems yet unclear. Relocated in Shelby County, he unsuccessfully ran for a seat in the Texas Congress. Jackson complained that his defeat was engineered by a fake-land-title cabal, which he bragged would be exposed to the General Land Office.

Still embittered, Jackson was accused of killing Joseph G. Goodbread, one of his enemies. When the 1840 trial date arrived, the crowd of Jackson supporters was so surly that Judge M. Hansford opened the proceedings by leaving an early morning note stating that he was "unwilling to risk my person in the courthouse any longer where I see myself surrounded by bravos and hired assassins . . ." excusing himself from further participation. Hansford had the right idea but was guilty of poor execution, as it were. Several days later he was found shot to death several miles outside Pulaski. The following year Jackson himself was bushwhacked and killed, prompting an expansion of hostilities between his Regulators and their opponents in the Regulator-Moderator War.

Rosa, 48-50; Tyler, *The New Handbook of Texas,* vol. 3, 894.

James, Alexander Franklin (Frank) (1843-1915)

Less notorious than his younger brother Jesse, Frank was born in Clay County, Missouri, on January 19, 1843. Frank also lived at various times in Oklahoma, Tennessee, Texas, and perhaps elsewhere. Frank participated in the Battle of Wilson's Creek near Springfield, Missouri, on August 10, 1861, as a Confederate regular. He was captured and paroled, then joined a band of guerillas led by William Quantrill which raided Lawrence, Kansas, on August 21, 1863, and staged another raid on October 6, 1863, near present-day Baxter Springs, Kansas, on the Indian Territory border. There, one hundred Union soldiers, including about ten unarmed band members and even a noncombatant newspaper correspondent, were killed.

His "banking and railroad" career, which began about 1866, involved commutes to Texas through Indian Territory. Frank married a young Kansas girl named Annie Ralston. After a series of successful raids, the James-Younger gang failed miserably in the September 7, 1876, bank raid at Northfield, Minnesota, their last robbery. After the James brothers escaped capture, Frank moved to Denison, Texas, in early June 1881. After Jesse was assassinated, Frank surrendered to Missouri governor Thomas J. Crittenden on October 4, 1882, and was acquitted of two charges. He owned a farm at Fletcher, Oklahoma, from 1909 to 1911, acquired while visiting his brother-in-law and fellow guerilla Allen Parmer in Wichita Falls, Texas. His honest occupations included shoe salesman in Dallas, horse race starter at county fairs, burlesque theater doorman, and a partnership in the James-Younger Wild West Show. Frank James died on the family farm in Missouri on February 18, 1915.

Selected Gunfights

Russellville, Kentucky, March 21, 1868

Frank James and seven others robbed a bank belonging to Nimrod Long of $12,000.

Gallatin, Missouri, December 7, 1869

Frank and Jesse James robbed the bank at Gallatin of several hundred dollars, killing proprietor John Sheets in the process.

Clay County, Missouri, December 15, 1869

The James-Samuel farm was home to Frank and Jesse and their

mother, Zerelda James Samuel. A four-man posse attempted to capture the brothers there, but the boys managed to escape, killing a horse belonging to Deputy Sheriff John Thomason.

Columbia, Kentucky, April 29, 1872

The robbery of the Deposit Bank netted about $600, but only after a teller, R. A. C. Martin, sounded an alarm and was killed by a single shot from one of the robbers.

Northfield, Minnesota, September 7, 1876

After years of successful raids, disaster struck the James-Younger gang while they were attempting to rob the First National Bank at Northfield. One bank employee who refused to open the bank's vault was shot to death. Another teller, A. E. Bunker, ran from the building sounding the alarm and was shot in the shoulder. A third citizen was killed as were robbers Clell Miller and William Stiles. A few days later Charlie Pitts was gunned down, and Cole, Jim, and Bob Younger were all wounded and apprehended. The James brothers escaped unharmed.

Smith, *Last Hurrah of the James-Younger Gang,* 10, 15-18, 22-23, 185, 212; O'Neal, *Encyclopedia,* 164-66; Nash, 182-83.

James, Jesse Woodson (Dingus) (1847-1882)

A frequent visitor to Texas, Jesse James became the most famous outlaw of the nineteenth century. Born on September 5, 1847, in Clay County, Missouri, he died on April 3, 1882, in St. Joseph, Missouri. At the age of seventeen, Jesse joined the infamous Confederate guerrilla band led by William "Bloody Bill" Anderson, a lieutenant of William Quantrill. After the Civil War, Jesse joined a bank and train robbing gang.

Jesse married Zee Mimms on April 23, 1874. Using many aliases, Jesse, his young bride, daughter, and son, lived in Missouri, Kentucky, and perhaps elsewhere. Scholars have no doubt that Jesse and perhaps his family visited the Sherman, Texas, area from time to time in the 1870s and afterwards since his younger sister taught school there and had married Sherman resident and former bushwhacker Allen Parmer and stayed in that area until her death in 1879. Jesse moved his family to St. Joseph, Missouri, in 1881. While there and in the midst of planning new robberies, Jesse was assassinated on

April 3, 1882, while straightening a wall picture in his own home. The assailant was Bob Ford, brother of James gang member Charlie Ford. Bob was at the James home, and the two were engaged in casual conversation when Jesse rose from his chair to straighten a picture on the wall. The Ford brothers had planned to collect the sizeable reward money on Jesse's head and an opportunity presented itself. Robert Ford shot Jesse in the back of the head, killing him instantly.

Selected Gunfights
Centralia, Missouri, September 27, 1864

Irregulars under the command of Bloody Bill Anderson, including Jesse James, participated in the Centralia raid. During that raid and in a skirmish following, more than 150 Union soldiers died. Union major A. V. E. Johnson led the charge against Anderson's men. Most scholars identify Jesse as Johnson's killer.

Russellville, Kentucky, March 21, 1868

Accompanied by Cole and Jim Younger and four others, Jesse and Frank James muffed this attempted robbery of the Southern Kentucky Bank. The bank president sounded the alarm and then proceeded to scuffle with Jesse in a back room. Nimrod Long received a glancing wound to his head from a shot fired by Jesse, but recovered in time to chase the bandits from the bank, dodging bullets the gang threw his way while racing out of town.

Gallatin, Missouri, December 7, 1869

While pretending to conduct a business transaction with bank owner John Sheets, one of the James boys pulled a pistol and shot the man to death. Teller William McDowell ran from the bank screaming and was shot once in the shoulder. Jesse and Frank were forced to flee on a single horse because one of the animals panicked when the shooting began. Jesse and his brother helped themselves to a large payroll despite the commotion. Some attribute the senseless and unprovoked killing of Sheets to the James animosity towards his service in the Union Army.

Kansas City, Missouri, September 26, 1872

The box office at the Kansas City State Fair was robbed by three men on horseback who took the contents of the money box. A ticket salesman wrestled with the robber, thought to be Jesse James, but the robber pulled a pistol and fired a single shot. The errant shot missed Wallace but struck a little girl in the leg. The robbers got away by charging into some nearby woods.

San Antonio, Texas, May 12, 1875

Jesse and Frank James, with the help of the Younger brothers, robbed a San Antonio stagecoach of $3,000.

Northfield, Minnesota, September 7, 1876

Eight members of the gang rode into town and followed a carefully planned robbery scheme. However, bank tellers Joseph L. Heywood and A. E. Bunker were uncooperative. Heywood was shot and killed, while Bunker was injured. Raiders Clell Miller and William Stiles were killed by the well-armed citizenry, while Cole, Jim, and Bob Younger were seriously injured. Town resident Nicholas Gustavson was gunned down by the gang in the street.

A posse killed gang member Charlie Pitts just a few days after the foiled robbery attempt. The Younger brothers were apprehended, while Jesse and Frank James made a clean escape.

Winston, Missouri, July 15, 1881

Jesse James and cohorts are widely believed to be responsible for this robbery of the Chicago, Rock Island and Pacific Railroad passenger train and its passengers. Conductor William Westfall chose to turn and run rather than surrender and was shot twice in the back and killed. The gunmen included a bearded man wearing a linen duster who was believed to be Jesse James. Passenger Frank McMillan was also shot and killed after other members of the gang began firing indiscriminately. The train was ordered to stop at a siding where two bandits entered the express car, pistol-whipped the messenger, and used his keys to unlock the safe. All the bandits then rode off into the darkness.

Smith, *Last Hurrah of the James-Younger Gang,* 10-223; O'Neal, *Encyclopedia,* 166-70; Metz, *The Shooters,* 54-55, 63; Nash, 173-74, 177, 182; Boswell, 41, 45, 138, 150.

Jennings, Napoleon Augustus (1856-1919)

Likely born in Philadelphia or New Hampshire, Jennings went to Texas at age eighteen. He worked at various occupations, including quartermaster's clerk for the U.S. Cavalry, before joining the

Texas Rangers in 1876. During the next two years, he participated in efforts to quell the Sutton-Taylor Feud under the leadership of L. H. McNelly and John B. Armstrong. He participated in a midnight Ranger attack against ten outlaws camping at Espantosa Lake near Carrizo, Texas, on October 1, 1876, and personally shot the only surviving outlaw in the jaw. Following his service with the Rangers, he took a variety of unrelated jobs farther west, then returned to the East, where he wrote for newspapers and magazines until his death.

Parsons and Little, 1, 28, 174, 220; Wilkins, *The Law Comes to Texas,* 115, 117-18; Nash, 191.

Jones, Frank (1856-93)

An Austin-born lawman, Jones assumed command of Company D of the Texas Rangers in 1886 after only about three years of prior service. Jones never would have been a candidate for ambassador to Mexico, given his habit of chasing outlaws across the Rio Grande without the usual legal niceties. Predictably enough, Jones died in action in Mexico.

Gunfights

Crockett County, Texas, October 1891

While chasing a gang of train and cattle thieves alongside a posse, the outlaws were encountered near Howard's well. Three of the four gave up, but the fourth led the posse on a tumultuous eight-mile chase, which ended when the discouraged and exhausted outlaw dismounted then shot himself.

Tres Jacales (Three Shacks), Mexico, June 30, 1893

Father-son cattle-thief team Jesus Maria and Severio Olguin led Jones, F. F. Tucker, Deputy Sheriff R. E. Byrant, J. W. Sanders, Ranger corporal Karl Kirchner, and Ed Aten across the Rio Grande into Tres Jacales, where a running gunfight began. The Olguins were wounded, but still game they fled three hundred yards to a house where the bandits found reinforcements among local citizenry. Jones was shot to pieces, then muttered, "Boys, I am killed," prompting the rest to gallop back across the border. Jones's body was retrieved and buried in Ysleta, Texas.

Webb, *Texas Rangers,* 438-44; O'Neal, *Encyclopedia,* 172; Metz, *Encyclopedia,* 135

Jones, John B. (1834-81)

John B. Jones was born in South Carolina on December 22, 1834. When he was four years of age, Jones's family moved to Travis County, Texas. Jones later attended Mount Zion College in Winnsboro, South Carolina. He served in the Confederate Army during the Civil War and in 1868 was elected to the Texas legislature. After his political stint, Jones joined the ranks of the Texas Rangers and was commissioned a major. He led the Frontier Battalion and quickly established a reputation as an effective combatant against outlaws and marauding Indians, often accompanying his men on daring raids and engagements. Jones reputedly restored order to Kimble County in April 1877 by simply arresting those individuals who could not give a good account of themselves. He was present during the questioning of captured and mortally wounded Sam Bass at Round Rock, Texas, thereby inspiring the later Ranger service of Ira Aten. Jones is credited with bringing the horrendous Horrell-Higgins Feud to its end. He died in Austin, Texas, on June 19, 1881.

Parsons, 42, 69-70; Webb, *Texas Rangers,* 312, 316, 325-39, 374-91; Metz, *Encyclopedia,* 242; Nash, 194.

Jones Brothers (d. 1900)

Originally from Dallas County, Missouri, brothers Jim and John Jones had humble beginnings as farmers. Sometime in 1892 they abandoned farming for outlawry. They left Missouri and wandered into Texas, where they were accused of killing the sheriff of Hamilton County. They then took their trade to Colorado, where they pestered local citizens by continually holding up stagecoaches and robbing banks. On August 11, 1900, the Jones boys robbed a Union Pacific train near Hugo, Colorado, where the take was small but the attention the act received was not. A large contingent of possemen stayed on track for several hundred miles, finally catching up to the two Jones boys at a small ranch house. The ensuing gun battle raged on for hours until the frustrated lawmen chose to burn the house down. Jim Jones shot himself in the head rather than be roasted alive or captured. Brother John dashed out the front door with a pistol in each hand, firing indiscriminately until a hail of bullets put an end to his foolishness.

Selected Gunfights
Colorado, August 11, 1900

At a small ranch house, brothers Jim and John Jones held off a large posse for hours in an exchange of gunfire before lawmen set fire to the house in which they had barricaded themselves. Jim Jones committed suicide inside the house. John Jones ran out through the front door and began firing at lawmen who shot him down.

Nash, 195.

Jones, William Daniel (Dub, Deacon) (1916-74)

Jones was a childhood friend of the Barrow boys whose family lived at the same West Dallas campgrounds where the Barrow family landed in 1922 after giving up farming. Neither family lived under a viaduct as some sources reported. Jones, usually called W. D., was born on May 12, 1916, and joined the Barrow gang at age sixteen, just in time for the cold-blooded Christmas murder of Doyle Johnson in Temple, Texas. Johnson had attempted to stop the theft of his automobile, which the gang casually dumped about a block away after the killing.

Jones was involved in at least three other Barrow gang killings and three kidnappings, then resigned to pursue other interests and spend more time with his family. Instead, he was arrested on a farm near Houston on November 18, 1933, then spent fifteen years in a Texas prison before his release. Later, he capitalized on the film *Bonnie and Clyde* by telling his version of Barrow gang adventures to a Houston reporter. The interview eventually appeared in *Playboy* magazine, giving Jones national exposure.

However, his outlaw past backfired on the widowed "Deacon" on August 20, 1974. That evening in Houston, Jones charmed a young lady he met in a bar. Later, she had Jones take her to the home of her ex-boyfriend, George Arthur Jones (no relation), whom she engaged in a shouting match at 10616 Woody Lane. Young George was apparently

William "Deacon" (W. D.) Jones in the Dallas County Jail. Jones was a cohort of Bonnie and Clyde. (Courtesy of the Dallas Public Library, Dallas, Texas)

not impressed by her empty boasts about her supposedly armed and dangerous Barrow gang connection, since he promptly shotgunned the unsuspecting and unarmed Barrow gang retiree. The Deacon was dead at age fifty-eight. Young George was convicted, appealed, and was awarded a new trial. Later, he killed himself with the same shotgun upon learning that he was about to be arrested on other charges.

Selected Robberies and Gunfights
West Dallas, January 6, 1933
Bonnie, Clyde, and W. D. Jones escaped a police trap at the home of Ray Hamilton's sister, Lillie McBride, but killed Deputy Sheriff Malcom "Lon" Davis as they escaped.
Joplin, Missouri, April 13, 1933
Jones and the two Barrow couples rented a garage apartment in Joplin for a short vacation. Instead, they were confronted by law officers, then killed Constable J. W. Harryman and policeman Harry McGinnis before escaping.
Alma, Arkansas, June 23, 1933
Clyde Barrow and W. D. Jones fatally wounded Alma town marshal Henry D. Humphrey north of Alma as Humphrey attempted to investigate a car wreck the pair had caused after robbing a Fayetteville grocery store.
Platte City, Missouri, July 18, 1933
Jones and the Barrows shot their way out of the Red Crown Tourist Court, where the authorities had surrounded them. They escaped, but Buck was mortally wounded.
Dexfield Park, Iowa, July 24, 1933
Surrounded by "the laws" again, Bonnie, Clyde, and Jones managed to escape, leaving Buck and Blanche Barrow to face the music. Blanche had suffered a permanent eye injury, and Buck died five days later in Perry, Iowa.

Helmer and Mattix, 179; Knight, 15, 200-203.

Kelly, Kathryn (Cleo Mae Brooks) (1904-85)
Kathryn Kelly was the wife, creative business partner, and self-appointed publicist for the gun-shy yet fearfully named George "Machine Gun" Kelly. She was born Cleo Mae Brooks in 1904, near Tupelo, Mississippi, to James Emory Brooks and Ora (Coleman) Brooks. Her mother divorced James Brooks and is said to have married Paradise, Texas, area resident and supposed small-time politico

Robert "Boss" Shannon in 1927. Kathryn moved to Oklahoma with her mother and stepfather, then married twice before becoming the wife of Texas bootlegger Charlie Thorne, whose later suicide in Coleman County was somewhat suspect.

Widow Thorne recovered nicely with an improved wardrobe and new appreciation of jazz learned in Fort Worth speakeasies. Her ship came in, as it were, one evening when her bootlegger boyfriend introduced her to a new business partner named George Barnes, formerly of Tulsa, Oklahoma, with whom she immediately started an affair. Soon a Methodist preacher recited the perfunctory nuptials in Minneapolis, leading to a new lifestyle based on a series of small-town bank robberies. Now calling herself Kathryn, Mrs. Barnes dreamed of bigger roadsters, more expensive clothing, and larger jewels, prompting a reinvention of her compliant, yet willing husband and partner.

She supposedly noted the distinct lack of government success in promptly solving the Lindbergh kidnapping. Soon Kathryn goaded George into the ill-fated 1932 kidnapping of Howard Woolverton of South Bend, Indiana, who lived large but was cash poor, due to Depression-era reversals. The hapless Woolverton was finally released with a stern warning after executing a $50,000 promissory note.

Chagrined but undeterred, Kathryn reached into the hat for another rabbit. First, she equipped George with a second-hand Thompson machine gun purchased at a pawnshop. Then she nagged him into constant target practice in the Texas countryside even though he apparently had little interest in weapons. Nevertheless, the Federal Bureau of Investigation tagged poor George "Machine Gun" Kelly, perhaps as a means of assuring that the public would appreciate their crime-fighting ways. One thing is certain: he never used the Thompson in anger.

Kathryn soon found a new kidnap target, Oklahoma City oil magnate Charles Urschel, business partner of wonder boy and Oklahoma wildcatter Tom Slick, whose widow Urschel had married. Extracted from his own front porch one evening, Urschel found himself blindfolded and in transit to the hardscrabble Shannon farm near Paradise, Texas. There he was detained in distinctly less-than-luxurious quarters only slightly better than a chicken coop.

Unbeknown to the kidnappers, Urschel had a highly developed

The Shannons feel the heat as federal lawmen grill them about the kidnapping of Oklahoma City millionaire oilman Charles F. Urschel. From left are: Robert G. "Boss" Shannon, his wife, Ora, his son Armon, and his son's wife, Oleta. (Courtesy of the Dallas Public Library, Dallas, Texas)

sense of observation and a photographic memory. Once his ransom was paid, the victim was dumped in Norman, Oklahoma, taxied home, then provided the FBI with sufficient detail to accompany law enforcement on a raid on the kidnapping lair. Although Kathryn and George Barnes were elsewhere, legendary thief Harvey Bailey was hiding at the Shannon place and soon found himself in silver bracelets.

When the Barneses were finally located, Kathryn pled ignorance, even though a substantial portion of the ransom money was found in the possession of her grandfather, T. M. Coleman of Stratford, Oklahoma. George died at the Federal Penitentiary at Leavenworth in 1954, while Kathryn was eventually released from prison and worked as a bookkeeper at the Oklahoma County Poor Farm, then essentially a hospital and nursing home. Following her 1974 retirement, she reportedly died in Tulsa about 1985, probably with all of her early dreams of fast cars, expensive clothing, and sparkling jewelry long forgotten.

Kemp, David (1862-1935)

David Kemp was sentenced to the gallows at a very young age for killing Doll Smith in Hamilton County, Texas, where he was born on March 1, 1862. He chose to fly rather than swing, jumping from the second story of the courthouse with two guards present. He managed to mount a nearby horse in spite of two broken ankles before concerned citizens surrounded and captured him. He made one more escape attempt, this at Huntsville Prison, before receiving a conditional pardon endorsed by Superintendent Thomas J. Goree, who had served as an aide to Lt. Gen. James Longstreet at the battle of Gettysburg.

Kemp left Texas and established a butcher shop at Eddy, New Mexico, now known as Carlsbad. He also bought an interest in a Phenix (*sic*), New Mexico, casino and received a full pardon for his Texas crime before defeating the older brother of Cochise County, Arizona, sheriff John H. Slaughter in a contest for sheriff of Eddy County. Kemp was known to work both sides of the badge, receiving his sheriff's pay while engaging in the gambling business, and, according to some, also cattle rustling. Eventually he left New Mexico for Globe, Arizona, but returned to Carlsbad and killed Les Dow, who had replaced Kemp as sheriff. Kemp was acquitted when the only witness to the shooting elected to move away. Kemp eventually returned to Texas and died of a heart attack on January 4, 1935, at his ranch near Booker, Texas, contrary to rumors that he had been killed by his sister.

Selected Gunfights

Hamilton, Texas, 1877

Kemp intervened in a fight between Doll Smith and his friend Dan Bogan and shot Smith to death. The sheriff ran to the scene, and Kemp attempted to shoot him too, but his weapon repeatedly misfired. Tom Mose seized Kemp for the sheriff.

Carlsbad, New Mexico, February 18, 1897

Kemp and a cohort named Will Kennon skulked around the post

office in which Sheriff Les Dow had entered. Dow and Kemp were longtime enemies. When Dow exited the post office with his nose buried in a letter he had received, Kemp thrust his pistol into the man's face and fired once. Dow died the next day. Kemp was later acquitted on grounds of self-defense.

Harkey, 39-45, 63-65, 74-75; O'Neal, *Encyclopedia,* 174-75; Nash, 197-98; DeArment, *Deadly Dozen,* 169-93.

Ketchum, Samuel W. (Black Jack) (1854-99)

One of two train robbing brothers who each lost an arm in their disasterous careers, Ketchum was born in Caldwell County, Texas, on January 4, 1854. In Western lore he shares the "Black Jack" nickname with his younger brother, Tom, as well as with William T. Christian. Sam was clearly a criminal by the mid-1890s, and during that time he formed a gang with his brother which may have occasionally included some members of the Wild Bunch. Like the Wild Bunch, Sam and his brother were known for robbing trains.

After robbing a Colorado and Southern train on Tuesday, July 11, 1899, near the same Twin Mountains location where Tom had robbed another train two years earlier, the Ketchum gang was pursued by a posse to Turkey Creek Canyon, in Colfax County, New Mexico. There, the gang killed Sheriff Edward J. Farr, lawman Henry Love, and Tom Smith. Sam Ketchum and Ellsworth Lay were injured, but the gang escaped to Ute Park. Sam's arm was amputated when it became infected with gangrene. He was captured soon after, and died on July 24, 1899, of blood poisoning in a Santa Fe prison.

Alexander, *Desert Desperadoes,* 245-46, 248, 251-52; Metz, *Encyclopedia,* 139; O'Neal, *Encyclopedia,* 176.

Ketchum, Thomas Edward (Black Jack) (1863-1901)

Ketchum was born in Saba County, Texas, on Richland Creek, on October 31, 1863, and now shares the "Black Jack" nickname with his older brother, Sam, and with William "Black Jack" Christian. Tom was known for his height and strong build, and spent his early years working as a cowboy in New Mexico and West Texas. His first known murder was on Thursday, December 12, 1895, when he killed John N. "Jap" Powers in Knickerbocker, Texas, with the assistance of Powers's wife. Ketchum fled to New Mexico, and Mrs. Powers was arrested. Tom joined his brother Sam and perhaps members of the Wild Bunch in train and coach robbery.

The Ketchum gang was strongly associated with the Wild Bunch, and members moved between them regularly, which caused some confusion among lawmen. The Ketchums purportedly robbed a train in Terrell County, Texas, on May 4, 1896. Later that year, while robbing the Texas Flyer the gang tried to open a strongbox with dynamite, relying on slaughtered beef carcasses to control and deflect the explosion. This attempt failed, reducing the box, and most of the money inside, to confetti. Gang member Ed Cullen was killed near the New Mexico-Arizona border in a December 1896 robbery by expectant Wells Fargo agents. Tom lost his brother Sam as a result of a July 11, 1899, train robbery.

Tom Ketchum's final train robbery occurred on August 16, 1899, near Folsom, Arizona, a crime which he attempted without any backup. His foolhardiness was rewarded with a shotgun blast to the right arm from a train conductor who saw Ketchum wound a mail clerk. For some reason, possibly because the wound was considered mortal, Tom Ketchum was merely thrown off the train. He had to flag down another train the next morning, and doctors eventually amputated his arm. He was found guilty of attempted train robbery, a capital offense in New Mexico at that time, and hanged on April 26, 1901, but not without complications. The executioners failed to consider the weight Tom had gained during his prison stay. Consequently, Tom was decapitated by the rope.

As the only man ever hanged for train robbery in the United States, he wrote these dubious words of advice for those who were to follow him: "My advice to the boys of the country is not to steal either horses or sheep, but to either rob a train or a bank when you have got to be an outlaw, and every man who comes your way, kill him; spare him no mercy, for he will show you none. This is the way I feel, and I think I feel right about it."

Selected Robberies and Gunfights
Near Folsom, Arizona, September 1898

Tom Ketchum, Sam Ketchum, and G. W. (George) Franks robbed a Colorado and Southern train. Some sources identify Franks as Will Carver. On July 11, 1899, the gang robbed the same train again.

Turkey Creek Canyon, July 12, 1899

Lawmen Edward Farr, W. H. Love, and Tom Smith were killed in an all-day gun battle with the Ketchums, Elzy Lay, and G. W. Franks. Sam Ketchum was mortally wounded and died after amputation of his arm.

Alexander, *Desert Desperadoes,* 245-48, 251-52; Metz, *Encyclopedia,* 139; O'Neal, *Encyclopedia,* 175-76.

Kilpatrick, Benjamin (the Tall Texan; Benjamin Arnold) (1876-1912)

Born into a large Texas family, Ben worked as a cowboy before joining Butch Cassidy, the Sundance Kid, and the Wild Bunch in the late 1890s. Ben was nicknamed the Tall Texan, but sometimes used the alias Benjamin Arnold. After serving a prison sentence for his role with the Wild Bunch during the Great Northern train robbery at Wagner, Montana, in 1901, Kilpatrick wasted no time in resuming his old ways about one year after being paroled in 1911.

Just prior to midnight on March 12, 1912, two masked men climbed onto the blind baggage car of the westbound Southern Pacific Sunset Flyer as it stopped for water at Dryden, Texas. When the train resumed moving toward Sanderson, the pair climbed across the coal tender and confronted the engine crew, forcing them to proceed to the express car. There, the engineer was forced to order young messenger David Trousdale to open the locked door. Once inside, Beck escorted the engine crew back to their stations while Kilpatrick began pilfering the car. Kilpatrick unwisely turned his back on Trousdale and bent to examine a package. Trousdale immediately seized the opportunity and struck Kilpatrick in the head with an ice mallet, crushing his skull. The Tall Texan soon died. Beck returned to the express car undoubtedly expecting a large payday. Instead, Trousdale killed the conveniently back-lit bandit with the very rifle Kilpatrick had dropped.

Pointer, 101, 181-82, 255-56; O'Neal, *Encyclopedia,* 190, 251; Nash, 200-202.

Kinney, John (ca. 1847-1919)

Probably born in Massachusetts in about 1847, Kinney enlisted in the Third U.S. Cavalry at Chicago on April 13, 1867. Much of his military time was spent fighting Apache Indians around Fort Seldon, near Mesilla, New Mexico. In 1873, Kinney was discharged while stationed at Fort McPherson in Nebraska. After serving the country, Kinney then began serving himself by amassing a cattle empire built solely on the unlawful acquisition of other people's cattle. The business was sustained by rustling in the Mesilla, Rincon, and Rio Grande areas. He and hired gunmen Jesse Evans opened and operated a butcher shop in Mesilla, using cattle Kinney had rustled.

On January 1, 1876, after Kinney returned to New Mexico, he found himself in a saloon brawl with soldiers. Kinney received a sound thrashing, prompting him to gather like-minded hooligans and shoot up the saloon, killing two of the six soldiers. In Dona Ana County, in 1877, Kinney was twice indicted by a grand jury: once for larceny, and then in November for the murder of Sheriff Ysabel Barela. Eventually, Kinney was acquitted of the second charge. Kinney had already moved by that time to El Paso with a bunch of hard cases he dubbed simply "The Boys." Soon he became enmeshed in the Salt War.

Following the conclusion of hostilities, Kinney opened a saloon in El Paso. This watering hole quickly became the resting place for thugs and thieves, prompting one area newspaper to write that Kinney's Exchange Saloon was "a hangout for the most parasitical." After his acquittal of the Barela murder charge, Kinney and The Boys traveled to Lincoln County for service as the "Rio Grande Posse" in the Lincoln County War. Kinney joined the Dolan-Murphy faction and was implicated in the torching of Andrew McSween's home during a five-day gun battle.

Kinney later returned to Rincon and to his cattle rustling business. When the governor ordered Col. Albert Jennings Fountain to investigate, Kinney felt the heat and tried to smuggle himself into Mexico by train from Lordsburg. He didn't make it as he was arrested before the train left the station. On March 5, 1883, he stood trial at Las Cruces for his illegal cattle operations. A jury took a scant eight minutes to reach a guilty verdict. Kinney was fined $500 and sentenced to five years in prison. He won an appeal in 1886, and moved to Prescott, Arizona, where he later contracted Bright's disease and died on August 25, 1919. A newspaper obituary heralded Kinney as "one of the most daring and courageous . . . of men who were sacrificing and unflinching to preserve law and order."

Nolan, 54, 62-65, 67, 146-48, 150-52, 155, 162, 164, 167, 200, 267, 315; Thrapp, *Encyclopedia,* II, 85-86; Metz, *Encyclopedia,* 143.

Kirchner, Karl (Carl) (prom. 1893)

Kirchner was among a force of Texas Rangers led by Capt. Frank Jones who was charged with arresting members of the Mexican outlaw family of Clato Olguin. The Olguins and a large number of other Mexican outlaws found refuge on an island that lay between Mexico and Texas created by a shifting Rio Grande River. As the Rangers and Deputy Sheriff R. E. Bryant approached the adobe home, Jones was shot and killed. The rest of his party never fired a shot but instead ran to the side of their fallen leader.

Selected Gunfights
Pirate Island, No Man's Land, Rio Grande River, June 30, 1893
A corporal in the Texas Rangers, Kirchner accompanied a small band of Rangers and a deputy sheriff to an area that was considered neither in Mexican territory nor in Texas, known as Pirate Island. As many as three hundred outlaw families made their homes there. Kirchner and the others were on the hunt for Jesus Maria Olguin and his son Severio when they and others opened fire on the Rangers, killing Capt. Frank Jones.

Utley, *Lone Star Justice,* 265-66; Metz, *Encyclopedia,* 143; Thrapp, *Encyclopedia,* II, 788; Wilkins, *The Law Comes to Texas,* 310-11; Nash, 245, 337.

Labreu, Jason (prom. 1880s)

Jason Labreu was already wanted in Texas and New Orleans on separate counts of murder when he brutally raped and murdered by drowning Leona Devere, an Arkansas farmer's daughter he had been courting. Labreu wandered into the Chickasaw Nation and went to work on the Jack Crow ranch where he was eventually arrested for the Arkansas murder due to the undercover work of Deputy Marshal H. D. Fannin. On the return trip to Arkansas, Labreu almost made good an escape attempt but the coolheaded Deputy Marshal Fannin put a stop to it with one well-placed rifle slug to the fleeing man's back. This proved nearly as troublesome for Fannin as it had for the escaping Labreu. In those days it was the responsibility of lawmen to pay for the funeral of their prisoners who died in captivity if no family appeared to claim the body. Fannin was charged sixty dollars for the funeral expenses and had to forfeit mileage fees and expenses as well.

Selected Gunfights
Near Fort Smith, Arkansas, 1880s

Deputy Marshal Fannin, with Labreu in tow, dismounted his horse while waiting for a train to pass by. Labreu, still seated on his mount, kicked the marshal's horse in such a way that its bucking caused the lead rope to snap, and Labreu galloped away. His freedom was short-lived, however, as Fannin put a slug in the middle of Labreu's back, killing him instantly.

Nash, 204.

Lake, Frank (1854-1919)

Texas associate and friend of Frank Canton, Frank Lake was born in Tennessee, the son of a Confederate prisoner confined with Canton's father at Alton, Illinois. After a boyhood in Texas, Lake homesteaded Canton's original Wyoming ranch, which he sold to Canton on December 1, 1887. Lake removed to Arkansas in 1889, moved again to Vernon, Texas, in 1890 to enter the livery business, then moved to Oklahoma Territory in 1893, ultimately homesteading near Pawnee.

Later, while Pawnee County sheriff and afterwards, he served as a deputy U.S. marshal with Frank Canton, with whom he had an ambivalent relationship dating back to their early days together in Texas. Deputy U.S. Marshal Charles Colcord once related that he found the inebriated pair in a Pawnee general store, in front of a potbellied stove, barely in time to keep an infuriated Canton from setting Lake's beard on fire. In August 1895, Lake arrested Jennie Stevens, better known as "Little Britches," for bootlegging. Jennie promptly escaped from a restaurant in Pawnee, but was soon recaptured. After years in law enforcement, Lake entered the real estate business in Sequoyah County, Oklahoma, and died at Siloam Springs, Arkansas, in 1919.

Selected Gunfights
Osage Hills, Indian Territory, June 1894
Sheriff Lake, U.S. Marshal E. D. Nix, and Deputy U.S. Marshals Canton and J. S. Burke tracked accused cattle rustler Ben Cravens to a cabin in the Osage Hills, where at daybreak Canton knocked the door open and drew down on Cravens, who simply dropped his own weapon and submitted to arrest. Later that month, Lake and Canton arranged for the Dunn brothers, fringe supporters of the Doolin gang, to betray the outlaws and provide information leading to their arrest.
Pawnee County, Oklahoma Territory, Fall 1896
After the Dunns killed two members of the Doolin gang, Canton and Lake suspected the brothers of returning to cattle theft. Even though the Dunns were serving as possemen for Heck Thomas, Lake and Canton tracked them for the purpose of making an arrest, but were unsuccessful, saving law enforcement from a bloody fraternal encounter.

DeArment, *Alias Frank Canton,* 30, 90, 150, 168, 173, 184, 186, 198, 296; Shirley, *West of Hell's Fringe,* 177; *Osage County News,* December 5, 1919.

Larn, John M. (1849-78)
Born in Mobile, Alabama, in 1849, Larn ran away while in his early teens and settled in Colorado, where he worked for a time as a ranch hand until he killed his boss in an argument over a horse. Larn fled to New Mexico, where he shot and killed a sheriff he believed to be tailing him. He then landed at Fort Griffin, Texas, and took a job as trail boss for Bill Hayes. Larn eventually married Hayes's daughter, and in 1876 was elected sheriff of Shackelford County.
During this period, Larn did his most proficient cattle rustling.

His schemes exposed, he was forced to resign on March 7, 1877, less than one year after taking office. Arrested for the ambush of a neighboring rancher named Treadwell, Larn was in jail the night of June 23, 1878, when a vigilante group Larn once led came to lynch the former lawman but found him shackled to the jail floor. They hastily formed a firing squad and executed him where he stood. His widow later married, then divorced, a preacher. She reflected years later that her experience had been that the cow thief had been the better man.

Selected Gunfights
Colorado, before 1871

Larn claimed that he shot and killed the owner of a ranch some eighty miles north of Trinidad. Larn had worked for the rancher, he claimed, but had not been paid. When Larn left with one of the rancher's best horses, and the rancher tried to stop him, Larn shot the man out of the saddle, or so he claimed.

New Mexico, before 1871

Larn claimed that while on the run after the Colorado shooting, he shot and killed a sheriff that he believed was tracking him.

Near the Pecos River, Texas, 1871

Larn and others shot two Mexican nationals to death, apparently for no reason other than racial animus or robbery. Larn and others claimed they dumped the bodies into the Pecos River "to feed the catfish," one source said.

Near Fort Griffin, Texas, June 1878

Larn ambushed one Treadwell, a local rancher whom he suspected of exposing Larn's rustling operations at the time he was sheriff. Larn fired too quickly, downing Treadwell's horse. Treadwell escaped the ambush on foot.

DeArment, *Bravo of the Brazos,* 7, 9-10, 26, 40, 43-45, 50, 57, 118, 120; O'Neal, *Encyclopedia,* 176-77: Nash, 205; Metz, *John Selman,* 52-89; Metz, *Encyclopedia,* 146; Interview with Candy Moulton, *Wild West Magazine,* August 2003.

Lee, Oliver Milton (1866-1941)

Born and reared in Buffalo Gap, Texas, at age eighteen, Lee and his half-brother, Perry Altman, traveled west to Tularosa Valley, New Mexico, where they homesteaded with their widowed mother. Lee was charged with the shooting death of neighboring rancher John Good's son, Walter. After serving time for the shooting, Lee improved his ranch, served as deputy sheriff, then deputy U.S. marshal. In the late 1890s Lee was implicated in two other murders. A trial at Hillsboro, Texas, won Lee's acquittal. He returned to ranching, selling out to a business consortium in 1914. Lee was twice elected to the Texas State Legislature. He died in 1941 of a stroke.

Selected Gunfights
White Sands Desert, New Mexico, mid-August 1888
　　Lee, accompanied by three accomplices, jumped Walter Good and shot him to death in retaliation for the death of Lee's closest friend, George McDonald.
Near Las Cruces, New Mexico, August 1888
　　John Good and fifteen relatives discovered the decomposed body of his son in the desert. Good and five others rode off toward Las Cruces when they saw Lee and his cohorts. After more than a hundred rounds were fired in the ensuing gun battle, not one man was wounded or killed. However two horses did die, and one was wounded.
Near El Paso, Texas, February 12, 1893
　　Trailing a herd of stolen cattle, Lee and Bill McNew caught up to the herd and its unauthorized drovers, Charley Rhodius and Matt Coffelt, near El Paso, Texas. After a brief firefight, both Rhodius and Coffelt lay dead. Lee traveled on to El Paso where he surrendered and won easy acquittal.
Dona Ana County, New Mexico, July 13, 1898
　　Oliver Lee and James Gilliland were believed to have murdered A. J. Fountain and his eight-year-old son. Pursued by a posse led by Pat Garrett, the suspects hid at Lee's Wildy Wells about thirty-two miles south of Alamogordo. Unable to roust the outlaws, the posse itself suffered injury and humiliation. Two lawmen were drenched when they took cover under a water tank that Lee and Gilliland then riddled with bullets. One posseman, Jose Espalin, had his boots filled with sand burrs after removing them for a quiet approach. Pat Garrett received a flesh wound to the rib cage. Only posseman Clint

Llewellyn was seriously injured, suffering a mortal gunshot wound. The chagrined posse was allowed to ride off to safety.
Dog Canyon, New Mexico, March 20, 1907
A battle for water rights led to a long-distance rifle battle when Lee discovered two men attempting to fence off the disputed area on his land at Dog Canyon Ranch. James R. Fennimore, one of the three men, took a slight wound to the hip from Lee's rifle.

O'Neal, *Encyclopedia,* 178-79; Nash, 208.

Lee, Robert E. (Bob) (d. 1869)
A prominent Grayson County, Texas, rancher and cattleman, Lee led a group opposing the Lewis Peacock faction and the Reconstruction-era Union League. His family had moved to Texas in about 1859, settling on the Hunt County-Fannin County line in North Texas. Lee was arrested by Reconstruction authorities and local hangers-on in about 1867 for reasons that are still unclear, but was offered his freedom in exchange for twenty dollars and the mule he was riding on. After Lee was shot and left for dead by another Unionist, he formed his own faction and initiated a feud that continued for about four years. Lee was ambushed near his home on Monday, June 25, 1869, prompting the killing of Lewis Peacock by Bob Lee associates Dick Johnson and Joe Parker at Pilot Grove, Texas. Peacock was murdered on June 13, 1871, as he went outside his home to gather firewood.

Selected Gunfights
Pilot Grove, Texas, April 1868
Lewis Peacock was wounded in a skirmish between his own faction and the forces led by Bob Lee following a series of ambushes and deaths.
Hunt County, Texas, June 15, 1868
Lee and his faction ambushed a Peacock crew near the Nance farm, reportedly killing three feudists.
Near Farmersville, Texas, December 1868
Peacock was ambushed again, this time in the company of Union soldiers, one of whom was killed.

Sonnichsen, *I'll Die Before I Run,* 9-18; O'Neal, *Encyclopedia,* 253-54; Metz, *Encyclopedia,* 151; Nash, 208.

Leroy, Kitty (1850-78)

Born in Texas, Kitty began a stage career by age ten and within ten years was the hottest ticket in Dallas. Leroy gave up her successful stage career, opting to become one of the best faro dealers and gamblers in the West. Expert marksmanship enabled her to abruptly end disputes with an accurately fired near miss. Kitty moved to Deadwood in the Dakota Territory with her fourth husband, opening the Mint Gambling Saloon. Kitty Leroy was murdered in 1878, by this husband, who then committed suicide, distraught when he learned of her earlier armorous adventures.

Metz, *Encyclopedia,* 153; Nash, 209; Thrapp, *Encyclopedia,* II, 848.

Leslie, Nashville Franklin (Buckskin Frank) (1842-ca. 1925)

A dashing gunman and ladies' man, Leslie worked in Texas, the Dakotas, and Indian Territory before engaging in a series of gunfights. Leslie was an Indian scout in Texas, Oklahoma, and the Dakotas in the 1870s He settled in Tombstone, Arizona, where he opened the Cosmopolitan Hotel and began seeing a married woman. On June 22, 1880, when the outraged husband showed up to protest, Leslie shot and killed him. Leslie and May Killeen, the bereft widow, were married one week later. Leslie rode with the Army during Apache unrest and worked for a time as a border customs agent along the Rio Grande River.

May divorced him after seven years, saying she grew weary of being used for his target practice, in which he would have May stand against a wall and then would trace her outline with bullets. On July 10, 1889, a drunken Leslie killed his love interest, Mollie Williams. After leaving prison, he went to Mexico and then the Alaskan gold fields. Leslie managed a pool hall in Oakland, California, then took the owner's pistol and simply disappeared in 1925.

Selected Gunfights
Tombstone, Arizona, November 14, 1882

Outside the Oriental Saloon, Leslie called out "Billy the Kid" Claiborne who had previously cursed Leslie. Claiborne was hidden behind a fruit stand in ambush but was taken by surprise when Leslie emerged through a side door. Claiborne turned and fired a wild shot. Leslie fired once, hitting Claiborne with a fatal shot to his left side that exited out his back.

Tombstone, Arizona, July 10, 1889

Leslie worked on Mike Joyce's ranch where he lived with Blonde Mollie Williams, an employee of the Bird Cage. Returning drunk from Tombstone, Leslie quarreled with Williams, then shot her to death. Young ranch hand Jim Neal witnessed the killing, was shot running away from Leslie, and then made his way to a neighboring ranch. Leslie thought Neal had died in the thick brush and returned to Tombstone to recite his usual self-defense plea. Neal's testimony sent Leslie to prison. Nearly thirty-five years later Neal offered Leslie a job running the pool hall from which Leslie disappeared.

O'Neal, *Encyclopedia,* 180-82; Metz, *Encyclopedia,* 153; Nash, 209-10.

Lindsey, Seldon Trullery (1854-1939)

A native of Minden, Louisiana, born on December 19, 1854, Lindsey moved to McLennan County, Texas, with his family in about 1870 and became a cowboy. Seldon was punching cows on the trail to Kansas at age sixteen. He once related that while buffalo hunting, he met Buffalo Bill Cody on two occasions. Lindsey was appointed a deputy U.S. marshal stationed at Paris, Texas, in 1890. His first assignment was to arrest one P. P. Barber, a Louisianan who had killed a former business partner. Barber was killed resisting arrest.

Lindsey was one of the lawmen who killed Bill Dalton near Ardmore, Indian Territory, on June 8, 1894. Lindsey died on March 29, 1939, in the Washita Valley near Ardmore.

Selected Gunfights
McLennan County, Texas, 1873

Seldon shot "Mr. Miller," a member of a local vigilante group known as the "White Caps," out of his saddle when Miller rapidly approached Seldon and his father, Benjamin Battle Lindsey, from behind, presumably for gunplay. Both Lindseys were jailed, but Seldon escaped and promptly robbed a stagecoach to obtain money for his father's pending trial, or so the story goes. Eventually, the Lindseys were acquitted of the killing.

Winn Parish, Louisiana, March 1890

Lindsey suspected that the accidental killing of Jesse McDonald near Berwynn in the Chickasaw Nation was not as accidental as his former business partner had claimed. After building a case that McDonald was killed for money, Lindsey tracked P. P. Barber to a house near Tullos, Louisiana, and killed him in a gunfight after a brief scuffle.

Near Mill Creek, Indian Territory, February 1891

Lindsey and a posse tracked the Hudgins Gang to a line house (outlaw hideout) near the mouth of Mill Creek. Lindsey sent for reinforcements, then, according to his own account, occasionally exchanged fire and insults with the outlaws, throughout the night. Gang leader Bill Hudgins was mortally wounded in an attempted escape, and the rest of the gang was captured. Lindsey suffered a grazing neck wound.

Near Purcell, Indian Territory, 1892

Seldon Lindsey, John Swain, and one Phillips cornered murder suspect Cornelius Walker. Walker dashed from the house and was shot by Lindsey. A second round fired by John Swain finished him off, seconds after Phillips was killed.

Near Ardmore, Indian Territory, June 8, 1894

Seldon Lindsey, W. H. Glover, Ed Roberts, and Loss Hart located Bill Dalton inside a home near Ardmore. Hart is credited in historical accounts as having killed Dalton. In later accounts, Lindsey said he killed the outlaw.

Near Eufaula, Indian Territory, 1895

Springing upon an outlaw camp, Lindsey and fellow lawmen shot and killed three of the sleepy outlaws. The fourth was cooking breakfast and escaped by jumping into nearby woods.

O'Neal, *Encyclopedia,* 182-83; Smith, *Daltons,* 169; Nash, 212; McCullough, 77-132.

Loftis, Hillary U. (Hill Loftis, Tom Ross, Charles Gannon) (1871-1929)

Loftis started working as a very young man at the Dan Waggoner ranch of Willbarger County. Loftis was a known associate of George "Red Buck" Weightman, Elmer "Kid" Lewis, and known murderer Joe Beckham. These four robbed both the Waggoner store and local post office on December 24, 1895, and were hunted down by a Texas Ranger sergeant leading a band of angry citizens. One of the men, Joe Beckham, was gunned down, but the posse was forced to retreat in the face of extremely cold weather.

After spending some time in Canada, Loftis, then operating under the name Tom Ross, returned to Texas, worked as a foreman, and established a ranch. This disguise would not last forever. When Sheriff Charles Tom and Capt. John H. Rogers attempted to arrest him, Loftis fled beyond the pistol range of the lawmen. When they found him later, he was sporting a Winchester, but only wounded Captain Rogers's horse. Milton Paul Good joined Loftis and killed Horace Roberson and Dave Allison in Seminole, Texas, on April 1, 1923, Easter Sunday, the day before they were to testify before a grand jury in a case regarding stolen cattle. Good and Loftis fled, but later surrendered and were imprisoned in Huntsville, Texas. They managed to escape after serving only two years, and parted ways in Oklahoma after a short crime spree. Loftis, by this time calling himself Charles Gannon, found work as a cowboy in Canada, where he killed a Chinese cook and then returned to the United States. After killing a ranch foreman in Browning, Montana, Loftis took his own life in a bunkhouse rather than face new murder charges.

Alexander, *Fearless Dave Allison,* 211-65; Metz, *Encyclopedia,* 98, 156.

Longley, William Preston (Wild Bill, Rattling Bill) (1851-78)

A thrice-hanged killer, Longley lived to regret his crimes. Mean enough to survive a lynching, he was legally hanged some nine years later on October 11, 1878, in Giddings, Texas. Bill was born in Austin County, Texas, on October 16, 1851, then moved with his family to Evergreen, Texas. Longley was one of many Texas lads who participated in Reconstruction violence. He killed a black Union soldier in 1867, killed three more blacks in later years, and even shot up a circus. Eventually he found work on a ranch owned by John Reagon in Karnes County, Texas, but found time for horse theft with Tom Johnson. A posse hanged them both at the Johnson home. Longley was cut down after the posse left, but seemingly learned nothing.

Following a brief stint with the Cullen Baker gang, he returned to Evergreen, then joined a cattle drive as a drover, terminating future employment in that occupation by killing his trail boss. Longley journeyed to Salt Lake City and other Western environs, finally finding new employment as a teamster at Camp Brown (later Fort Washakie), where he schemed with a crooked quartermaster to defraud the government, then killed his business partner in an apparent dispute over the division of profits. This escapade ended in a thirty-year prison sentence, which Longley avoided by escaping to Indian Territory and safe haven with the Utes. The year 1876 found poor Bill on the run from Indian Territory to Arkansas and Texas. Ultimately, he was captured in Louisiana, returned to Texas, and sentenced to hang again. Longley complained to the governor that the noted killer John Wesley Hardin had merely received a long prison sentence. Since disparity in sentencing was not yet a concern to anyone, the plea went unanswered, leaving the killer time to ponder his fate and the gallows.

The second hanging failed as well. When the trap door sprang, the six-foot, five-inch Longley dropped to a knee-banging collision with the ground. Poor Bill was hoisted up and hanged again.

Selected Gunfights
Evergreen, Texas, 1867

Longley shot to death a black soldier with whom he had quarreled on a road alongside the Longley farm. He then hid the body in a shallow ditch.

Near Evergreen, Texas, December 1868

Longley trailed three black men, with whom he had argued earlier, to their camp. One of the men fired at Longley. He returned fire, striking the soldier in the head, then fled.

Yorktown, Texas, 1869

Longley shot and killed an army sergeant in a case of mistaken identity. The soldier had believed Longley was Charles Taylor of the Sutton-Taylor Feud. Longley apparently believed he was being arrested for one of his previous murders.

Indian Territory, 1869

Longley shot and killed his domineering and exacting trail boss, a Mr. Recto, following an argument over Longley's herd management skills.

Leavenworth, Kansas, 1870

Longley shot to death another soldier after a saloon argument. Longley hopped a train to St. Joseph, Missouri, where he was apprehended.

Parkersville, Kansas, 1872

Young Charles Stuart picked the wrong cowboy with whom to discuss the rules of cards. Longley pulled a pistol and killed him, prompting Stuart's father to post a $1,500 reward, which went uncollected.

Comanche County, Texas, 1874

Defending the honor of one Mrs. Forsythe, Longley found the man who insulted her and shot him twice in the head.

Bastrop County, Texas, April 1, 1875

Longley killed his old friend Wilson Anderson at Wilson's home after learning that Anderson had killed Longley's cousin.

Delta County, Texas, 1876

Longley mortally shotgunned Rev. Roland Lay, for whom Longley had been working shares on a farm. The poor reverend had left his own shotgun nearby on a fence post, but was just too slow to reach it.

Tyler, *The New Handbook of Texas,* vol. 4, 282; O'Neal, *Encyclopedia,* 192-95; Metz, *Encyclopedia,* 159; Nash, 216; Eckhardt, 86.

Lowe, Joseph (Rowdy Joe) (Red Joe) (ca. 1845-99)

Rowdy Joe Lowe was born in New York to an English father and an Irish mother who had moved to Dimmick Township, LaSalle County, Illinois, by 1850. The family lived near Troy Grove, Illinois, the boyhood home of Wild Bill Hickock. Lowe joined the Union Army during the Civil War, participated in one engagement, and then joined in the Powder River Indian Expedition against the Sioux and Cheyenne before his honorable discharge on Christmas Day

1865. Lowe was a saloon proprietor in several Kansas cattle towns, notably Ellsworth, Newton, and Wichita. After killing his competitor and rival Edward T. Beard on October 27, 1883, in Wichita, he escaped from custody to avoid related charges.

Lowe was arrested for breaking jail in St. Louis, but released on a writ of habeas corpus under suspicious circumstances, while carrying more than $8,500 in cash. The spring of 1874 found Rowdy Joe and his paramour Kate (last name unknown, but called Kate Lowe) headed for Denison, Texas, then a two-year-old frontier town. By December 1874 they had moved on to Luling, Texas, then an important railroad terminus. One observer of the time noted that Joe and Kate established the first saloon in that burg. Nevertheless, by March 1875 the twosome were dividing their time between Luling and San Antonio, where Joe was convicted of assaulting the lovely Kate. One account of early San Antonio days states that Lowe ran a casino and saloon at the corner of Main Plaza and Soledad, which came to be known as "The Fatal Corner" after a series of killings in that locale, culminating with the death of Ben Thompson and John King Fisher in 1884.

Still greener pastures beckoned at Fort Worth, where Joe finally proposed marriage, but not to Kate. Joe married Mollie Field, the first of the two wives he formally married. Jilted but undeterred, Kate bolted for northwest Texas, was last reliably observed running a bawdy house at Big Springs in 1886, then simply disappeared. Joe in the meantime had transitioned into the theater business, but left Fort Worth for Colorado in December 1878 or perhaps early the next year.

He was killed by former policeman Emmanuel A. Kimmel, with whom he had quarreled on February 1, 1899, in Denver.

Selected Gunfights
Newton, Kansas, February, 19, 1872

A. M. Sweet, owner of the renowned Through Ticket Saloon, spirited "Rowdy Kate" Lowe away from Joe, her common-law husband, after the lovebirds quarreled. Kate and Mr. Sweet were secluded at the home of one Fanny Gray when Joe found them. Sweet pulled his own revolver, but not quickly enough. Joe responded to the threat by mortally wounding Sweet with two pistol shots. Lowe was later acquitted.
Wichita, Kansas, October 27, 1873

Edward T. Beard, whose family founded Beardstown, Illinois, was better suited to saloonkeeping than more mercantile enterprises. He competed with Rowdy Joe when they both ran saloons in Newton, Kansas, and had recently started a new saloon next to Lowe's place on Delano Street in Wichita. The evening of October 27, 1873, found Beard in his cups and ready for trouble. He fired his pistol into Lowe's saloon, chased Josephine McDermott into Lowe's place then and mistakenly shot Lowe employee Annie Franklin. Lowe fired at Beard but missed, then chased Beard into the street and mortally wounded him with a shotgun. Beard suffered wrist and hip injuries and died about two weeks later of infection. Lowe was acquitted in the death of Beard, but bar denizen Billy Anderson, who was shot during the gunfight, sued for damages and had Lowe arrested for attempted murder. Rowdy Joe escaped from custody and eventually migrated to Texas.

Denver, Colorado, February 11, 1899

Police found Lowe's horse neglected and unfed, then impounded it. After paying a fine, Lowe proceeded to a saloon, where he ridiculed the police force in the presence of former policeman Emmanuel A. Kimmel. After the two quarreled, Lowe reached into his pocket, prompting Kimmel to shoot Rowdy Joe once near the heart. The saloonkeeper died in a few minutes. Kimmel was acquitted of all charges. Lowe had been unarmed.

Rosa and Koop, 8-9, 43, 54, 74-88, 93-118, 155; Miller and Snell, 255-72; Selcer, 26, 48, 293; O'Neal, *Encyclopedia,* 195-97; Metz, *Encyclopedia,* 235.

McCarty, Henry (William H. Bonney, Henry Antrim, Kid Antrim, Billy the Kid) (ca. 1859-81)

Overshadowed in Western lore only by Jesse James, if anyone, McCarty was a regular visitor at Tascosa, Oldham County, Texas, where he sold horses of questionable provenance.

Although his traditional birth date of November 23 is most certainly a fabrication, he was probably born around 1859 to Irish-American parents. The place of his birth was most likely New York City, the impression of a postal inspector who interviewed him at Santa Fe in early 1881 and noted the remnants of a Manhattan street dialect. He may have been baptized Patrick Henry McCarty at the Church of St. Peter in lower Manhattan.

Military pension records, city directories, and real estate records are persuasive that by about 1868, Henry, his widowed mother, and brother were living in Indianapolis, where they met William Henry Antrim, with whom Mrs. McCarty purchased Wichita real estate in 1871. She married Antrim in Santa Fe in 1873, with Henry and his brother serving as witnesses, eventually journeying to Silver City, New Mexico.

Using the name Antrim and William H. Bonney, Henry (by then called Billy) eventually found himself in the Lincoln County War, a mercantile affair pitting Scotsman Alexander McSween and Englishman William Tunstall against Irishmen Lawrence "Larry" Murphy, James "Jimmy" Dolan, Johnny Riley, and others whose retail establishment dominated Lincoln County affairs.

Forsaking heritage for friendship, Billy joined Tunstall's Regulators, whose ranks included Frederick T. Waite, from the vicinity of present-day Pauls Valley, Oklahoma, and Big Jim French, most likely a native of the Choctaw Nation. Another Regulator, John Middleton, according to at least one authority, died in 1885, the very year a John Middleton associated with Belle Starr drowned, or was murdered in the Choctaw Nation.

According to some scholars, Waite was Billy's closest friend, with whom he dreamed of starting a farming operation. Some evidence exists that at the conclusion of the Lincoln County War, Waite offered to help Billy establish himself in the Chickasaw Nation. Instead, the young man known today as Billy the Kid chose to stay in New Mexico. He was killed by Pat Garrett on July 14, 1881, at Fort Sumner, and thus became a legend.

Selected Gunfights
Fort Grant, Arizona, August 17, 1877

Blacksmith Francis P. "Windy" Cahill provoked McCarty into an altercation at George Atkin's saloon, which McCarty resolved by mortally wounding Cahill with a pistol shot to the belly. Soon thereafter, McCarty became William H. "Billy" Bonney.

Steel Springs, New Mexico, March 9, 1878

William Morton, a prime suspect in the killing of rancher John

Tunstall, was apprehended by the Kid and other Regulators, along with fellow Dolan-Murphy factionist Frank Baker, following a lengthy horseback chase. The pair was killed attempting to escape, or simply in cold blood, along with William McCloskey, a Dolan-Murphy hireling who had joined the posse but vowed to protect Morton to the very end.

Lincoln, New Mexico, April 1, 1878

Responding to the urgings of Alexander McSween, Billy Bonney, Frank McNab, and four other Regulators rose from behind a high wooden gate behind the Tunstall store and ambushed Sheriff William Brady, who was on his way to post a notice at the courthouse. Brady and his deputy George Hindman died on the spot.

Blazer's Mill, New Mexico, April 4, 1878

Andrew L. "Buckshot" Roberts encountered several Regulators at Dr. Blazer's place, then soon found himself in a gunfight. Roberts traveled to Blazer's Mill hoping to get a check for the sale of his Ruidoso ranch. Instead he was confronted by the Regulators but managed to kill Dick Brewer before Roberts died of a mortal wound sustained during the course of the gunfight.

Fort Sumner, New Mexico, January 10, 1880

Joe "Texas Red" Grant provoked Bonney into a gunfight, not knowing that Bonney had anticipated the duel and had set the hammer on the pistol Grant was using to fall on an empty chamber. Grant drew down on Bonney as the Kid turned away from him, then heard the click of the hammer falling on an empty chamber right before Bonney drilled him with three bullets in the chin. Looking down at the corpse, the Kid observed, "Joe, I've been there too often for you," then walked away.

Near White Oaks, New Mexico, November 27, 1880

That day the Kid, Dave Rudabaugh, and Billy Wilson had escaped a posse, but boldly strode into White Oaks, where they traded shots with Deputy Sheriff James Redman. Later that night a posse tracked the gang to the Jim Greathouse Ranch, about forty miles from White Oaks. The next morning, during negotiations, the gang traded Jim Greathouse for Deputy Sheriff James Carlyle, who attempted to escape late in the day only to be killed by the gang or his own posse.

Fort Sumner, New Mexico, December 19, 1880

The Kid rode with Tom O'Folliard, Charlie Bowdre, Tom Pickett, and Billy Wilson into Fort Sumner for some rest and recreation. Instead, they were challenged by Pat Garrett and a posse demanding surrender near the old fort hospital. O'Folliard was mortally wounded by gunfire, then died cursing Pat Garrett as the rest of the Kid's posse escaped.

Stinking Springs, New Mexico, December 23, 1880

Garrett tracked the gang to a small stone cabin, then began an assault early the next morning. Charlie Bowdre was mortally wounded as he stepped outside the small cabin. Eventually, the gang surrendered.

Lincoln County courthouse, April 28, 1881

Thursday evening, at about 6:00 P.M. Lincoln County deputy Bob Olinger took three accused murderers across the street to the Wortley house for dinner, leaving the Kid under the supervision of former Texan James Bell. The Kid asked to be taken to the privy. When returning, he reached the top of an interior staircase ahead of Bell, then quietly slipped his small hands through the handcuffs. Bonney quickly overpowered Bell, taking his pistol, with which he shot Bell in the back as the deputy bounded down the staircase. The Kid then found Olinger's fully loaded shotgun and waited. Olinger heard the commotion from across the street, then ran to the courthouse, where he was greeted with a view of his own shotgun pointing toward him from a second-floor window. "Look up, old boy, and see what you got!" the Kid said, just before he peppered Olinger with his own shotgun, sending the hapless lawman into the next world.

Fort Sumner, July 14, 1881

Pat Garrett, Tip McKinney, and Frank Poe arrived in Fort Sumner looking for the Kid. That evening, Garrett visited prominent Fort Sumner citizen Pete Maxwell to see if Maxwell knew the whereabouts of Bonney. While Garrett and Maxwell talked, the Kid backed into the room, while he looked at Garrett's posse on the front porch, asking, *"¿Quién es?"* ("Who is it?"), giving Garrett the advantage he needed. The first shot found its mark, and the Kid fell with a small groan to the floor, then quickly died. And so, the twenty-something gunfighter who in myth killed one man for each of his years, died with only a dull, worn butcher knife in his hand.

Wallis, 6-17, 147, 171-79, 196-201, 234, 247, 249; Rasch, 4-5, 10, 15, 153-56; Adams, *More Burs Under the Saddle,* 72; Utley, *High Noon in Lincoln,* 43, 143, 166; Metz, *Encyclopedia,* 21; Tower, "Fred Tecumseh Waite"; Nolan, 49-58, 101-4, 124-33, 193-215, 237-46; Utley, *Billy the Kid,* 12-14, 56-60, 63-68, 172-74.

McGeeney, Patrick Sylvester (1873-1943)

A San Antonio resident, McGeeney was a native of Tyrone County, Ireland. Brought as an infant to Newton, Kansas, a rousing cattle town, by 1892 young Pat worked for the Sante Fe Railroad as a brakeman. According to his memoirs, his "other duties as assigned" included acting as a guard on trips from Kansas through Oklahoma Territory.

In such capacity, he helped thwart several robberies, including an effort on November 8, 1892, by Ed Newcome, Earnest Lewis, and others near Wharton (now Perry). In May 1893, he thwarted a robbery by Henry Starr, and was commissioned a deputy U.S. marshal, perhaps the youngest in history. He gained further notoriety by helping thwart a train robbery being conducted by half-wit future congressman Manuel "Manvel" Herrick, between Round Pond and Perry, on June 29, 1893. Manvel had received the commission from Flora Quick, but claimed that he worked for the Doolin Gang.

These and other exploits brought him in contact with Bill Tilghman, Chris Madsen, Charles Colcord, and others. Fate or coincidence placed him at the Acme Saloon, in El Paso, Texas, on August 19, 1895, as an eyewitness to the killing of John Wesley Hardin by John Selman, Sr. McGeeney settled in San Antonio, and was a successful pioneer filmmaker, concentrating on what he knew best, stories of law enforcement in the Old West. Responding to a desperate request, he salvaged the production of *Debtor to the Law,* a film biography of Henry Starr produced by a Tulsa film company. Regrettably, he could do nothing about cost overruns, which occurred before he joined the project and which doomed the enterprise to financial failure. A bitter Henry Starr soon returned to crime and was mortally wounded at Harrison, Arkansas, while robbing a bank.

McGeeney became a stalwart of the Irish-American community in San Antonio, joined his children in Los Angeles late in life, and died on October 15, 1943.

Shirley, *Purple Sage,* 1-190.

McNelly, Leander H. (1844-77)
A former Confederate Army captain, McNelly joined the Texas

Rangers in 1874. He was assigned the task of quelling the long-running Sutton-Taylor Feud in DeWitt County, Texas. Later he was stationed along the Mexican border combating the bandit army of Juan Cortina, and was successful in ending that band's cattle rustling forays. He resigned from the Rangers in February 1877, suffering from tuberculosis. He died on September 4, 1877.

Capt. Leander H. McNelly of the Texas Rangers, circa 1872, probably photographed in Canada. (Courtesy of the Texas Ranger Hall of Fame and Museum, Waco, Texas)

Parsons and Little, 129-35, 137-58, 163-65, 190-204; O'Neal, *Encyclopedia,* 26, 125, 170; Metz, *Encyclopedia,* 165, 243; Nash, 224.

Manning, James (ca. 1845-1915)
A native Virginian, James Manning, along with four of his five brothers, fought for the Confederacy during the Civil War. James, Doc, Frank, and John vowed never to shave until the South rose again. The four brothers drifted to the Texas Gulf Coast where they built a sloop and sailed to Mexico, fighting with Emperor Maximilian. Returning to Texas, they finally settled in El Paso, in 1881. James Manning was embroiled in a feud with Sheriff Dallas

Stoudenmire, whom he later killed. Manning owned saloons in El Paso and Seattle, Washington. A fire claimed the Seattle enterprise in 1889, and after a brief stint in Anacosta, Washington, Manning moved to Arizona where he invested in mining operations. He succumbed to cancer and died in 1915 while residing in Los Angeles, California.

Selected Gunfights
East Texas, ca. 1875

During a cattle drive the Mannings made an enemy who shot and killed the youngest brother, William, from ambush. The other brothers chased the assailant down and shot him to death.

El Paso, Texas, February 14, 1882

While managing his Coliseum Variety Theater, Manning found himself confronted by Doc Cummings, a brother-in-law of Sheriff Dallas Stoudenmire with whom the Mannings had been feuding. The inebriated Cummings insisted on a fight in spite of Manning's earlier refusals and quickly had more trouble than he bargained for. Cummings was shot by Manning and the bartender, then staggered into the street and died.

El Paso, Texas, September 18, 1882

James came to the rescue of his brother Doc Manning, who was engaged in a gunfight with Dallas Stoudenmire. While Stoudenmire concentrated on subduing Doc, James shot Stoudenmire behind his left ear, which killed him immediately.

Tyler, *The New Handbook of Texas,* vol. 4, 445-46; O'Neal, *Encyclopedia,* 213-14; Metz, *Encyclopedia,* 235; Nash, 225-26.

Marlow, Boone (1865-89)

One of four brothers, Boone Marlow was not a gunslinger but ran afoul of the law when he killed a man in Wilbarger County, Texas, in 1886. The entire family moved to Colorado, where brothers Charley, Alf, George, and Epp, and their father, farmer and doctor, sought new beginnings. They eventually returned to Texas, settling at Vernon. An attempt was made to arrest Boone on murder charges, but he escaped. His brothers were arrested.

Boone on the other hand avoided arrest for days by burrowing into a haystack and outfitting his hideout with many comforts of home. He then escaped, only to be fatally poisoned, then shot twice in the forehead for good measure, by his prospective brother-in-law, G. H. Harbolt, and two others for a $1,500 reward. The deed was done on Hell Roaring Creek, near Fort Sill, Oklahoma Territory, in late January 1889, with the apparent collusion of Boone's young but financially astute sweetheart.

Selected Gunfights
Wilbarger County, Texas, 1886
Fueled by either rage or liquor, a man named James Holden began shooting at Marlow as he rode up to his sister's house. Marlow returned fire, killing his assailant.
Near Vernon, Texas, December 16, 1888
Dinner was unexpectedly interrupted when Deputy Sheriff Tom Collier and Sherriff Marion Wallace burst into the home to arrest Boone. Shots were exchanged, mortally wounding Wallace, but Deputy Sheriff Collier turned and bolted into the night. Boone Marlow had drawn a bead on him and ordered him to come back, which he did. Boone was ready to shoot the lawman dead, but his brother, who was cradling the dying Wallace's head, persuaded him otherwise.

Shirley, *The Fighting Marlows*, 3, 10, 41-50, 153-55; Thrapp, *Encyclopedia*, II, 942-43; O'Neal, *Encyclopedia*, 214-15; Nash, 226; DeArment, *Life of the Marlows*, 1-20, 38-95, 119-37.

Marlow Brothers (prom. 1880s)
The story of the Marlow family was the basis for the John Wayne film *The Sons of Katie Elder*. The Marlow Boys were the sons of Dr. Williamson Marlow, born about 1804, and his wife, Martha, a direct descendent of Daniel Boone. They were from Tennessee but eventually settled on the western border of the Chickasaw Nation between Hell Roaring Creek and Rush Creek. Previously they had lived in Cooper County, Missouri, in Texas, and in the gold fields of California. Son William (b. 1853) died

Martha Jane Marlow, mother of the Marlow boys. (Courtesy of the University of Texas at Austin, Robert K. DeArment Collection)

about 1879 in Colorado, but George (b. 1855), Charles (b. 1860), Epp, Alfred, and Boone (b. 1864/ 1865), and the rest of the family lived about seven miles from Rush Springs by 1880, at a site later called Marlow.

Some eight years later Deputy U.S. Marshal Ed Johnson swore out a warrant claiming that the boys had stolen nineteen horses from a Caddo Indian. The inevitable shoot-out occurred on December 17, 1888, at a cabin near Fort Sill, resulting in the death of Sheriff Wallace some seven days later. The boys were arrested, taken to a jail at Graham, Texas, and escaped a mob through the good offices of Sheriff Johnson, but were then ambushed on January 19, 1889, just outside of Graham, at the hands of a hooded mob, which may have included law enforcement officers, as loosely portrayed in the *The Sons of Katie Elder.*

Boone Marlow was fatally poisoned for reward money in January 1889, but the surviving boys lived relatively long lives and sometimes assisted law enforcement officials as possemen. George was even elected president of his local school board in 1899.

Shirley, *The Fighting Marlows,* 3, 10, 153-55.

The Marlow brothers on horseback. Left to right: George, Boone, Alfred, Llewellyn (Epp), Charles, taken about 1887. (Courtesy of the University of Texas at Austin, Robert K. DeArment Collection)

Massey, Robert (1863-83)

A Grayson County, Texas, native, on December 1, 1881, Massey murdered cattle partner Edmond Clark of Comanche County, Texas, in the Chickasaw Nation on the South Canadian River, about 225 miles west of Fort Smith. Massey relieved the corpse of cattle sales proceeds obtained in the Dakotas. He was apprehended some months later by Clark's father, some twenty-five miles from Fort Sill. Clark's pistol was found in the possession of another man with whom Massey had traded. Massey's claim that he had shot Clark in the back of the head in self-defense went unheeded. He was hanged on April 13, 1883.

Harman, *Hell on the Border,* 172, 233-36; Nash, 226.

Mason, Bernard (Barney) (1848-1916)

A Texas cowboy, posseman, deputy sheriff, and saloonkeeper, Mason was best known for his association with Pat Garrett in the pursuit of Billy the Kid. Born on October 29, 1848, to Irish parents in Richmond Virginia, he drifted to Texas and on to New Mexico Territory. There, on December 29, 1879, he killed former Mason

County War partisan John Farris (Faires) at Fort Sumner, suggesting Mason's own possible participation in that Texas feud. Mason became associated professionally and personally with Pat Garrett, the Lincoln County sheriff. He became a deputy sheriff and joined Garrett in a double wedding on January 14, 1880, at Anton Chico, where the gentlemen married Juanita Madril and Apolonaria Gutierres, respectively.

Mason participated with Garrett, Jim East, Lee Hall, and Tom Emory in the siege of Billy the Kid at Stinking Springs, New Mexico, which began at dawn on December 23, 1880, at a small windowless rock shed near the Wilcox-Brazil house in Lincoln County. Garrett, according to one version, had instructed the posse that, if possible, they should kill the Kid, who would be wearing a Mexican hat. Inside the house were the Kid, his horse, Charlie Bowdre, Billy Wilson, Dave Rudabaugh, and Tom Pickett. Three horses were tethered nearby.

According to posseman Louis Bousman, when hapless Charlie Bowdre came out to feed the horses, the posse mistook him for the Kid and simply blew Bowdre back into the shed in a bullet blizzard. On the other hand, Cal Polk, another participant, stated that Bowdre was shot feeding the horses, then charged the posse and died nearby.

Later, at about 4:00 P.M., the gang was enticed out by the smell of food. Barney Mason famously pulled his gun and started to kill the "slippery" Kid, but Jim East and Lee Hall stopped him. Incredibly enough, Billy later missed a perfect opportunity to take revenge on Mason, some six miles from Fort Sumner near Arroyo Taiban. Perhaps because Mason was with his family, the disguised but easily identifiable Kid passed Mason on the road but did nothing.

Subsequently, Mason served as Lincoln County deputy sheriff under Sheriff John Poe, homesteaded in New Mexico Territory, then worked on Arizona water projects. He moved on to Bakersfield, California, and died there of natural causes on April 11, 1916.

Nolan, 177, 230-31, 277.

Masterson, William Bartholomew (Bat) (1853-1921)

William Bartholomew (he later changed it to William Barclay) Masterson was one of seven children born to Thomas and Catherine Masterson. "Bat" as he would become known, was born on

November 26, 1853, and baptized as "Bertholowmiew" (*sic*) in the parish of St. George, Henryville, county of Iberville, province of Quebec, Canada. His baptismal name was later anglicized to Bartholomew. He died in New York City on October 25, 1921.

Scholars debate the origin of his nickname to this day. Some say his parents called him "Bat" as a contraction of Bartholomew, while others attribute the name to his use of a cane to subdue street rowdies while a law officer in Wichita. When Bat was about fourteen, his large family migrated south and settled on a claim near Wichita, Kansas, at Sedgwick.

Bat and an older brother left the family farm in 1872, taking work on the Atchison, Topeka and Santa Fe Railroad, but Bat left that job and was soon hunting buffalo on the Western prairie. Bat found himself in the company of about a dozen other such hunters on July 27, 1874, headquartered at Adobe Walls in the Texas Panhandle. The party was under attack by Quanah Parker and a large contingent of Indian warriors. Bat left buffalo hunting shortly after the incident at Adobe Walls, then joined the ranks of Gen. Nelson A. Miles's troop where, for seventy-five dollars a month, he served as a scout for about three months.

Masterson's whereabouts between his discharge and his return to Dodge City, Kansas, in 1877 are somewhat hazy, although it is widely believed that Bat participated in a fatal saloon gunfight in Mobeetie, Texas, in early 1876.

Masterson opened a saloon in Dodge City, but managed to get himself summarily pistol-whipped by the city marshal while aiding a jailbreak. Nevertheless, he was elected Ford County deputy sheriff and quickly made a name for himself.

Two years after his election and shortly after his appointment, this time as deputy U.S. marshal, Bat joined the Atchison, Topeka and Santa Fe Railroad as a detective. He joined in the company's dispute over rail passage rights through Raton Pass, New Mexico, and Royal Gorge, Colorado, against the Denver and Rio Grande Railroad.

Masterson then traveled through Colorado, New Mexico, and Nebraska before returning to Tombstone, Arizona, for a meeting with old friends Luke Short and Wyatt Earp in 1880.

Masterson had returned to Dodge City by December 1880 and assisted his brother Jim by starting a gunfight with his brother's adversaries almost the moment he stepped from the railcar. Next, Bat sojourned in Fort Worth, Texas, where he lived large while promoting horse racing and prizefighting.

Bat married Emma Walters in Denver, and by 1902 the couple was in New York, where Bat began a writing career. He penned sports stories for the *New York Morning Telegraph* for nearly twenty years. President Theodore Roosevelt commissioned Masterson as a part-time deputy U.S. marshal in 1905, but Bat soon gave up the badge. The aging gunfighter died with his boots on and writing pen firmly in hand on October 25, 1921, while writing a prizefighting article.

Selected Gunfights

Mobeetie, Texas, January 24, 1876

Officially the death of Sergeant King of the Army's Fourth Cavalry was caused by a shot fired by "a citizen" at the Lady Gay Saloon. Although several variations of the incident exist, most historians of the West accept that Bat Masterson killed King in a saloon gunfight over the affections of one Molly Brennan, who was apparently killed by King accidentally.

Dodge City, Kansas, September 25, 1877

Masterson shot several times at A. C. Jackson as he shot up the town, after being ordered to stop. Bat missed the unruly cowboy but shot the horse dead.

Dodge City, Kansas, April 16, 1881

Bat's brother, Jim Masterson, held a partnership in the Lady Gay Dance Hall and Saloon with A. J. Peacock. An already unstable business relationship was made even worse after Peacock refused Jim's many requests to fire ill-tempered bartender Al Updegraff, who was Peacock's brother-in-law. Jim wired Bat for assistance. No sooner had Bat stepped from the train than he observed Peacock and Updegraff walking together. Bat called them to turn and fight, and the battle was on. Bat dove behind some stacked wood near the station while Peacock and Updegraff ran for cover behind the corner of the city jail.

The battle raged until a pall came over the streets while the shooters reloaded. In the silence, Sheriff Fred Singer and Mayor A. B. Webster appeared in the clearing gunsmoke with guns of their own and stopped the fight. That evening Jim Masterson and Peacock dissolved their partnership before the Masterson brothers departed Dodge City on an evening train, with Bat having paid a small fine. Updegraff suffered a bullet wound to the chest, but survived.

DeArment, *Bat Masterson,* 3-86, 206-9, 325-26; Tyler, *The New Handbook of Texas,* vol. 4, 550-51; O'Neal, *Encyclopedia,* 219-22; Nash, 227-29; Adams, *Burs Under the Saddle,* 500; Adams, *More Burs Under the Saddle,* 20.

Mather, Dave H. (Mysterious Dave) (1845-ca. 1887)

A Connecticut native with a bad case of restlessness, Mysterious Dave's formative years remain a mystery. Some sources state that he was born David Allen Mather on August 10, 1851, the son of Ulysses Mather and Lydia Mather. Ulysses was a sea captain distantly related to the noted divine Cotton Mather. Mysterious Dave supposedly left Connecticut after his mother's death in about 1868, eventually landing in New Orleans. Mather was supposedly rustling cattle by 1873 in Arkansas and later Wise County, Texas.

Mather resided in Texas from time to time during a ten-year period beginning in 1873, when Mather, Milton Yarberry, and Dave Rudabaugh fled Arkansas to avoid cattle rustling charges. Three years later, it is known, Yarberry lived in Decatur, Texas, raising the possibility that Mather resided there as well, although undetected. One observer of the times, Jim McIntire, improbably claimed in his own memoirs that during his time as town marshal of Mobeetie, Texas, Mather was associated with Wyatt Earp in a treasure hunting scam there.

During the same ten-year time period, Mather drifted to Dodge City where, after suffering a knife wound to the stomach, he moved to New Mexico. Mather purportedly killed a man in the Texas Panhandle town of Mobeetie, near Fort Elliott. Mather found his way to New Mexico by 1879 and was arrested on suspicion of a train robbery near Las Vegas, but was released for lack of prosecution. He was cleared of the charge and almost immediately won appointment as deputy city marshal.

Leaving there, he toured through San Antonio, Dallas, and Fort Worth. In December 1881 he was partnered with Georgia Morgan, madam of the Long Branch and an associate of future Tombstone lynching target John Heath, who kept a saloon at the corner of Leonard and Commerce. Perhaps as a consequence of a love triangle gone sour, Morgan accused Mather of stealing an expensive silk dress and jewelry, followed him to Fort Worth, and arranged for his three-month sojourn in the Dallas County jail.

Following his acquittal, Mather traveled to El Paso, where some say he disguised himself as Dave Melasky. One bounty hunter claimed he located a "Mysterious Dave" in Manchaco, Texas, but the Kansas governor knew of no outstanding warrants for such a person. Moving to Dodge City, Kansas, in 1883, Mather secured an appointment as deputy city marshal. He ran for constable in February 1884, but was defeated. An old feud with his replacement, Deputy Marshal Tom Nixon, ended in Nixon's death a few months later.

Mather moved back to Dodge City, Kansas, where in May 1885 he shot and killed a man. Mather jumped bail and moved on to New Kiowa, Kansas. He was reportedly appointed city marshal there on August 14, 1885, but some sources note that this account contradicts information later published indicating that one Mike O'Shea was city marshal in the same time period. More certainly, Mather was present in New Kiowa when his associate Dave Black shot and killed infantryman Julius Schmitz (Schmidt) on Main Street. Law enforcement authorities jailed Black, then moved him to Wellington, thus avoiding a lynching at the hands of Schmitz partisans. The same authorities notified Mather of his own prospective lynching at the hands of the same crowd, prompting his prompt exodus. Left to face the music, Dave Black complained to the Barber County, Kansas, District Court that "a pretended friend" had absconded with a $300 defense fund raised by his friends. That would be Dave Mather.

Court documents confirm that in any event, Ford County, Kansas, officials believed by November 9, 1887, that Mysterious Dave was no more. So stated the Ford County attorney in a motion to dismiss charges against his bondsmen. Nevertheless, like Jesse James, Billy the Kid, and Butch Cassidy, Dave Mather was reported to be alive for many years after his official albeit nonconclusive death. Mather, it seems, reinvented himself as a customs official, a homesteader, and even a member of the Royal Canadian Mounted Police. Others say that by 1887 Mysterious Dave had moved on to Long Pine, Nebraska, where he took employment at a hotel and soon faded into obscurity.

Selected Gunfights

Las Vegas, New Mexico, January 22, 1880

Although the record is far from clear, some accounts state that Mather took the part of Town Marshal Joe Carson in a saloon shooting. The fracas occurred at Close and Patterson's Variety Hall. The marshal was killed outright, while his cowboy opponent, William "Big" Randall was mortally wounded.

Las Vegas, New Mexico, January 25, 1880

Constable Mather shot and killed Joseph Castello, a railroad worker who threatened to shoot the lawman while Mather was quelling a disturbance Castello and two cronies had started in a saloon.

Dodge City, Kansas, July 18, 1884

Assistant city marshal Tom Nixon fired an errant shot at Mysterious Dave after the two quarreled near Mather's saloon. Nixon had recently replaced Mather as assistant city marshal. Nixon was disarmed by the sheriff but claimed that Mather had waved a pistol at him. The shot splintered some nearby woodwork, and Nixon had to post $800 bail. Three days later, Mather shot Nixon to death in the presence of numerous witnesses about 10:00 P.M., outside the Opera House.

Dodge City, Kansas, May 10, 1885

Mather and his brother Josiah killed twenty-three-year-old Ashland, Kansas, grocer David Barnes after Mysterious Dave became upset over his losses to Barnes at a game of Seven-Up. Mysterious Dave suffered a grazing scalp wound during the gunplay, but continued firing. Two bystanders suffered leg wounds. Sheriff Sughrue (*sic*) arrested the Mather brothers who posted a $3,000 bond, jumped bail, and never returned.

DeMattos, 11-20, 81-125, 159-72; O'Neal, *Encyclopedia*, 222-24; Nash, 229.

Meador, William D. (prom. 1870s)

A Sutton faction adherent, Meador was accused of complicity in the deaths of Dr. Phillip H. Brassell and his son George T. Brassell on September 19, 1876, in DeWitt County, Texas, for reasons unknown. Previously, Meador had been involved in the September 11, 1876, killing of one Joe DeMoss by Jake Ryan.

Before his death, George Brassell had identified Meador, Ryan, and

Joe Sitterlie as members of the Sutton mob. Two days after indictments were issued on December 20, 1876, McNelly Ranger lieutenant Jesse Lee "Leigh" Hall and others attended and participated in a DeWitt County wedding party. The host had asked the officers to arrest the groom and several other suspects only after the party was over.

Although guilty verdicts were obtained against some of the participants in the Brassell killings, in the end no one was punished. Only David Augustine was sentenced, but he was pardoned by Governor J. S. Hogg before he even arrived at Huntsville Prison.

Parsons and Little, 281-90.

Methvin, Henry (Scar Neck) (1912-48)

A Barrow gang stalwart, Methvin, along with his father, arranged the demise of Bonnie and Clyde in 1934. Henry Methvin was a car thief doing time at Eastham Prison Farm when he escaped with Raymond Hamilton, Joe Palmer, and others on January 16, 1934, leaving prison guard Major Joseph Crowson mortally wounded. Methvin was directly involved in three killings and at least six bank robberies while in the Barrow gang, notably the cold-blooded killing of two motorcycle patrolmen at Grapevine, Texas, on April 1, 1934.

Methvin received de facto immunity from prosecution for his Texas crimes, but was returned to Oklahoma for prosecution in the Commerce, Oklahoma, death of Cal Campbell. He was released from an Oklahoma prison in 1942. Incredibly, Methvin outlived most of the Barrow gang, only to be killed accidentally crawling under a Southern Pacific passenger train near Sulphur, Louisiana, on April 19, 1948. Some two years earlier, his father died under suspicious circumstance, which some believed was prompted by the Methvins' role in the deaths of Bonnie and Clyde.

Selected Robberies, Kidnappings, and Gunfights
Rembrandt, Iowa, January 23, 1934
Henry Methvin, Clyde Barrow, Ray Hamilton, Hilton Bybee, and Joe Palmer robbed the First National Bank of $3,800, in the maiden voyage, as it were, of the second Barrow gang.
Poteau, Oklahoma, January 26, 1934
Someone robbed the Central National Bank of some $1,500,

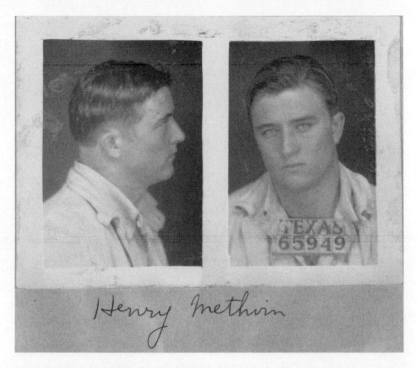

Book-in profile and mug shot of Henry Methvin. (Courtesy of the Dallas Public Library, Dallas, Texas)

two days after the Rembrandt, Iowa, crime. Some attribute this robbery to the second Barrow gang, omitting Hilton Bybee from the list of thieves.

Knierim, Iowa, February 1, 1934

Clyde Barrow, Henry Methvin, and Ray Hamilton robbed the State Savings Bank, netting $307 from the bank and a luckless customer. Earlier, Hilton Bybee had quit the gang, and Joe Palmer had begun a brief vacation in Joplin, Missouri. Methvin intermediary John Joyner met with lawman Frank Hamer some ten days later to negotiate a Texas pardon for Methvin, in return for information leading to the capture or death of Bonnie and Clyde.

Lancaster, Texas, February 27, 1934

Barrow, Hamilton, and Methvin robbed the R. P. Henry and Sons bank of about $4,100, then quarreled about the split. Hamilton left the gang shortly thereafter.

Gladewater, Texas, March 29, 1934

Clyde Barrow, Henry Methvin, and Joe Palmer kidnapped Wade Hampton McNabb, a furloughed inmate with whom Palmer had prison difficulties. Palmer killed McNabb near Waskom, Texas, reportedly in revenge for beatings suffered at McNabb's hands.

Near Grapevine, Texas, April 1, 1934

Clyde Barrow, Henry Methvin, and Bonnie Parker were parked on a dirt road near Highway 114, reportedly waiting to meet gang member Ray Hamilton, when their car was approached by two Texas State Highway motorcycle patrolmen, E. B. Wheeler and H. D. Murphy. Clyde told Methvin to "take them," supposedly meaning to apprehend the officers and take their weapons. Instead, Methvin opened fire with a Browning automatic rifle, mortally wounding both officers, then shot Murphy again as he lay helpless on the ground.

Near Commerce, Oklahoma, April 6, 1934

Commerce constable Cal Campbell and police chief Percy Boyd encountered gunfire from Clyde Barrow or Henry Methvin on a dirt road just outside town. Campbell was killed, but the wounded Boyd endured a lengthy kidnapping which ended with his ejection from the Barrow gang car at Fort Scott. The gang treated surviving hostages pleasantly enough, and Boyd was no exception. The gang offered condolences for Campbell's death, then provided Boyd transportation money before roaring off. Bonnie Parker did insist that the press be told that in spite of certain photographs published nationally, she did not smoke cigars.

Stuart, Iowa, April 16, 1934

Barrow and Methvin stole some $1,500 from the First National Bank, while Bonnie Parker waited outside.

Everly, Iowa, May 3, 1934

Barrow, Methvin, and Palmer took some $700 from the Farmers Trust and Savings Branch, Barrow's last confirmed bank robbery. Methvin invited Bonnie and Clyde to hide near his parents' home in Bienville Parish, Louisiana. He then confirmed his deal to give up Bonnie and Clyde with Texas authorities through his parents on May 21, just two days before their fatal ambush.

Milner, 60-160; Knight, 128, 132-33, 135-36, 138, 158, 163, 181, 189, 200-203; Helmer and Mattix, 213, 239; Phillips, 138-39, 157, 309; Simmons, 129.

Middleton, David (Doc, Gold Tooth Charley, Texas Jack) (1851-1913)

Middleton was born James M. Cherry on February 9, 1851, at Bastrop, Texas, to Nancy Cherry who was an unmarried teenager at the time. Seventeen months later, Nancy married J. B. Riley, and her three children took Riley's surname. James Riley was indicted for horse theft on May 16, 1866, in Gillespie County, Texas, and again on October 13, 1872, in Coryell County.

Although neither charge was ever prosecuted, finally on July 22, 1875, James and his cousin Lewis Bell were confined at Huntsville Prison following conviction for three counts of horse theft in Cooke County on the Indian Territory border.

Riley escaped from Huntsville Prison on April 1, 1876, changed his name to David C. Middleton, then joined a cattle drive to Dodge City, Kansas. His biographer speculated that Middleton named himself for David Crockett and used his grandmother's maiden name. Middleton was asked late in life to reveal the origins of the name but declined to do so. One legend has it he was nicknamed "Doc" while treating the broken leg of another cowboy on a cattle drive.

On Sunday, January 14, 1877, Middleton shot and killed a Pvt. James Keefe from nearby Sidney Barracks in a Sidney, Nebraska, dance hall, then promptly moved on to Fort Robinson, in far northeast Nebraska, long before his indictment for second-degree murder was issued. Eventually he journeyed to the ranch of William Irvine on Horse Creek in Wyoming, where Middleton repaid Irvine's hospitality by stealing some horses. Middleton, George Smith, and Texan Edgar Scurry aggregated Irvine's horses with others which they drove toward Kansas, but were intercepted by detective William Lykens, then jailed at Sidney, Nebraska, six days after Christmas. Doc promptly escaped and reputedly formed his own gang of horse thieves the next year along the Niobrara River in Nebraska, near the Morris crossing, gaining something of a Robin Hood reputation, whatever his motivations.

In May 1879 he married teenager Mary Richardson in Holt County, Nebraska, apparently without divorcing Mary Edwards, whom he had married on June 23, 1870, in Hays County, Texas. Doc was lured into an ambush on July 20, 1879, with the promise of a pardon and work as a cattle detective. Middleton escaped but was captured nine days later at his hideout on Wyman Creek, about seven miles from the Morris crossing of the Niobrara. He pleaded guilty to the theft of three horses, then was imprisoned, but released on June 18, 1883, only to learn that his second wife had remarried. Unfazed, Doc married the teenaged sister of his second wife. Doc opened a series of saloons, served as a deputy sheriff, and even reportedly performed briefly in the Buffalo Bill Cody Wild West Show. He was arrested again on November 11, 1913, on a charge of operating an illegal saloon. Middleton contracted erysipelas, a contagious disease that proved fatal. Doc carried the legacy of being "an outlaw of the worst kind, a horse thief, a handsome cuss."

Hutton, 8-27, 39-57, 129-48; Metz, *Encyclopedia,* 207; Nash, 232; *Lincoln Journal Star,* "Doc Middleton, One of Nebraska's Most Infamous Outlaws," April 14, 2002.

Middleton, John (of Indian Territory) (d. 1885)

Perhaps a cousin of Jim Reed, the Arkansas native murdered J. H. Black, the sheriff of Lamar County, Texas, on November 16, 1884, allegedly at the behest of former sheriff G. M. Crook. Middleton may have also become a lover of Belle Starr. He was found dead near Keota on the banks of the Poteau River in the Choctaw Nation. Sam Starr was his suspected killer.

Harmon, *Hell on the Border,* 586; Shirley, *Belle Starr,* 175-76, 178, 180, 247-48, 256.

Middleton, John (of New Mexico)

Little is known of the John Middleton who rode with Henry McCarty during the Lincoln County War. One historian, Ramon Adams, states that after separating from McCarty at Tascosa, Texas, in 1878, the John Middleton of New Mexico went to Barber County, Kansas, where he ran a grocery store. Another authority states, however, that the John Middleton of New Mexico died in 1885, the very year that a John Middleton associated with Belle Starr died in the Choctaw Nation, Indian Territory.

Adams, *More Burs Under the Saddle,* 72; Utley, *High Noon in Lincoln,* 166.

Miller, George Daniel (Hookey) (1861-1923)

A Dallas County, Texas, native and amputee, George "Hookey" Miller overcame his handicap to become a skilled gunfighter. Miller served six months as a Texas Ranger, under Capt. George Baylor, but resigned and drifted into unsavory pursuits. Consequently, he sported a hook in lieu of the right hand he lost while fighting on March 5, 1896, at the side of notorious outlaw George "Red Buck" Weightman. Red Buck had been expelled from the Doolin Gang for unprofessional conduct when he murdered an old preacher for no reason at all. Eventually Miller joined the ranks of law enforcement and was killed with Two Gun John Middleton while attempting to arrest an oil field troublemaker in Oklahoma.

Selected Oklahoma Robberies and Gunfights

Near Arapaho, Oklahoma Territory, February 14, 1896

George and Red Buck killed informant W. W. Glover, according to a grand jury indictment returned in April 1896. No trial was conducted.

Canute, Oklahoma Territory, March 5, 1896

About five miles north of Canute, on March 5, 1896, Hookey lost his right hand and parts of three fingers on his left hand while Red Buck was killed, in a gunfight with Deputy Sheriff Joe Ventioner and posse. George was incarcerated in the Texas Prison System, which fitted him with a prosthesis, perhaps in the vain hope he would become a farmer when paroled. Instead, when released in 1900, George developed the ability to shoot effectively in spite of his missing right hand. Little is known of his whereabouts until 1905.

Southeastern Pottawatomie County, Oklahoma Territory, early July 1905

Employed as a bartender at the Corner Saloon on the dividing line between the Chickasaw and Seminole Nations, Hookey killed Ed Hendricks, reputedly in a dispute over liquor sales. Hookey disappeared again until 1923, when he became a Kay County deputy sheriff assigned to work with Two Gun John Middleton at Three Sands, a booming oil town.

Three Sands, Oklahoma, July 21, 1923

Hookey and Two Gun John Middleton (no apparent relation to nineteenth-century men of the same name) were each wounded in a gunfight with Jackson Burns, whom Middleton had previously arrested. The two lawmen entered a restaurant to confront Burns. Middleton ran out the door as soon as the shooting started. Miller's poignant last words while poised on the edge of eternity were that his only wish was to live long enough to kill Middleton. The wish was unfulfilled, but Middleton died anyway.

Butler, *Oklahoma Renegades,* 176-83.

Miller, James B. (Killin' Jim, Killer Miller, Deacon) (1866-1909)

Miller was born on October 24, 1866, in Van Buren, Arkansas. While still a very young boy, Jim moved with his family to Franklin, Texas. His murderous tendencies began just eight short years after his birth. After his parents' death, he lived with his grandparents in Evant, Texas, at least until he was detained for their murder. Although he was ultimately released, the stigma lingered long with the young man.

Miller next found shelter in the home of his sister and her husband, John E. Coop, near Gatesville, Texas. When Miller was seventeen, he

"Deacon" Jim Miller, seated at gambling table wearing white hat. Photo taken in an El Paso saloon. Miller would later be lynched in Ada, Oklahoma, by an angry mob in 1909. (Courtesy of the Nina Stewart Haley Memorial Library, Midland, Texas, Robert N. Mullin Collection)

Miller and friends hang out together in Ada. From left: Jim Miller, Joe Allen, Berry Burrell, Jesse West. (Courtesy of the Nina Stewart Haley Memorial Library, J. Evetts Haley Collection)

was accused of killing his brother-in-law. After his acquittal, Miller went to work as a cowhand on the ranch of Mannen Clements in McCulloch County. After his employer was killed, Miller allegedly located the assailant and ambushed him. He spent at least two years prowling the Mexican border around San Saba where he ran a saloon and then started wearing the badge. As town marshal at Pecos, Miller often boasted of the large number of Mexican men he had killed, allegedly in the line of duty, while they were supposed to have attempted escape. He was once quoted as boasting, "I have lost my notch stick on Mexicans that I killed out on the border."

By 1891, Miller married Mannen Clements' daughter, Sallie, and took up the Methodist faith. He was so consumed by his newfound religious fervor that he was given the nickname "Deacon." When he wasn't speaking at or at least attending prayer meetings, Deacon Miller could be hired out as a $150 assassin, or so the rumors said. One of Miller's alleged victims was famed lawman Pat Garrett. A later assassination, that of Ada, Oklahoma, rancher Angus A. "Gus"

Bobbitt, so riled the local populace that Miller was quickly sought by extradition from Texas. Miller was so confident of acquittal that he waived extradition, but was promptly lynched by a mob with the three men who had hired him, on rumors that highly successful defense lawyer Moman Pruiett would represent them.

Selected Gunfights

Plum Creek, Texas, July 30, 1884

Miller allegedly crept up on his sleeping brother-in-law, John Coop, at the latter's farm near Gatesville, and shotgunned him to death. He was convicted of murder, but was later released on a technicality. A second trial was never conducted.

Near Ballinger, Texas, 1887

Mannen Clements, an employer of Miller, was shot and killed by Ballinger city marshal Joe Townsend on March 29, 1887. Townsend was ambushed not long afterward along a dark road with a single shotgun blast. Townsend recovered, but his left arm was amputated. Miller was never charged, much less convicted.

Pecos, Texas, April 12, 1894

Miller was freed after being arrested by Sheriff Bud Frazer for mule theft. One theory has it that Frazer feared retaliation by the renowned quick-tempered, quicker trigger-fingered Miller and took a pot shot at Miller. Miller returned fire but missed Frazer, instead hitting a bystander, Joe Kraus, in the hip. Frazer kept firing until he had emptied his six-gun into Miller's chest and Miller went down but not for long. Miller regularly wore a steel breastplate for just such an occasion.

Pecos, Texas, December 26, 1894

Frazer again pulled a sneak attack on Miller. This time he spied his quarry outside a blacksmith shop and opened fire on him. Miller was hit twice but worked his six-gun in the direction of the sheriff. Two of Frazer's rounds glanced harmlessly off Miller's breastplate. Frazer, perhaps seeing the uselessness of further effort, ran off.

Toyah, Texas, September 14, 1896

Frazer left Texas after the last Pecos debacle of 1894, and landed in Carlsbad, New Mexico. He tempted fate by returning to the greater Pecos area for a visit with his mother and sister at the small village of Toyah. Deacon Miller found Frazer catching up with old friends in a saloon, where Miller blew away most of Frazer's head with his favorite shotgun. When the sister berated Miller back in Pecos, he offered to shoot her too.

Coryell County, Texas, 1899

Miller allegedly shot the only witness to testify in the Frazer killing at Toyah. Joe Earp was ambushed about three weeks after the prosecution was unsuccessful in convicting Miller. Supposedly, Miller spurred his horse on a hundred-mile gallop to establish an alibi.

Ward County, Texas, summer 1902

Claiming to have encountered cattle rustlers near the Pecos River, Miller shot and killed two men and wounded a third who managed to stay atop his horse and escape.

West Texas, ca. 1903

While hired to guard a cattle herd near the Mexican border, Miller came upon two Mexicans butchering a stolen steer, and shot and killed the pair.

Near Lubbock, Texas, ca. 1904

Taking up his old profession as contract killer, Miller received $500 to eliminate Lubbock lawyer James Jarrott, who had raised the ire of area ranchers by winning court cases for nesters. Miller did kill Jarrott, but only after having to shoot him four times, prompting the assassin to complain, "He was the hardest damn man to kill I ever tackled."

Fort Griffin, Texas, 1904

Miller stalked Frank Fore into the restroom of the Hotel Westbrook where he coolly shot the man to death. Upon returning to the hotel lobby he saw lawman Dee Harkey and attempted to surrender himself to the lawman. But Harkey had been talking with two of Miller's associates, Jenks Clark and Tom Coggin, and said he wanted nothing whatsoever to do with the incident. Clark and Coggin later testified that they saw the whole thing and that Miller was forced to shoot Fore in self-defense.

Near Emet, Indian Territory, August 1, 1906

Miller was indicted but never convicted in the shooting ambush and death of U.S. Deputy Marshal Ben Collins. In 1903 Collins had shot Port Pruitt, partially paralyzing him, and family members swore their

Jim Lee, Wayne Brazil, and Will Craven, around 1900. Brazil (center) was present when Pat Garrett was assassinated while stopping to relieve himself along a dirt road. Brazil initially took blame for the murder, but it is still widely accepted that Jim Miller did the deed. (Courtesy of the University of Texas at El Paso Archives, Hal Cox Collection)

revenge. Three years later, on August 1, 1906, Collins was nearing his home when a load of buckshot hit his stomach. Collins fell from his saddle but managed to empty his six-gun in the direction of his assailant before he was killed with a second load of buckshot to the face.

Near Las Cruces, New Mexico, February, 29, 1908

The most renowned of Miller's alleged victims was the legendary lawman Pat Garrett. Garrett was riding with fellow ranchers Wayne Brazil (Brazel) and Carl Adamson, when Garrett stopped the buggy and stepped out to relieve himself. He was shot in the back of the head with a .45-caliber bullet, and as he spun on his heels in the direction of the shooter he received a second slug to the belly. He died at the scene. Brazil inexplicably confessed to the murder but was cleared, leaving wide speculation that Miller was the hit man.

Ada, Oklahoma, February 26, 1909

Once again crossing the Red River to accept a contract, Miller ambushed Gus Bobbitt who was returning home driving a supply wagon. An employee of Bobbitt's, Bob Ferguson, was driving a second wagon and raced around the deadly scene. Miller was tracked to Fort Worth and waived extradition, but before a trial could be conducted Miller was hanged, along with his three employers, in a livery stable in Ada on April 19, 1909.

O'Neal, *Encyclopedia,* 230-33; Metz, *Encyclopedia,* 172; Metz, *Pat Garrett,* 234, 239, 242-48; Nash, 233-34; Shirley, *Shotgun for Hire,* 1-32, 34-40, 59-116.

Morales, Lopez (d. 1925)

A murder suspect, Morales was killed on March 26, 1925, in Abilene, Texas, by Police Chief Robert Burch, Deputy Chief Lige Jennings, and other bystanders while resisting arrest. Morales had killed Howard County sheriff W. W. Satterwhite and Young County constable George L. Reeves while resisting arrest on March 24, 1925. Morales had wounded both law enforcement officers in a gunfight, then dispatched each in cold blood. Morales himself was dispatched by a crowd "assisting" the Abilene officers.

Hatley, *Texas Constables,* 136; Tise, 269.

Musgrave, George (ca. 1874-1947)

Musgrave was born in Texas and raised in New Mexico, where he joined the outlaw gang of Black Jack Christian. Early during his outlaw career, Musgrave was betrayed in a cattle rustling scheme by his associate George T. Parker. He would later kill Parker at a Diamond A roundup wagon on the Rio Feliz, southwest of Roswell, New Mexico, on October 19, 1896. Between the time of the betrayal and the settling of that score, Musgrave found work on ranches throughout Arizona using many aliases, including Jeff Davis, Jesse Miller, Jesse Johnson, or Jesse Williams.

Musgrave eventually joined the notorious Christian brothers, Bob and Bill, and their gang, the "High Fives." After the death of Black Jack, Musgrave continued to ride with Bob Christian. The two of them were arrested in 1897 at Fronteras, but released due to lack of evidence. Musgrave maintained a low profile for several years until he was recognized and arrested at North Platte, Colorado, on Christmas Day 1909, then charged with the shooting death of his one-time cattle rustling pal, George Parker. Acquitted once again, Musgrave was released on June 10, 1910. He died on August 15, 1947.

Thrapp, *Encyclopedia*, II, 1035-36; Metz, *Encyclopedia*, 177; Tanner and Tanner, 25-69, 105-253.

Newcomb, George (Bitter Creek, Slaughter's Kid) (d. 1895)

Newcomb left his Fort Scott, Kansas, home while still a youth. He traveled to Texas and went to work on C. C. Slaughter's ranch, prompting those who knew the boy to dub him Slaughter's Kid. In 1883 Newcomb hit the dusty trail once again, finding work as a cowboy in the Cherokee Strip ranching country of Indian Territory (Oklahoma). He received the nickname "Bitter Creek" by repeating the lyrics to a song, which were, "I'm a wild wolf from Bitter Creek." Newcomb changed careers soon afterwards, becoming a criminal and riding with both the Doolin and Dalton gangs.

Newcomb was present with the Doolin gang at Ingalls, Oklahoma Territory, in September 1893, when that gang came under attack by a posse. Newcomb was injured in the wild exchange of gunfire but escaped. A year earlier, in July 1892, Newcomb was with the Dalton gang when that bunch robbed the train station at Adair, Indian Territory, and exchanged shots with lawmen on an incoming passenger train.

Newcomb was killed when he and fellow bandit Charlie Pierce stopped at Rose Dunn's family home for a hasty visit. Rose's brothers welcomed them with a hail of bullets. It seems the $5,000 reward on Bitter Creek's head was just what the Dunn brothers needed to put an end to their sister's affair with the outlaw. It wasn't until the next day that the bodies were loaded into a wagon and hauled off to town where the brothers were expecting to receive the reward money. The wagon ride held one surprise, however, in that Bitter Creek wasn't dead and moaned that he wanted some water. The startled Dunn brothers answered his plea with a bullet, or so the story goes.

Smith, *Daltons*, 49; O'Neal, *Encyclopedia*, 93, 242-43; Metz, *The Shooters*, 71; Nash, 241-42.

Newton Boys (prom. 1920s)

The Newton Boys, featured in a 1998 movie of the same name,

were Texans from Cottonwood, near Dallas, who claimed to have robbed more than eighty banks and six trains. They conducted the largest train robbery in United States history in 1924, netting $3 million ($32,556,103 today) in an Illinois job. The record still stands. Willis served six years at the federal prison in Leavenworth, Kansas, was supposedly pardoned at the suggestion of FBI director J. Edgar Hoover, and thereafter owned two Tulsa clubs, the Buckhorn and the Music Box. Brothers Jess and William "Doc" Newton reputedly resumed small-time criminal careers after prison, but Joe Newton went straight. Doc Newton capped his career by robbing a bank at Rowena, Texas, at age seventy-seven, earning a brief return to prison.

Newton and Newton, 1-47, 95-104, 181-202, 267-321; Interview, *Tulsa World,* January 1, 2000; Helmer and Mattix, 21.

O'Folliard, Thomas (Tom) (1858-80)

O'Folliard was born in Uvalde, Texas. His parents were Irish immigrants who moved to Mexico just prior to the Civil War and later died of smallpox in Monclova, Mexico. O'Folliard returned to Uvalde where he was raised by relatives. At age twenty, O'Folliard left Texas for New Mexico, where he began stealing horses.

One of his victims, Emil Fritz, was a member of the Murphy-Dolan faction, and O'Folliard soon found himself in the Lincoln County War, mentored by Billy the Kid. After the Lincoln County War had concluded, O'Folliard, Billy the Kid and others continued their lawlessness by stealing horses throughout New Mexico and the Texas Panhandle. O'Folliard was killed by Pat Garrett and perhaps others on December 19, 1880, at Fort Sumner.

Selected Gunfights
Lincoln, New Mexico, July 15-19, 1878

A four-day war between the Regulators and the Murphy-Dolan faction ended only when U.S. Cavalry troops toting cannon and a Gatling gun entered the besieged town, siding with Murphy. O'Folliard and Billy the Kid were trapped in the besieged McSween house. O'Folliard was wounded while fleeing, Billy escaped unscathed, but McSween and others were shot and killed.

Lincoln County, New Mexico, December 1880

Pat Garrett and an exhausted posse came across O'Folliard on open ground and gave chase. Garrett's tired horses, just brought down from a rugged mountain pass, were no match for the rested, faster horse from which O'Folliard fired his rifle as he galloped into the distance.

Fort Sumner, New Mexico, December 19, 1880

O'Folliard, the Kid, and four other desperados rode into Fort Sumner and were spotted by the Garrett posse, which had bunked at the abandoned post hospital. O'Folliard received a rifle slug to the chest just below the heart. Unable to fight or ride, the outlaw rode toward Garrett and asked the lawmen to take him down from his saddle. He died several hours later, cursing Garrett. He was buried in the Fort Sumner cemetery where his friend Billy the Kid would soon join him.

O'Neal, *Encyclopedia,* 244-45; Metz, *Pat Garrett,* 75; Nash, 244.

Olguin Family (prom. 1890s)

A family of thieves, the Olguins lived in Tres Jacales, Mexico, near their patriarch Clato Olguin, who was content to live in peaceful retirement having spent a lifetime as a criminal. His sons, Antonio and Jesus Maria, carried on their father's work of cattle rustling, train robbing, and any other pursuit that called for the unlawful liberation of someone else's hard-earned stock, money, or other possessions. They became such a nuisance along the Texas-Mexico border that the Texas Rangers were summoned to assist with the arrest of Antonio, Jesus Maria, and his son, Severio. But an across-the-border shoot-out resulted in the death of Texan and company commander Frank Jones, who had led the Rangers into the desperados' den. The Olguins made a clean escape.

Selected Gunfights

Tres Jacales, Mexico, June 30, 1893

In search of cattle thieves Jesus Maria Olguin and his son Severio, the Texas Rangers led by Capt. Frank Jones, a native Texan, met with disaster after chasing the pair into a settlement there. Barricaded, the Olguins, joined by Jesus' brother, Antonio, opened up on the posse, killing Jones. The Olguins managed to sneak away to safety following the confusion of the Rangers at the death of their commander.

O'Neal, *Encyclopedia,* 172-73; Utley, *Lone Star Lawmen* 265-66; Nash, 245.

Olive, Isom Prentice (Print) (1840-86)

Olive lived in Williamson County, Texas, on his father's ranch when the Civil War began. Olive joined the Texas Volunteers. After the war he returned to Williamson County to resume ranching interests. He later became both revered and reviled in his quest to build his ranching empire. He was known for less than tolerant means of dealing with rustlers. He brutally killed those who were found with Olive cattle in their possession without a proper bill of sale. In time, the hatred that Print Olive aroused in decent folk forced him to move to three different states before he was shot to death by a lonesome loser who owed the former cattle baron ten dollars.

Selected Gunfights
Trail City, Colorado, Monday, August 16, 1886
As Olive pushed open the swinging doors of his favorite saloon he was met with a gun blast from the weapon held by Joe Sparrow, a blowhard and part-time badman who owed Olive ten dollars. Apparently Olive made several threats earlier in attempts to motivate the lackluster cowboy to repay the loan. Instead, the threats only served to motivate Sparrow to kill the lender.

Tyler, *The New Handbook of Texas,* vol. 4, 1145-46; Metz, *Encyclopedia,* 183; Nash, 246.

Outlaw, Baz (Bass) (1855-94)

Reportedly the son of a respectable family, the unfortunately named Texas Ranger joined up in 1885, but ran afoul of rules prohibiting drinking on guard duty. He resigned and became a deputy U.S. marshal and engaged in two alcohol-fueled gunfights, ultimately leading to his death in El Paso on April 5, 1894.

Camp Rioletas. Texas Rangers' camp at a spot called Rioletas while on patrol. Left to right: Walter Durbin, stirring fire; Ernest Rogers, eating; John Hughes, sitting on ground; Dude Johns, on stool; E. R. Goff, making bread; Frank Smith at Dutch oven; Wood Sanders, to right of Smith; Bass Outlaw, raising tin cup; Cal Aten, brother of notable Texas Ranger, Ira Aten, seated to right of Outlaw; Capt. Frank Jones, seated and looking at photographer. The man standing is not identified. (Courtesy of the Nina Stewart Haley Memorial Library, Midland, Texas, J. Evetts Haley Collection)

Gunfights

Sierra Del Carmen, Coahuila, Mexico, 1889

During a break from his security work at a silver mine, Outlaw found time to kill a miner who had threatened him with a knife, then bolted for the border.

Near Vance, Texas, December 25, 1889

Outlaw and fellow Rangers Ira Aten, John Hughes, and Deputy Sheriff Will Terry ambushed the Odle brothers, ruining their last Christmas.

El Paso, April 5, 1894

While waiting to give trial testimony, Outlaw became inebriated during an afternoon bar crawl, then killed Texas Ranger Joe McKidrick before being mortally wounded by Constable John Selman. "Where are my friends?" Outlaw wailed, just before dying some five hours later. Apparently, he had forgotten that he had just killed one.

Metz, *John Selman,* 139-50, 203, 223; O'Neal, *Encyclopedia,* 248.

Palmer, Joseph Conger (Joe) (1904-32)

Quiet, no-nonsense, Texas-born Joe Palmer was an old friend of Clyde Barrow. He became an integral part of the Barrow gang after the January 16, 1934, breakout from Eastham Prison Farm by Palmer, Ray Hamilton, and others. Palmer certainly knew how to carry a grudge. Wade McNabb, with whom he had quarreled in prison, discovered this trait the hard way. Unbeknown to McNabb, Palmer had arranged for McNabb to enjoy a sixty-day furlough, at the end of which Palmer murdered him on March 29, 1934, near Waskom, Texas, as revenge for prison beatings, with the connivance of Ray Hamilton and Clyde Barrow.

Earlier, Palmer had mortally wounded prison guard Major (given name) Joseph Crowson during the 1934 Eastham breakout. Later, Palmer related that he had warned Bonnie and Clyde to stay out of Louisiana, shortly before submitting his resignation from the gang at Wichita in early May. Palmer learned of their deaths while lounging in the lobby of the Hutchins Hotel in Oklahoma City. He then traveled to Dallas by a circuitous route through Tulsa and attended Barrow's funeral unrecognized. Soon recaptured, he escaped Huntsville Prison with Ray Hamilton and Blackie Thompson on July 22, 1934, only to be apprehended again at Paducah, Kentucky, on August 11, 1934.

Palmer was electrocuted just before Ray Hamilton on May 10, 1935. The pair had been prepared for death by irrepressible prison chaplain Father Hugh Finnegan, whose admonitions apparently had a salutary effect on the cold-blooded killers. Only a few years before, Hamilton and Palmer had quarreled bitterly about the division of Barrow gang spoils and nearly had a gunfight. Yet in the end, Palmer accommodated Hamilton's fears by volunteering to be executed first. Hamilton was later observed crossing himself before riding Old Sparky.

Selected Robberies and Gunfights
Eastham Prison Farm, Texas, January 16, 1934

During a prison break engineered by Clyde Barrow and Floyd

Hamilton, Palmer mortally wounded Major Joseph Crowson, who died eleven days later.

Rembrandt, Iowa, January 23, 1934

Palmer, Ray Hamilton, Hilton Bybee, and Henry Methvin robbed the First National Bank of $3,800.

Poteau, Oklahoma, January 26, 1934

The same crew (except Bybee) robbed the Central National Bank of $1,500.

Everly, Iowa, May 3, 1934

Joe Palmer, Henry Methvin, and Clyde Barrow robbed the Farmer's Trust and Savings Branch, taking at least $7,000. This was the last confirmed bank robbery of the Barrow gang.

Knight, 125, 132-34, 142, 154, 156-58, 161, 175, 187-88, 190, 202-3; Helmer and Mattix, 15, 217, 221, 229; Milner, 102-6, 114, 116, 122, 159.

Parker, Bonnie (1910-34)

Born in Rowena, Texas, Bonnie was, according to family stories, a bright and happy child. She became a study in divided loyalties, contradictions, and an American tragedy during hard times in tough West Dallas, Texas, where the Depression started in the twenties. She married Roy Thornton, an alumnus of the juvenile reform school at El Reno, Oklahoma, in 1926, and was faithful to him in her own way. Although he was in prison during her years on the criminal road with Clyde Barrow, she refused to divorce Thornton and was wearing his wedding ring when she died. Even though she had no problem associating with trigger-happy Clyde Barrow, Oklahoma's Ray Hamilton, and other stone-cold killers, she was kind to children, pets, family members, and hostages.

Loyal to Barrow to the end, she refused his entreaties to turn herself in, sharing his death as she had predicted in a fabled poem.

Her first known criminal act was smuggling a weapon to Clyde Barrow in prison to aid an escape. She committed her first robbery with Barrow at Kaufman, Texas, east of Dallas, on April 19, 1932. She participated in numerous holdups thereafter, but always waited in cars while Clyde and others collected the cash. Perhaps her

Bonnie Parker and Clyde Barrow pose standing together in an apparent rural setting. (Courtesy of the Dallas Public Library, Dallas, Texas)

fate was sealed when a press report incorrectly portrayed her as the killer of two motorcycle patrolmen shot by Henry Methvin and Clyde Barrow at Grapevine, Texas, Easter Sunday, April 1, 1934. She died with Clyde on May 23, 1934 in a Louisiana ambush. Her family and some 10,000 curious onlookers participated in her funeral ceremonials in Dallas, Texas.

Steele and Scoma, 37, 50; Milner, 17, 31; Knight, 3, 142, 147, 194.

Peacock, Lewis (d. 1871)

Lewis Peacock led a band of post-Civil War Reconstruction Union League soldiers and Unionists throughout North Texas. One rival group, led by Bob Lee, was in repeated conflict with Peacock and his men. The ensuing four-year feud went on, although Lee was killed in 1869, two years before the end of the violence. Peacock was gunned down while retrieving firewood one evening at his home in Pilot Grove (also known as Lick Skillet), Texas, in 1871.

Selected Gunfights
Pilot Grove, Texas, April 1868
The Lee and Peacock factions faced off against each other in Pilot Grove. Peacock was wounded in the fray, but no fatalities occurred.
Hunt County, Texas, June 15, 1868
While seeing to their mounts at the Nance farm, Peacock and his men came under attack. Lee's men fatally wounded three of Peacock's men. The Lee force escaped without injury.
Near Farmersville, Texas, December 1868
Peacock narrowly escaped injury again, while leading some of his own men and a contingent of Union soldiers on a hunt for Lee. The Peacock contingent was ambushed, resulting in the death of one soldier and the injury of a Peacock partisan.
Pilot Grove, Texas, June 13, 1871
Even though Lee was killed in 1869, his friends Dick Johnson and Joe Parker nevertheless watched Peacock's home and waited for an opportunity to kill him. They did so as Peacock stepped outside his home in Pilot Grove to fetch firewood.

O'Neal, *Encyclopedia,* 253-54; Sonnichsen, *I'll Die Before I Run,* 22-25, 28, 30-33; Metz, *Encyclopedia,* 151.

Pickett, Tom (1856-1934)

Tom Pickett, whose father became a Confederate officer, was born on May 27, 1856, in Wise County, Texas. Tom served briefly as a Texas Ranger before becoming a Kansas gambler and earning his mark in Western lore during the Lincoln County War in New Mexico. Pickett apparently accompanied Dave Rudabaugh from Kansas to New Mexico. Following brief stints as a peace officer in Las Vegas and White Oaks, Pickett entered the moonlight cattle market with fellow rustlers Charlie Bowdre, Henry McCarty (Billy the Kid), and Tom O'Folliard. After O'Folliard's death, Pickett drifted on to Arizona, married in 1888, and served in the administration of President Woodrow Wilson before dying in Pinetop, Arizona, on May 14, 1934. His claim to fame was the fabled Stinking Springs shoot-out pitting Billy the Kid and other Regulators against Pat Garrett and a posse. The Regulators were trapped in an abandoned cabin, but surrendered after Bowdre was killed. Pickett posted a three-hundred-dollar bail and soon bolted for Arizona.

Nolan, 213, 247-48; O'Neal, *Encyclopedia,* 254.

Place, Etta (Ethel Place) (b. ca. 1879)
    Etta (or Ethel) Place was supposedly a schoolteacher identified by the Pinkerton Detective Agency as a prostitute from Texas who became the love interest of Harry Longabaugh, known to the world as the Sundance Kid. Etta traveled with Longabaugh and his partner Robert LeRoy Parker (Butch Cassidy) to South America. She may have participated with the outlaw pair in several bank robberies there before she returned to the United States and anonymity in about 1907.

Pointer, 3, 6, 16, 18, 162-63, 195-98, 200-202, 205, 207-8, 212-13, 217, 256-57; O'Neal, *Encyclopedia,* 191; Metz, *Encyclopedia,* 40, 41; Ernst, *Women of the Wild Bunch,* 59-77.

Poe, John William (1850-1923)
    Poe was born on a farm in Mason County, Kentucky, but left home at a very young age. He put down roots in Fort Griffin, Texas, around 1872 and began hunting buffalo, and at one time claimed to have killed 20,000 of them. Poe became a lawman in 1878, serving as city marshal in Fort Griffin. About a year later he was deputy sheriff in Wheeler County. He spent some time as a

U.S. deputy marshal before (or maybe while) serving the Canadian River Cattle Association as a private detective. He walked right by Billy the Kid on July 14, 1881, failing to recognize him, mere minutes before the Kid was killed.

Poe investigated Pat Coughlin in Tularosa, New Mexico, on suspicion of assasination, and managed to have him formally indicted. He was sheriff of Lincoln County in 1882, where he got married. He resigned that post about two years later and moved to Roswell, New Mexico. He became a prominent citizen there, founding two banks, served on the Board of Regents of the New Mexico Military Institute, and as president of the New Mexico State Tax Commission. He died on July 17, 1923, in Battle Creek, Michigan.

Metz, *Encyclopedia,* 198; Nolan, 173, 230-31, 277.

Post, Wiley Hardeman (1898-1935)

Today, few Southwesterners are aware that the heroic, world-renowned aviator and friend of Will Rogers had an earlier, less admirable career. He was born on November 22, 1898, at Grand Saline, Texas, to Irish-American Mae Quinlan Post and William Francis Post, a Scot. The family had lived in Oklahoma earlier and migrated to Rush Springs in 1907. Trained as an automobile mechanic and employed as an oilfield roughneck, Wiley eventually tried his hand at highway banditry. In early April 1921, the *Chickasha Star* reported his capture. He had been hijacking cars near Ninnekah that spring. Arrested, brought to Chickasha, and convicted of robbery on April 21, 1921, he was sentenced to ten years in the state reformatory at Granite. Paroled by Governor J. B. A. Robertson on June 3, 1922, he went on to become a distinguished aircraft pioneer, associating with such aviation leaders as oilman Frank Phillips, aviatrix Amelia Earhart, and others involved in the fledgling industry. Within ten years of his parole, his exploits setting records aboard the *Winnie Mae* won him worldwide acclaim. He met two presidents and numerous other luminaries before his tragic death with Will Rogers near Point Barrow, Alaska, on August 15, 1935, brought to a close perhaps the most prominent story of personal redemption in Southwestern history.

Burke, 19-25, 186.

Pruiett, Moman (1872-1945)

Born on July 12, 1872, at Alton, Illinois, the son of a Confederate veteran, Pruiett knew much about criminality first hand. Convicted of forgery in December 1887, he served eight months of a two-year sentence. In Paris, Texas, he was convicted of robbery, serving two years for this offense. He swore that he would return and defeat the judicial system, or so the story goes. After parole, he returned to Paris, Texas, where he worked in a cotton warehouse by day and studied law by night, gaining admittance to the Texas bar in 1895.

He then established his practice at Pauls Valley, Oklahoma Territory, and was known for exonerating clients at any cost. Possessing a violent streak, he supposedly once shot a man for borrowing his father's dress coat without permission. On another occasion, Pruiett and a client brawled during jury deliberations. Pruiett later stood proudly by his bandaged client as the jury foreman intoned "not guilty."

Pruiett won acquittals in 303 of the 343 death penalty cases he tried, often with dubitable evidence. His reputation for success at any cost was so potent that four men, including notorious assassin Jim Miller, were lynched at Ada on the rumor that Pruiett would defend them on murder charges. Pruiett died on December 12, 1945, in Oklahoma City.

Gunfight
Oklahoma City, October 1921
Pruiett killed Oklahoma City bootlegger and gambler Joe Patterson in a gunfight at Patterson's home. A coroner's jury decided the killing was justified.

Butler, *Oklahoma Renegades*, 142-50; Shirley, *Shotgun for Hire*, 96-97, 114.

Quantrill, William (1837-65)

William Quantrill was a guerrilla leader of Western Missouri who occasionally forayed into Texas and Indian Territory. One authority places him in Indian Territory in August 1861, where he joined Cherokee Confederates en route to the battle of Wilson's Creek, Missouri. In October 1863 Quantrill and his forces massacred eleven members of the First Indian Home Guard near the Creek Agency. Another source states that in 1864 Quantrill led his forces, which included Frank James and Jim and Cole Younger, through the Choctaw Nation, capturing and killing twelve Union troopers near Perryville. Earlier the raiders had slaughtered some ten unarmed musicians near Baxter Springs, Kansas, on October 6, 1863.

Quantrill headquartered in Northern Texas, near Sherman, in the spring of 1864. Discipline among Quantrill's followers was less than exemplary. Perturbed Confederate commanders, including Generals Sterling Price and Henry McCulloch, met little success reining in the Missourians, who simply rode out of Texas on April 10, 1864. Quantrill returned to Missouri in December, then traveled with some thirty partisans to Kentucky. He was mortally wounded in Spencer County, about five miles south of Taylorsville, by forces under the command of Capt. Edward Terrell. The guerilla leader died in a prison hospital at Louisville on June 6, 1865, after converting to Catholicism.

Milligan, 115; Yeatman, 46; McCorkle, 144-45; Castel and Goodrich, 33-36.

Raidler, William F. (Little Bill) (1865-ca. 1905)

Raidler was an educated man who hailed from a Pennsylvania Dutch family. He spent some time as a cowboy in Texas, then Oklahoma Territory, where he met Bill Doolin and the two became fast friends. Raidler joined the gang, which committed many of their holdups in Oklahoma Territory. Raidler was shot six times while resisting arrest by possemen led by noted lawman Bill Tilghman. Raidler survived, was imprisoned, and married after famed Deputy U.S. Marshal Bill Tilghman facilitated his release. Poor health attributable to wounds suffered during his arrest resulted in Raidler's death several years thereafter.

Selected Gunfights
Near Dover, Oklahoma Territory, spring 1895
Raidler and other Doolin gang members escaped the surprise attack of a posse upon the outlaw camp. Only the outlaw Tulsa Jack Blake was killed in the forty-five-minute gun battle.
Southwest City, Missouri, May 20, 1895
The Doolin gang, having just robbed a bank, was met with heavy gunfire from the guns of angry citizens. As Raidler was galloping out

of town he let loose an imprecise barrage of bullets. One passed through Oscar Seaborn, a citizen who was barely injured. His brother Joe was not so lucky. As Joe stepped outside the Seaborn store to see the commotion, the same bullet killed him instantly.

Near Bartlesville, Indian Territory, July 1895

Raidler was hiding in a cave near town when he was located by lawman Heck Thomas and two Osage Indian scouts. Raidler opened up on the trio with his rifle. Thomas fired back, and one bullet slammed into Raidler's right hand. Raidler left his rifle as he scampered into nearby brush and amputated the two mangled fingers of the injured hand. He successfully escaped capture by hiding in a tree.

Near Elgin, Kansas, September 6, 1895

Raidler found refuge from the authorities at the Sam Moore ranch about eighteen miles south of Elgin, Kansas. At least until the evening of September 6, 1895, when deputy U.S. Marshal Bill Tilghman found him. During the gun battle that followed, Raidler was again shot in the hand. Unable to shoot, he turned and ran right into the path of Deputy U.S. Marshal W. C. Smith, who blasted him with a load of buckshot. Wounded in both sides of his body, the neck, the hand, and twice in the head, Raidler collapsed. After Sam Moore and his wife tended his wounds he was taken into custody. Raidler served time in prison, but with the help of Tilghman he was granted early parole.

Shirley, *West of Hell's Fringe,* 186, 191, 267, 273, 276, 318-20, 324; O'Neal, *Encyclopedia,* 258-59; Nash, 263.

Ratliff, Marshal (the Santa Claus Robber) (d. 1929)

Marshal and Lee Ratliff planned a rather unusual costume party and holiday heist for December 23, 1927, at Cisco, Texas. The brothers had been injudiciously released after serving one year of their respective lengthy sentences for robbing a bank at Valera. Lee was re-arrested before the Cisco job, requiring the gang to replace him. Other gang members included Henry Helms, his relative Louis Davis (who replaced Lee Ratliff), and Robert Hill.

Marshal Ratliff borrowed a Santa suit from his landlady Midge Tellett, and walked toward the targeted bank, drawing a throng of excited children along the way. Patrons and staff alike saw the cranky side of Santa very quickly. His elves drew weapons inside the bank, enabling St.

Nick to grab cash from the teller, then force his way into the safe.

Meanwhile, Chief of Police G. E. "Bit" Bedford and other well-armed citizenry gathered outside, perhaps enticed by the $5,000 reward recently offered by the Texas Bankers Association for each unquestionably dead bank robber delivered. The excited crowd aimed gunfire into the bank, prompting the Bearded One and his staff to attempt an alleyway escape. While doing so, the suspects mortally wounded Chief Bedford and his deputy, George Carmichael.

During the confusion, the gang attempted to swap the original getaway equipment for the Harris family Oldsmobile, leaving mortally wounded Louis Davis behind to face the music. Somehow, the escaping gang also managed to leave behind every single penny of the stolen loot. Their third getaway car was stolen and promptly wrecked near Putnam.

Soon the gang was ambushed by Sheriff J. B. Foster of Young County and Texas Ranger Cy Bradford while attempting to cross the Brazos River at South Bend. The trio were captured and recovered from their wounds sufficiently enough for Helms to be executed on September 6, 1929. The shock of it all pushed Marshal Ratliff "over the edge," that very day, or so he convinced jail guards, who even cared for his personal toilet needs. Ratliff rapidly recovered at an opportune moment on November 18, 1929, and mortally wounded one of the very guards who had catered to his every whim, only to die the very next evening at the hands of a lynch mob angry enough to hang him twice for good measure. The kind jailer also died that night.

Tyler, *The Handbook of Texas,* vol. 5, 883.

Reed, James C. (Jim Reed, James Black, William Jones, Robert Miller) (1844-74)

A Texas outlaw, Reed was born near Rich Hill, Vernon County, Missouri, in 1844. The quiet, previously religious young man became a Confederate guerilla during the Civil War. Jim met Myra Maebelle Shirley (Belle Starr) in Carthage during the war, then renewed the acquaintance afterwards in Scyene, Texas, where Belle had moved with her parents in the summer of 1864. Contrary to legends placing the love-struck couple in a horseback wedding officiated over by an outlaw,

Belle and Jim were married by an authentic preacher on November 1, 1866. Jim initially worked as a Dallas salesman, but soon returned with his wife to Missouri, working a Bates County farm with his brothers.

The year 1868 heralded the birth of Rosie "Pearl" Reed, in Missouri, but also the death of Belle's brother Ed Shirley, who was shot off of his horse near Dallas. While Belle remained in Bates County, Jim engaged in horse racing in Fort Smith, as well as more nefarious matters in Indian Territory. Reed became part of the Tom Starr gang, which, among other crimes, stole cattle in the Choctaw Nation for delivery to Texas cattle buyers. While so engaged he met Cole Younger, for whom an admiring Tom Starr had named his place Younger's Bend as early as 1866.

Younger, it is said, asked Reed to join in a bank robbery at Russellville, Arkansas. Reed declined at Belle's insistence, or so the story goes. Reed reportedly purchased forty acres in Bosque County, Texas, which he eventually sold before moving to Sycene. His reported accomplices in the November 19, 1873, robbery of Watt Grayson in the Indian Territory were Texans Dan Evans and W. D. Wilder. He also reportedly robbed the San Antonio-Austin stage with "Cal H. Carter" and Jack Rogers four miles north of San Marco on the Blanco River.

Reed also involved himself in the Shannon-Fisher feud in and near Evansville, Arkansas, on the Indian Territory border. On June 2, 1870, Jim Reed and John Fisher ambushed Shannon adherents, N. C. Fitzwater and one Stout. Fitzwater was killed and Stout mortally wounded, drawing the unwelcome attention of law enforcement.

These difficulties spurred a move west to California, where Belle and Jim lived for about two years. A second child, Edwin "Eddie" Reed was born there in 1871. Charges that Jim had passed counterfeit money soon prompted a return to Texas. Land records show that Jim purchased land on Coon Creek in Bosque County, Texas, where he was known as an amiable young man whose neighbors suffered unexplained losses of livestock.

In February 1873 Dick Cravey was robbed and murdered at his home some sixteen miles from Meridian, Texas, by four men, two of whom were identified as brothers Solomon "Sol" Reed and Jim Reed. Six months later, a Reed gang member and informant named Wheeler was murdered, apparently by the Reed brothers, who also removed Wheeler's tongue. The governor of Texas offered a five-hundred-dollar reward for each of the Reeds, encouraging their sudden departure from the Lone Star State. Sol returned to Missouri, while Jim sought other opportunities in Indian Territory. Following two robberies there and a stagecoach holdup near Blanco, Texas, carried out with the assistance of former Fisher gang members, Reed was killed by John T. Morris, a distant relative and friend, sixteen miles northwest of Paris, Texas.

Selected Robberies and Gunfights
Near North Fork Town, Indian Territory, November 19, 1873

James Reed, Texans W. D. Wilder, J. Marion "Burns" Dickens, and perhaps others robbed former Creek Supreme Court justice Watt Grayson of more than $30,000 in gold he was holding for the tribe. Grayson was hanged twice, but only revealed the location of the gold after the gang threatened his wife. Fisher gang alumni Calvin H. Carter (Charles Farmer) and Charles Bush (John Boswell) were initially suspected but eventually eliminated as suspects.

Court documents later provided by Belle Starr established the true identity of Reed's accomplices. Contrary to popular legend, Belle did not participate in the robbery, although she witnessed the division of the proceeds. Wilder was captured in Bosque County, Texas, convicted of the robbery on December 8, 1874, and sentenced to serve one year at the federal penitentiary at Little Rock. Court documents indicate that J. Marion Dickens died before November 27, 1874, at a place and time now unknown. Reed and Belle fled to Texas. The bandits spent virtually all the money on gambling.

Near Blanco, Texas, April 7, 1874

Eleven passengers on the Austin-San Antonio stagecoach were stopped about two miles east of Blanco, by at least three men. About $4,000 and assorted mail was stolen by suspects later identified as Jim Reed, William Boswell, and Calvin H. Carter, the last two being former residents of the Butler, Missouri, area. The gang took the stagecoach horses then departed, leaving the passengers to fend for themselves. Rosa McCommas and J. Marion Dickens were later charged, but no further action was taken since they were not participants. Rosa was an eighteen-year-old from Dallas whom Reed seduced and took to San Antonio just before the robbery.

Near McKinney, Texas, May 23, 1874

Jim Reed was rumored to be visiting the home of John T. Morris, a distant relative and friend, in order to see Rosa McCommas, who had returned from San Antonio. A posse of twenty-five surrounded the home and, due to an error, began firing at it, mortally wounding Deputy U.S. Marshal Herseberg. Reed fled a campsite nearby after hearing the gunfire.

Going Snake District, Cherokee Nation, July 13, 1874

Calvin Carter, Bill Fisher, Jim Reed, and five others traveled to the William Harnage residence. Three gang members asked to spend the night and were later joined by the others who stole more than $1,600 and looted the house of saddlebags and weapons. Later, the gang was surrounded by deputy U.S. marshals and Cherokee police near Muskogee, but escaped.

Near Paris, Texas, August 6, 1874

John T. Morris, specially appointed as a deputy U.S. marshal and Collin County deputy sheriff was tasked to bring in his friend, distant relative, and some say former bandit partner, Jim Reed. Instead, Morris shot and killed Reed at a farmhouse about sixteen miles northwest of Paris where the pair had stopped for lunch. Following custom, Reed and Morris left their weapons on their horses when they entered the home. Soon however, Morris made excuses, returned to his horse, then attempted to arrest Reed, who was mortally wounded in a dining room scuffle. Reed admitted his part in the stagecoach robbery near Blanco just before he died.

O'Neal, *Encyclopedia,* 260-61; Shirley, *Belle Starr,* 51-129; Drago, 95-96, 103.

Reed, Edwin (Ed, Eddie) (1871-96)

Bandit turned lawman, Edwin Reed was the only son of Myra Maebelle Shirley (Belle Starr). Eddie was born in California, but spent his early years in Dallas County, Texas, with his parents, Myra Shirley Reed (Belle Starr), Jim Reed and sister "Pearl." He went to federal prison in August 1889 for receiving stolen goods, but was pardoned through the toil of his soiled-dove sister Pearl in 1893. After an initial bootlegging foray into Indian Territory in 1894, he hired on as a railroad detective, and eventually became a deputy U.S. marshal at

Wagoner, Indian Territory. He married Jennie Cochran of Claremore. Soon, he tangled with former deputy U.S. marshals Zeke and Dick Crittenden, both of whom he sent to the Promised Land on October 25, 1895, at Wagoner. He then joined them himself, courtesy of bootleggers he attempted to arrest on December 14, 1896, in Claremore. Reed apparently suspected them of selling bad whiskey to his father-in-law.

Shirley, *Belle Starr,* 93, 130, 182-83, 251-56; Steele, 76.

Reed, Nathan (Texas Jack) (1862-1950)

Born on March 23, 1862, in Madison County, Arkansas, Reed was orphaned and went west at an early age, working in Colorado, Wyoming, Idaho, and Texas. Eventually, he became a ranch hand in Oklahoma. Reed claimed to have committed seven robberies between 1885 and 1892, none of which distinguished author Glenn Shirley has been able to verify. It is known for certain that by the summer of 1895, Reed was living at federal expense in Fort Smith, courtesy of Judge Parker, having participated in his only fully verified crime, the robbery of a Katy train at Blackstone Switch, near Muskogee, Indian Territory, on November 13, 1894, with Tom Root, Buss Luckey, and Will Smith. The bandits collected $460, but missed $60,000 hidden by guards. Shot and captured by Deputy U.S. Marshal James Franklin "Bud" Ledbetter in the Boston Mountains of Arkansas, he used his time "in stir" to plot the downfall of informant Jim Dyer, who was convicted of the same offense, but later shown to be at a horse race in Wagoner at the time of the robbery. Reed was believed to be the last train robber to face Judge Parker.

Reed's claimed additional crimes included an April 1891 bank robbery at Brownsville, Texas, and an escape some two months later from Texas Rangers into Indian Territory, supposedly earning him the sobriquet "Texas Jack." Reed had his memoirs printed in Dallas some two years before his last claimed bank robbery at Riverton, Texas, in 1898.

Later, he became an evangelist and outlaw exhibitionist, producing *Texas Jack, Train Robber.* The old outlaw was often seen peddling his book on the downtown streets of Tulsa and Oklahoma City. Reed died peacefully in downtown Tulsa on January 7, 1950.

Shirley, *Fourth Guardsman,* 25-33, 35-41, 43, 171; Reed, 1-84.

Reeves, Bass (ca. 1840-1910)

Bass Reeves was born a slave in the household of William Steele Reeves of Crawford County, Arkansas. During a newspaper interview about nine years before he died, Reeves elaborated that he became a body servant of Col. George Reeves of Grayson County, Texas, a son of William S. Reeves. Though the details are unclear, Bass and Col. Reeves had a falling out during the Civil War, perhaps over a card game. Reeves reportedly escaped to the Seminole Nation or Creek Nation, where he learned local dialects.

Reeves became the first black deputy U.S. marshal west of the Mississippi upon appointment in May 1875 by Judge Isaac Parker of Fort Smith. Reeves's strength, stealth, and ability to make arrests by the use of disguises were legendary. Reeves reportedly made more than three thousand arrests by 1901, including that of his own son for killing an unfaithful wife. A controversial figure, Bass was once accused of killing his own trail cook, among other alleged transgressions. In fact, the cook was killed accidentally when Reeves's weapon misfired. After working for the U.S. Marshal's service, he served with the Muskogee Police Department, and died of Bright's disease on January 12, 1910.

Selected Gunfights

Washington-McLish Ranch, Chickasaw Nation, 1883

Texas cowboy and foreman Jim Webb confronted Rev. William Steward, a black preacher and small rancher who had accidentally started a spring grass fire that spread onto the Washington-McLish Ranch. Webb terminated the argument by killing the divine. Later, Reeves and posseman Floyd Wilson (himself killed years later by Henry Starr) approached the ranch without identifying themselves and attempted to arrest Webb. When Webb resisted, Reeves was forced to choke Webb with one hand while exchanging gunfire with Webb associate Frank Smith. Webb then submitted to arrest and was taken to Fort Smith, but Frank Smith died at Tishomingo of wounds sustained in the gunfight. Webb later jumped bail, forfeiting $17,000.

Near Sacred Heart Mission, Indian Territory, June 15, 1884

Assisted by posseman John Cantrell, Reeves investigated reports that escaped murder suspect Jim Webb could be found at the

Bywater store, a site in present-day Woodford, Oklahoma. Cantrell scouted the store, then motioned for Reeves to come forward, prompting Webb to run for the bush, then begin exchanging fire with Reeves, cutting a button from the deputy U.S. marshal's coat. Reeves's Winchester found Webb, who, according to one account, gave his revolver to Reeves before expiring.

Delaware Crossing, Red River, 1889

Accompanied by rustling victim George Delaney of Texas, Reeves waited in hiding for the Story gang to cross the river into the Lone Star State after selling stolen livestock in Indian Territory. Tom Story and Perry Kincheon "Kinch" West crossed into Texas with two of Delaney's prize mules, then resisted a demand for surrender. Story was killed on the spot, while West lived at least seven years to tell the tale.

Seminole Nation, Indian Territory, April 1890

Bass Reeves captured Greenleaf, a Seminole outlaw and bootlegger who newspapers reported had murdered three whites and four Indians. Greenleaf was arrested and taken to Fort Smith, where he was convicted of selling whiskey. The murder charges were not pursued, perhaps due to insufficient evidence.

Burton, *Black, Red and Deadly,* 202; Burton, *Black Gun, Silver Star,* 82-89, 139, 147, 149, 157-58, 163-67, 170-76.

Reynolds, N. O. (Mage) (1846-1922)

Reynolds was a Texas Ranger with a mysterious past. He was called "Mage" after capturing a Confederate major during the Civil War. He claimed to be from Missouri, but census records suggest a possible Pennsylvania origin. Reynolds commanded Company E of the Texas Rangers in 1878, helped end the Horrell-Higgins Feud, and warned Rangers at Round Rock of an impending attack by Sam Bass.

Wilkins, *The Law Comes to Texas,* 72, 74-76, 80, 83, 124, 131-32, 134, 148-50, 153, 164-66, 168-69, 177, 189-90.

Riggs, Barney (d. 1892)

The West Texas son of a violence-prone clan, Riggs first came into historical focus when he ambushed Richard Hudson who had bragged of seducing Riggs's wife. He was sentenced to life in prison, but won parole under very unusual circumstances. While he was serving in the Yuma Territorial Prison in 1887, seven prisoners tried to escape. The guards killed six, but the seventh took Thomas Gates, the prison superintendent, hostage with a knife. Thinking quickly, Riggs retreived a gun from the floor and shot the convict twice. In gratitude, the governer granted him pardon on the condition that he never return to Arizona. He settled in Pecos, Texas, soon after.

He married Annie Stella Frazer Johnson, a sister of George A. "Bud" Frazer, who soon became sheriff of Reeves County, Texas. Riggs later involved himself in a feud involving Sheriff Bud Frazer and noted assassin "Deacon" Jim Miller. On the morning of March 3, 1896, two associates of Miller, John Denson and Bill Earhart, entered R. S. Johnson's saloon. Earhart immediately opened fire on Riggs but missed, and was killed when Riggs retaliated. Denson fled but was gunned down by Riggs in the street just outside the door. Riggs was killed at Fort Stockton, Texas, about four years later in a family dispute with the husband of his stepdaughter.

Shirley, *Shotgun for Hire,* 22-26, 33-36, 41-46; O'Neal, *Encyclopedia,* 261-62; DeArment, *Deadly Dozen,* 134-51.

Ringo, John Peters (ca. 1850-82)

The death of former Texan John Ringo in Arizona in July 1882 has intrigued historians for years. Traditional stories relate that he was born in Ringoes, New Jersey, or perhaps Missouri, where, a myth states, he attended William Jewell College. More probably, he was born on May 3, 1850, in Greenfork, Wayne County, Indiana, to Martin Ringo and Mary Peters Ringo and received only a rudimentary education. The family moved to Liberty, Missouri, where some members of the Ringo clan already lived. John Ringo's aunt, Augusta Peters, married Col. Coleman Younger, uncle and namesake of the notorious train and bank robber Thomas Coleman "Cole" Younger. According to the journal of Mary Peters Ringo, 1864 found Martin Ringo, his wife, and five children in a wagon train headed west. Martin was killed in a gun accident along the way on July 30, leaving Mary to take the young family on to San Jose,

California, where they arrived in October 1864. John Ringo reputedly left California in 1869, perhaps joining some of his father's kinsmen who had settled in Texas.

About six years later, Texas newspaper accounts indicate that John associated with Scott Cooley in the "Hoodoo War," a Mason County conflict between families who had supported the Confederacy and Unionists largely of German descent. Cooley's sole interest in the feud was obtaining revenge for the death of Tim Williamson, his former employer and mentor, who had been killed by German factionist Peter Bader with the collaboration of former Mason County deputy sheriff John Worley (Worhle). Cooley found, killed, and scalped Worley at Mason, Texas, in 1875. Ringo apparently participated in two more Mason County War killings, those of a German faction hireling named Cheyney, and poor Charley Bader, who may have been mistaken for his brother Peter Bader, the presumed murderer of Tim Williamson.

The Bader killing resulted in Ringo landing in the Travis County, Texas, jail in 1877. Fellow inmates included Bill Taylor, John Wesley Hardin, and Mannen Clements, all participants to one degree or another in the Sutton-Taylor Feud. Ringo reportedly escaped, then briefly served as a Loyal Valley, Texas, constable before seeking his fortune in New Mexico. His first publicly reported introduction to Arizona society about two years later was less than promising. Ringo took offense when saloon denizen Louis Hancock refused to accept a proffered drink, then pummeled and shot him, leaving poor Hancock seriously wounded on December 14, 1879.

That very year prospector Ed Schieffelin founded a small town in the Arizona desert near his three mines, the Lucky Cuss, Toughnut, and Contention. Ed Seiber, chief of Army scouts had told the prospector that all he would find in the desert would be his tombstone, thus inadvertently suggesting a name for the most fabled town in the American West.

Although nothing is known of Ringo's arrival in Tombstone, his nemesis, lawman Wyatt Earp, settled there shortly after the town was founded. He was soon joined by his brothers Virgil, James, and Morgan, as well as Earp loyalist Doc Holliday. The visibly Republican Earp faction soon tangled with John H. "Johnny" Behan, a much maligned Democrat who had developed a quite respectable public record before coming to Tombstone. Accurately or not, Behan has traditionally been identified as an ally of the Cowboy faction, whose most prominent luminaries included Billy Claiborne, the Clantons, and the McClaury brothers, reputed cattle rustlers all. Behan replaced Earp as Pima County sheriff in November 1880, then was appointed sheriff of newly created Cochise County early the next year. Ringo associated himself with the Cowboy faction, along with Curly Bill Brocius, another man of mystery who started life in Missouri as William Graham, punched cattle in Texas, then drifted through New Mexico into Arizona.

Ringo figured among the most likely suspects in the December 28, 1881, shotgun shooting that left Virgil Earp crippled for life, since witnesses had observed Ringo and other Cowboy factionists toting shotguns around Tombstone the evening in question. Later investigations by Wells Fargo agent Fred Dodge suggested that Johnny Barnes, a cowboy later mortally wounded by Wyatt Earp at Iron Springs, was a much more viable suspect. Ringo further aggravated the Earp faction by challenging Doc and Wyatt to a gunfight the evening of January 17, 1882, on Allen Street, prompting Deputy Sheriff William M. Breakenridge to place Ringo in jail, perhaps for his own protection.

These events placed Ringo on the short list of cowboys the Earp faction pursued following the murder of Morgan Earp at the Bob Hatch Saloon on the evening of March 18, 1882. Wyatt Earp apparently suspected Ringo in both shootings but was unable to locate him. Curly Bill Brocius, Florentino "Indian Charlie" Cruz, and former Cochise County deputy sheriff Frank Stilwell were not so lucky. The Earps killed Stilwell in the Tucson train yards three days after Morgan was killed, then Cruz two (or three) days afterward in a woodcutter's camp near Tombstone. On March 24, Wyatt Earp and his posse stumbled into Curly Bill Brocius, Johnny Barnes, and others at Iron Springs, a distinctly uninviting watering hole about thirty-five miles west of Tombstone. Wyatt killed Curly Bill outright and mortally wounded Johnny Barnes.

Some four months later, Ringo, Buckskin Frank Leslie, and Billy Claiborne had taken to drink in Tombstone a few days before the trio wandered off into the mountains near Turkey Creek Canyon. Ringo's body was discovered on July 14, by a passerby. The previous day, an area resident had heard a single gunshot at about 3:00 P.M. The resulting inquest ruled that Ringo committed suicide, but doubts have lingered until this very day.

Ringo was either scalped intentionally or by the bullet that killed him, his cartridge belt was on upside down, and an old undershirt covered his feet. Rumors swirled as to who might have shot and killed Ringo. Cowboy factionist Billy Claiborne placed the blame at Leslie's feet, but Ringo's friend Pony Deal insisted that gambler Johnny O'Rourke was responsible. Other suspects included Lewis W. "Lou" Cooley (no relation to Scott Cooley). Some theorize that Cooley was hired by Gen. Henry C. Hooker, whose Sierra Bonita Ranch was said to have been heavily rustled by Curly Bill and John Ringo. Eventually, even Wyatt Earp joined the short list of potential killers by claiming he killed Ringo in retaliation for the ambush and murder of his brother Morgan. Whatever the facts, they remain Ringo's secret. Pony Deal followed his own convictions, tracked down O'Rourke (known as "Johnny-behind-the-deuce") and killed him, or so the story goes.

Selected Gunfights

Crystal Palace Saloon, Safford, Arizona, December 14, 1879

Drinking heavily, as was his custom, Ringo bashed in the skull of patron Louis Hancock with his pistol then wounded him with a gunshot to the throat. Historians Leon Metz and Jay Robert Nash say that Ringo was agitated by a disparaging remark Hancock made about a street prostitute. However, contemporary newspaper accounts attributed the shooting to Hancock's refusal to accept a drink Ringo had offered, an inconsequential act by modern standards, but an insult in the Old West.

Tombstone, Arizona, December 28, 1881

Ringo was one of several avowed Earp clan enemies. On this night he and three other known Earp detractors were seen carrying shotguns around town. As Virgil Earp left the Oriental Saloon he was ambushed by men using shotguns. Because of this act, Ringo was one of several Cowboy factionists suspected of having participated in the attack. Virgil was crippled for life, but survived. Ringo was also suspected in the subsequent assassination of Morgan Earp on March 18, 1882.

O'Neal, *Encyclopedia*, 263-64; Metz, *The Shooters*, 250-51; Nash, 270; Tanner, *Doc Holliday*, 195-98, 294 n. 42; Burrows, 3-81, 129-205; Alexander, *John H. Behan*, 9, 149-50, 191, 204.

Roberts, Andrew L. (Buckshot, Bill Williams, William Albert Roberts, Bill Roberts) (d. 1878)

The origins of Buckshot Roberts are somewhat obscure, but include unverified stories relating his supposed experience as a soldier and Texas Ranger before seeking his fortune in New Mexico. It is known with relative certainty that Roberts was in the posse that killed rancher John Tunstall, generally considered the opening event of the Lincoln County War.

On April 4, 1878, Roberts encountered Tunstall adherents Dick Brewer, Charlie Bowdre, Billy the Kid, John Middleton, Frank Coe, and his brother George at Blazer's Mill. Roberts has been portrayed more than once as an aggressor who supposedly decided to collect rewards for the heads of the Regulators. Less dramatically but more likely, Roberts was wary of the Regulators, who had a warrant for his arrest, but stumbled onto them during his second visit to the mill that day. Roberts was looking for mail that contained a check for the sale of his Ruidoso farm, but found eternal rest instead. After Roberts refused an offer of safe passage and arrest tendered by his neighbor Frank Coe, a gunfight ensued. Roberts took a last stand in an adobe building, then killed Dick Brewer with a head shot before receiving his own mortal wounds. He died later that night in Dr. Emil Blazer's home.

O'Neal, *Encyclopedia,* 264-65; Nash, 270-71; Nolan, 127.

Roberts, Judd (d. 1887)

Texas bred, Texas born, Texas dead, Judd Roberts was born in Williamson County, Texas. Roberts first came to the attention of the Texas Rangers after he and a gang of four robbed and murdered one Brautigen in Fredericksburg, Texas, in 1885. Captured with one of his henchmen, Roberts sojourned briefly in the local jail. Suspecting a possible lynching, authorities spirited the grateful suspects to San Antonio. Soon, a posse captured another Roberts gang member and returned him to the Fredericksburg jail, which was promptly consumed by a mysterious fire, bandit and all. Properly motivated, Roberts escaped the San Antonio bat cave to pursue a new career as a Texas Panhandle horse thief. Texas Ranger Ira Aten and soon-to-be Ranger John Hughes killed Roberts in a July 1887 Williamson County gunfight.

Selected Gunfights
Liberty Hill, Burnet County, Texas, June 1887

Only two months after being wounded by Ira Aten at the George Wells ranch in Williamson County, Roberts decided to settle a disagreement with young rancher John Hughes by ambush. Instead he was surprised again by the seemingly ever present Ira Aten. During the gunplay, Roberts was hit in the hand twice, then rode painfully toward the Texas Panhandle.

Texas Panhandle, July 1887

Roberts found more than work on a Panhandle ranch soon after the Liberty Hill fiasco. However, his romantic interlude with his employer's daughter was interrupted by the irrepressible Ranger Ira Aten and the very John Hughes whom Roberts had earlier sought to murder. Roberts supposedly tilted his six-gun in its holster and blasted away at his pursuers. Aten and Hughes peppered him with six bullets from chest to groin. Judd confessed to the Brautigen killing, then died in his lover's arms, or so the story goes.

O'Neal, *Encyclopedia,* 266-67; Nash, 271-72; Thrapp, *Encyclopedia,* IV, 19.

Roberts, William Henry (Brushy Bill) (1859-1950)

Roberts was one of several individuals who claimed to be Billy the Kid. According to his own account, William Henry Brushy Bill Roberts was born near Buffalo Gap, Texas, on December 31, 1859, to Kentucky parents. In about 1872, after a disagreement with his father, "Wild Henry" Roberts, he went to Indian Territory, worked as a cowhand, then supposedly met Belle Starr and the James and Younger brothers near Briartown. Roberts and his supporters claim that he then went to New Mexico, after a stop in Kansas, and became "Billy the Kid," the legendary outlaw who fought in the Lincoln County War against the Murphy-Dolan "house" and for John Tunstall.

Pat Garrett killed the wrong man, or so the story continues, at Fort Sumner on July 14, 1881. One Billy Barlow, a look-alike friend of Brushy Bill, had gone to the Pete Maxwell place for beef that fateful evening and found the bullet that was intended for Brushy Bill. Just after the killing, Brushy Bill and Pat Garrett had a gunfight, which no one else remembered or recorded. Brushy Bill claimed that he then returned to Oklahoma, where he worked for the Anti-Horse Thief Association in Southeastern Oklahoma, becoming known as the "Hugo Kid."

After stints as a deputy U.S. marshal for Judge Issac Parker, a rancher in Old Mexico, and a member of Teddy Roosevelt's Rough Riders, he began trading horses and cattle in Oklahoma, Arkansas, and Texas. Shortly before his death, William V. Morrison "discovered" Brushy Bill and unsuccessfully petitioned the governor of New Mexico for a pardon. Among those present at the hearing was prominent statesman Patrick J. Hurley, who served as secretary of war in the Hoover administration and United States ambassador to China. Hurley was reportedly a nephew of the John Hurley who fought in the Lincoln County War. The request was denied, of course, and Bill died shortly thereafter on December 27, 1950.

Brushy Bill supported these claims with some Bible records, a knowledge of Lincoln County War occurrences of which few were aware, and five affidavits by elderly Lincoln County residents who swore Brushy Bill and Billy the Kid were one and the same person. More recently a photo-comparison study by the well-regarded Texas Laboratory for Vision Studies showed that six of nine significant facial characteristics portrayed in the only authenticated photograph of Billy the Kid were numerically identical to the facial characteristics of Brushy Bill. Nevertheless, Brushy Bill is still considered an imposter by most professional historians, leaving nothing more to say until the Texas findings are corroborated by one or more laboratories of equal stature.

Jameson, 21-23, 35, 44, 50, 54, 58, 61.

Rudabaugh, David (1840-86)

Rudabaugh was a thief and no-account of the first order. He began his nefarious career in the late 1870s in Texas, leading a gang in robberies and cattle rustling. Rudabaugh moved his operations to Kansas by 1878. After one train robbery on Sunday, January 27, of that year, Rudabaugh and fellow thief Edgar West were captured by Bat Masterson. John Joshua Webb, a member of Masterson's posse, kept Rudabaugh from shooting it out by getting the better of the outlaw on the draw. Rudabaugh eventually won his release when he sold his compatriots down the river, turning state's evidence. He righteously vowed to go straight and earn a legal living, but by 1879 Rudabaugh was right back at his former career.

During a six-month period, Rudabaugh and a ragtag gang of thieves pestered Las Vegas, New Mexico, with thieving and confidence games. The gang was seemingly immune from the town's laws of the time. City marshal and former Masterson posse member John Joshua Webb, who first arrested Rudabaugh, allowed the gang's activities to flourish. That all changed in 1880 when Marshal Webb was arrested for murder. After attempting to break Webb out of jail, which succeeded only in the death of a lawman, Rudabaugh was again on the run.

He was with Billy the Kid in 1880, when Pat Garrett and posse cornered and arrested the Kid and several other gang members. In September 1881 Rudabaugh, Webb, and others attempted to shoot their way out of jail but failed. Two months later Rudabaugh and Webb with five other prisoners managed to tunnel their way to freedom. Rudabaugh and Webb rode back to Texas and then on to Mexico.

Webb vanished shortly after he crossed the border, but Rudabaugh took a job on a ranch belonging to the governor of Chihuahua. That job came to a halt once Rudabaugh became suspected of rustling some of his boss's cattle. Rudabaugh made his way to Parral, Mexico, where on February 18, 1886, he was in a cantina arguing with a couple of locals over a card game. The heated exchange grew worse until both Rudabaugh and the other player stood up facing each other across the table. That's when Rudabaugh drew his gun and put a bullet in the forehead of his card-playing opponent. A second local reached for his gun and managed a frantic shot that missed, allowing Rudabaugh to fire one round into the man's chest. Rudabaugh left the cantina and apparently hoped to find his trusty steed tied to the rail outside, but the horse wasn't there. Rudabaugh deliberately walked back into the cantina in which all lights had been extinguished and was overpowered by a mob that cut off his head.

Selected Gunfights

Las Vegas, New Mexico, April 30, 1880

Rudabaugh attempted to break former Las Vegas sheriff and murder suspect John Joshua Webb out of jail. Deputy Sheriff Lino Valdez drove Rudabaugh off, but not before being mortally wounded. Rudabaugh rode to Fort Sumner where he joined Billy the Kid.

Near White Oaks, New Mexico, November 27, 1880

Regardless of having escaped the long arm of the posse the day before, Billy the Kid, Rudabaugh, and Billy Wilson returned to town. There they were spotted by Deputy Sheriff James Redman, and one of the gang fired at the lawman. The errant shot missed Redman who took cover behind a saloon. A large crowd gathered and, seeing what happened and emboldened by their number, chased the outlaws out of town a second time. Later that night a posse tracked the gang members to the ranch of Jim Greathouse about forty miles from White Oaks.

The next morning the posse tightened its circle on the ranch house, but the outlaws traded their associate, ranch owner Jim Greathouse, for Deputy Sheriff James Carlyle during a parley. Later that night, Carlyle attempted to escape by jumping out a window, but he was shot dead either by the gang or by his fellow lawmen who believed they were firing on an escaping bandit.

Fort Sumner, New Mexico, December 19, 1880

Rudabaugh, the Kid, Wilson, Tom Pickett, Tom O'Folliard, and Charlie Bowdre rode into Fort Sumner expecting to find some rest and recreation. Instead Pat Garrett and a posse demanded the outlaws' surrender. The gun battle that followed resulted in O'Folliard and Pickett being wounded, O'Folliard fatally. Although Rudabaugh's horse was killed, he was rescued by Billy Wilson during his galloping retreat. The gang got as far as Stinking Springs where they found refuge in an abandoned stone cabin.

Stinking Springs, New Mexico, December 23, 1880

Respite in the stone cabin was short-lived as Garrett and posse had little trouble tracking the men by the prints their horses left in the snow. The posse encircled the cabin but waited for daylight to make their move. At dawn Charlie Bowdre blithely stepped into the sunlight from the cabin where waiting lawmen riddled him with lead, mortally wounding him. The others inside maintained a daylong gun battle, but with the only way out blocked by a dead horse, Rudabaugh displayed an impromptu white flag, and the gang surrendered.

Las Vegas, New Mexico, September 19, 1881

Rudabaugh and his former boss, Sheriff John Joshua Webb, shared a cell at Las Vegas. Rudabaugh managed to have a pistol smuggled to him and, together with Webb, Thomas Duffy, and H. S. Wilson, attempted a breakout. Rudabaugh fired one shot at jailer Florencino Marches. Hearing the shot, another jailer, Herculano Chavez, shot and mortally wounded Duffy, prompting Rudabaugh to throw down his weapon in surrender. By November, Rudabaugh, Webb, and five others successfully escaped by digging through the walls of the jail.

Parral, Mexico, February 18, 1886

While playing cards with two Mexican locals, accusations of cheating soon led to gun play. Rudabaugh shot one of his accusers in the forehead and another through the heart, killing both men instantly. He went outside the cantina where he hoped to escape on his mount, but the horse was nowhere in sight. Rudabaugh went back into the cantina but was overpowered by other Mexican men who had witnessed the shooting. During the struggle Rudabaugh was decapitated by the enraged citizens, who impaled his head on a pole.

O'Neal, *Encyclopedia*, 269-71; Nash, 273-74; Nolan, 205, 213-14, 233-34, 323 n. 19; Thrapp, *Encyclopedia*, III, 1247.

Russell, John

A Pecos, Texas, native who became sheriff of Okmulgee County, Oklahoma, "Big John" often acted first and asked questions later. A minor Oklahoma bandit named Ben Rosekans and a character who only identified himself as "Snakeye" discovered this the hard way when they attempted to escape from Russell, who had tracked them to the Pecos area. The sheriff shot them both on the spot and was promptly exonerated. Earlier, Russell had killed Wilbur Underhill associate Ike Akins, who was resisting arrest near Okmulgee on February 12, 1926.

Morgan, 42-48.

St. Leon, Ernest (Diamond Dick) (d. 1898)

St. Leon was raised in San Antonio, Texas, having immigrated to the United States with his French parents. Abandoning the study of law, St. Leon joined the cavalry and attained the rank of sergeant.

Sometime in the 1880s, St. Leon left the cavalry and joined the Texas Rangers. He was assigned to Company D, but left the service in disgrace due to a drinking problem. Before his untimely retirement, St. Leon was dubbed Diamond Dick because of his showy diamond-studded clothing. Later, Texas Ranger John Hughes gave Diamond Dick an undercover work assignment somewhat attuned to his avocation. St. Leon masqueraded as a miner in order to successfully infiltrate a diamond theft ring. Consequently, he was reinstated as a Ranger. Nine years later, St. Leon was killed in a senseless saloon brawl.

Selected Gunfights
Shafter, Texas, 1889
St. Leon hired on as a miner-turned-thief in order to arrest three diamond thieves. Texas Rangers John Hughes and Lon Oden intercepted St. Leon and his unsuspecting associates, then shouted for surrender. St. Leon turned on the three thieves and killed them at close range.

Texas, 1891
St. Leon and a deputized citizen had three cowboys in custody. Inexplicably, St. Leon freed them and took the entire crowd to a nearby saloon and ordered a round. Although St. Leon had no hard feelings, the suspects apparently did. Following an argument, St. Leon and his deputy were gunned down. The deputy died on the saloon floor, and St. Leon lingered until the following day.

Utley, *Lone Star Justice,* 35 n. 24; O'Neal, *Encyclopedia,* 272; Hatley, *Bringing the Law to Texas,* 124; Wilkins, *The Law Comes to Texas,* 309, 312, 334; Nash, 276.

Scarborough, George Adolphus (1859-1900)

Born in Natchitoches Parish, Louisiana, sometime in 1859, Scarborough moved to McCulloch County, Texas, in 1874, where he married and had seven children, one of whom would follow in this father's footsteps, however imperfectly. Scarborough was elected sheriff of Jones County in 1884 and served in that capacity until he was tried for the murder of the outlaw A. J. Williams and lost his reelection bid. He worked as a financial detective until 1893, when he became a deputy U.S. marshal.

Jeff Milton (left) and George Scarborough. They posed for this photograph in El Paso sometime around 1895. (Courtesy of the Nina Stewart Haley Memorial Library, Midland, Texas, J. Evetts Haley Collection)

Scarborough was involved in the 1895 killing of outlaw and cattle rustler Martin Morose (Mrose). Martin was hiding in Mexico, but sent his wife north to enlist the services of lawyer John Wesley Hardin. Scarborough, Jeff Milton, Frank McMahon, and possibly John Selman killed Morose, and all but Selman were tried for murder. They were not convicted, but Scarborough lost his job as a deputy U.S. marshal.

In El Paso on April 5, 1896, Scarborough killed John Selman. He was again aquitted, but once again lost his job as a deputy U.S. marshal. Scarborough then ranched near Fort Davis, Texas, before resuming police work in Deming, New Mexico. Scarborough was mortally wounded near San Simon, Arizona, in April 1900, and died during surgery, mainly from blood loss, exactly four years to the day after Selman's death.

Selected Gunfights and Robberies
Haskell, Texas, Saturday, October 15, 1887
Jones County sheriff George Scarborough and his brother Will

Jeff Milton poses with lawmen. Jeff Milton (seated far right) rose through the ranks of El Paso's constabulary to become that city's top cop in the late 1890s. Here he poses with other lawmen of the day. The others are: standing, left to right: Charles Wise, Capt. Jim White, Beverly G. Thomas; seated, left to right: Frank P. Clark and Col. Abner Tibbetts. (Courtesy of the El Paso Public Library, Aultman Collection)

were confronted in the Q.T. Saloon by a cattle rustler whom Scarborough had previously captured. The rustler drew his pistol, but not quickly enough. Later, George and Will were acquitted after a five-minute jury deliberation.

El Paso, June 21, 1895

As previously agreed, Martin Morose met Scarborough on a bridge between Texas and Mexico and turned toward El Paso, with the hope of meeting his estranged wife. Instead, Morose was killed in a fullisade from law officers J. D. Milton, Scarborough, and Texas Ranger F. M. McMahon.

El Paso, April 5, 1896

On April 1, 1896, John Selman, Jr., married the fifteen-year-old daughter of Jose Maria Ruiz. The couple eloped to Juarez, where John, Jr., was arrested. Four days later, on Easter Sunday, in the early hours, John Selman, Sr., and Scarborough met at the Wigwam Saloon and eventually wandered into an alley nearby. There, Selman asked Scarborough to help rescue John Selman, Jr., from the Mexican authorities or, alternately argued over money supposedly taken from Martin Morose the previous year. Although stories conflict as to the underlying reasons for the gunfight, Scarborough shot Selman four times before Selman could even draw his weapon, then three more times. The mortally wounded Selman died the next day after surgery.

Near San Simon, New Mexico, April 3, 1900

Summoned by Walt Birchfield, manager of the Triangle Ranch, Scarborough began pursuit of several cattle rustlers in Triangle Canyon, some twenty miles southwest of San Simon. Following an initial stand-off, Scarborough was mortally wounded by a high-powered rifle as he and Birchfield looked for a better vantage point. Scarborough died early in the evening of April 5, 1900. The outlaws were never found, but suspicion fell upon associates of Ben and George Kilpatrick.

Metz, *Encyclopedia,* 214; DeArment, *George Scarborough,* 34-38, 108, 156, 222-24.

Scarborough, George Edgar (Ed) (1879- ca. 1945)

Ed Scarborough shared his father's penchant for trouble, yet lived to a somewhat riper age. Born into the family of a legendary El Paso lawman, Ed followed the family profession, beginning as a posseman for his father George. Young Scarborough then served as a deputy sheriff of Grant County, New Mexico Territory. He was also commissioned as a Grant County Cattleman's Association detective, briefly serving with the first contingent of the Arizona Rangers before his early dismissal for malfeasance. Scarborough tracked, then arrested Tod Carver, whose true name was T. C. Hilliard, a Texas suspect in the killing of Ed's father. Eventually Carver was released for insufficient evidence, then a common occurrence.

Perhaps embittered by this experience, Scarborough turned to less virtuous pursuits, soon finding himself charged with robbery and horse theft, yet never convicted of either crime. Returning to Arizona in 1915, he settled a grazing rights dispute by shooting rancher John Clinton, drawing a life sentence in May 1916, but soon escaped to Mexico. He was known to be alive there as late as 1945.

Selected Gunfights and Suspected Robbery
Near Silver City, New Mexico Territory, September 3, 1900
Newly captured murder suspect Ralph Jenks attempted to escape from Scarborough at about 9:00 P.M., near Duck Creek, while riding into Silver City. Jenks grabbed Scarborough's shotgun and attempted to use the weapon while Scarborough asked him to surrender. When Jenks refused, Scarborough rapidly shot him three times, terminating the arrest attempt. Jenks, his brother Roy, and Henry Reinhart were suspects in the ambush killing of Grant County deputy sheriff W. D. "Keechi" Johnson.
Deming, New Mexico, August 20, 1904
A man dressed in a Mother Hubbard dress robbed the Harvey House Restaurant, taking the paltry sum of twenty-four dollars. Later, Ed was arrested at the scene of the crime while dining. The dress and other gear used in the robbery were found in his makeshift quarters in the back room of a pool hall. Scarborough was charged along with purported accomplice Lester Noal. Later, the case was transferred to Grant County on a change of venue, then dropped.

DeArment, *George Scarborough,* 245-61; Metz, *Encyclopedia,* 214-15.

Selman, John, Sr. (1839-96)
Born on November 16, 1839, in Madison County, Arkansas,

John Selman, Sr., late 1890s El Paso lawman/gunslinger. (Courtesy of the El Paso Public Library, Southwest Collection)

Selman was the son of an English immigrant who moved on to Grayson County, Texas, before the Civil War, Selman joined the Confederate cavalry and was stationed in present-day Oklahoma before deserting and returning to the Lone Star State, where he married in 1865. After a brief sojourn with in-laws in Colfax County, New Mexico, he established roots some eight miles from Fort Griffin, Texas. There he became embroiled with reputed soiled dove Minnie Martin and met a cast of notables, including Wyatt Earp, Bat Masterson, Doc Holliday, and the durable Killin' Jim Miller.

Operating a saloon and rustling business with former Shackelford County sheriff John Larn, he attracted the unwelcome attention of the Texas Rangers, motivating a relocation to Lincoln County, New Mexico, in about 1878. The moonlight cattle business in Texas beckoned within a year, leading to the impromptu hanging of his brother Tom and yet another relocation, this time to Chihuahua, Mexico. After a brief return to New Mexico, Selman became a John Deere salesman.

Learning that all was forgiven, or at least forgotten, in Texas, he moved to El Paso in about 1888 and took a sixteen-year-old as his third wife, having outlived two prior spouses. Donning the badge of a city constable, he managed to kill two notorious Texas shootists in two years before himself falling before the six-shooter of George Scarborough on April 5, 1896.

Selected Gunfights
Fort Griffin, 1877
While assisting Shackelford County sheriff John Larn, Selman shot one "Hampton" a half-deaf suspect who resisted arrest by walking away when ordered, perhaps in a whisper, to halt.
Lincoln County, New Mexico, 1878
Selman seized control of the Hart gang while the pair was in a cabin. The next month, Selman killed a rebellious gang member on the Pecos River.
El Paso, Texas, April 5, 1894
City constable Selman and Frank Collinson encountered an inebriated deputy U.S. marshal, Bass Outlaw, and all three visited a sporting house. There, Outlaw killed Texas Ranger Joe McKidrick for no apparent reason, then handicapped Selman for life before Selman killed him.

El Paso, August 19, 1895

Coming to the belated defense of his fellow constable John Selman, Jr., Selman shot and killed John Wesley Hardin from behind in the Acme Saloon. Hardin had threatened both Selmans after Junior had arrested Hardin love interest and legal client Beulah Morose, widow of Martin Morose, a former Hardin client. Some sources theorize that after the killing of Martin Morose, Hardin had removed some money, perhaps owed on account, from his dead client's pockets, drawing the ire of Selman.

El Paso, April 5, 1896

Apparently foregoing Easter sunrise services, an inebriated Selman encountered fellow officer George Scarborough. The two stepped from a saloon into an alley, for discussion of Selman's contention that Hardin and Scarborough split money extracted from poor dead Martin Morose without doing the right thing and dealing Selman in. Perhaps remembering the manner in which Hardin died, Scarborough wasted no time treating Selman to a four-shot fusillade. Like Hardin, Selman died without drawing his weapon.

Metz, *John Selman*, 179-80, 197-203, 229; O'Neal, *Encyclopedia*, 214-15.

Sherman, James D. (Jim Talbot) (d. 1896)

Sherman likely adopted the alias "Talbot" in order to keep his dubious reputation as a Texas brawling bully from preceding him. Talbot took his wife and two children along on a cattle drive to Caldwell, Kansas, where he set up a new home for his brood in 1881. Talbot was forced to go on the lam for fourteen years after he killed a former lawman, Mike Meagher. During the ensuing years, Talbot sent for his family to join him on a California ranch. In 1894, Talbot was arrested on a possible murder charge of a Mendocino County man, but acquitted of that murder and the murder of Meagher in 1895. His freedom was short-lived, however, because on a night in August 1896 an assassin's shotgun blast to the back killed him on the spot. Two theories exist as to the identity of the assassin. One suggests the shooter was John Meagher, the brother of the slain Mike Meagher. The second theory, and the one most widely accepted, is that during Talbot's year in jail, his wife took a lover, and it was her new carnal companion who "done him in."

Selected Gunfights

Caldwell, Kansas, December 17, 1881

After wresting Tom Love and Jim Martin from the clutches of the local authorities, Talbot turned on his pursuers, who chased him and his companions as far as the Opera House, and opened fire on them with his Winchester, striking Meagher in the chest. Meagher died within the hour. Angry townspeople then took up arms against the rowdy cowboys, chasing them into Indian Territory (Oklahoma) before the fugitives wounded W. E. Campbell. The fervor of the civilian posse waned, allowing the murderers to slither away into the darkness.

Ukiah, California, August 1896

Talbot was just riding up to his gate with a sack of flour on his saddle at his California ranch one Tuesday evening in August when from a secluded spot someone sprang out behind him and fired a shotgun blast, severing the former Texan's spinal chord, killing him instantly. The ambush resulted in speculation that the brother of the murdered Mike Meagher, John Meagher, used the occasion to get even with Talbot. A more universally accepted theory is that Mrs. Talbot, feeling a loss of sorts during the absence of her husband as he sat in jail for more than a year, took a lover, and it was the lover who killed Talbot from ambush under the cover of darkness.

Miller and Snell, 62-63, 498, 500-502, 504-5, 648; O'Neal, *Encyclopedia*, 281-82; Nash, 280-81.

Shirley, Myra Maebelle (Belle Starr) (1848-89)

A small-time horse thief, Shirley was transformed by the *National Detective* into "The Bandit Queen." She was born on February 5, 1848, about four miles southeast of Medoc, a small community near Carthage, Missouri, in an even smaller community known later as Georgia City. Myra Maebelle, or Belle, was the daughter of Virginia native John Shirley and his second wife, Kentuckian Elizabeth (Pennington) Shirley. About 1858, John

Shirley acquired the Carthage Hotel, which was situated on the town square. In the summer of 1864, Belle moved with her family to Scyene, Dallas County, Texas; her brother Preston living nearby in Collin County. She married James C. Reed on November 1, 1866, in Collin County, Texas, and bore him two children, Rose "Rosie" Reed, called "Pearl," born in September 1868, in Missouri, and Edwin "Eddie" Reed, born three years later in California. The Reeds moved to California after legal difficulties in Texas. Counterfeiting charges in California soon prompted a move back to Texas. However, James ranged over Indian Territory and became involved in robberies, notably the November 19, 1873, robbery of Watt Grayson in the Choctaw Nation. Reed was killed on August 6, 1874, some fifteen miles northwest of Paris, Texas, by Deputy U.S. Marshal John T. Morris.

Kansas records reflect that Belle married Bruce Younger, a cousin (or uncle) of Cole Younger in Chetopa, Kansas, on May 15, 1880, but soon discarded him for Sam Starr, whom she married at Catoosa, then known as the hell hole of Indian Territory. She moved with him to the Starr place at Hi-Early Mountain in the bend of the Canadian River, known as Younger's Bend due to Tom Starr's admiration of Cole Younger. One source, Ramon Adams, states definitively that Belle was visited by Jesse James in 1881. Belle and Sam Starr were arrested in 1882 for horse theft and sent to prison in February 1883. The experience did little to reduce Belle's outlaw associations or notoriety. In early 1886 she had her picture taken with convicted murderer Blue Duck, whom she did not know, at the request of Duck's attorney.

During an interview with the *Dallas Morning News* on June 7 of that year she famously described herself as "a friend to any brave and gallant outlaw," then appeared in a staged robbery with Judge Parker and others at the Seventh Annual Fair of Western Arkansas at Fort Smith in October. Her husband Sam was killed some two months later during Christmas week near Whitefield, Indian Territory, in a gunfight with Cherokee policeman Frank West, who also died. Her other supposed love interests included John Middleton of Arkansas, who was found dead in 1885, and Jim July, whom she apparently married and persuaded to call himself Jim July Starr.

Three years after her famous interview, Belle was killed two days before her forty-second birthday. On February 3, 1889, she accompanied Starr part of the way to Fort Smith for a court appearance. She was knocked off her horse by a shotgun blast, then finished off at close range. Suspicion fell upon Edgar Watson, a tenant with whom she had differences. Jim July Starr accompanied Watson to Fort Smith at gunpoint and then preferred charges, which were eventually dismissed by a U.S. commissioner (modern term U.S. magistrate) for insufficient evidence. Suspicion also fell on Starr himself, John Middleton's brother Jim, and even Belle's son, Eddie.

The mysterious circumstances of her death and her rumored but apparently unfounded romance with Cole Younger made her life a focus of many national stories. She became famous as a result of a series of articles in the *National Police Gazette.* More significantly, she became a principal subject of a groundbreaking book, *The Female Offender,* written by Caesar Lombroso, often considered the father of modern criminology.

Smith, *Last Hurrah of the James-Younger Gang,* 23-24; Shirley, *Belle Starr,* 72-73; O'Neal, *Encyclopedia,* 260-61; Metz, *Encyclopedia,* 232; Block, 215; Steele, 51.

Short, Luke (1854-93)

Short but dapper, Luke Short was born on February 19, 1854, near Lamar, Mississippi, and moved with his family to Grayson County, Texas, at age two. Family stories related that in about 1867 he stabbed another boy, then fled to Kansas. There and in Nebraska he peddled whiskey and even scouted for the U.S. Army. He worked as a cowboy early in life, but became an inveterate gambler and voracious reader as well. According to Wyatt Earp, he also became a Shakespearian expert of sorts, capable of quoting the Bard on a moment's notice.

About a hundred miles north of Sidney, Nebraska, sometime in 1876, Short joined whiskey peddlers who dealt with the Sioux Indians. He worked briefly as a dispatch rider in Sidney, Nebraska, then wounded a man named Brown in a Leadville, Colorado, gambling argument. Short drifted through Tombstone, Arizona, before moving on to Dodge City, Kansas, where he killed a man

Dodge City Peace Commission. Standing, left to right: W. H. Harris, Luke Short, Bat Masterson. Seated, from left: Charles E. Bassett, Wyatt Earp, Frank McLain, Neil Brown. (Courtesy of the Nina Stewart Haley Memorial Library, Midland, Texas, Robert N. Mullin Collection)

while working as a card dealer in the Oriental Saloon.

After being released from custody, he starting working in the Long Branch Saloon, and was a participant in the 1883 Dodge City War. The war started when newly elected mayor Larry Deger declared prostitution illegal and reduced prostitutes to the status of vagrants, a shocking development in the early Kansas cow towns. This reform spelled trouble for the Long Branch Saloon, in which Short had an interest. Several Long Branch "dancers" were arrested, and Short himself was charged with shooting at local lawman Lewis Hartman, then banished from Dodge. Eventually, the state militia was requested because of rumors that Short would return to town with other gunfighters. On June 6, Short returned to Dodge with Wyatt Earp, Charlie Bassett, Frank McLaine, and Bat Masterson. In response, Mayor Deger called the governer for help. Gen. Thomas Moonlight negotiated an agreement with the self-described Dodge City Peace Commission. The Long Branch Saloon was sold, and Short moved to Fort Worth with his partner.

Now located in Texas, Short tangled with former law officer

Longhair Jim Courtright, who was reputed to be running a protection racket fronting as the TIC Detective Agency. Traditional stories relate that Courtright approached Short for a cut of the Keno game Short was running on the second floor of the White Elephant Saloon. Others, including Bat Masterson, suggested that a cash-strapped Courtright approached Short for a security position, only to be told that Short would rather pay him to stay away. Yet another version, viewed by most as improbable, poses Short as a lovesick puppy who coveted Courtright's wife Betty. Whatever the cause, there is very little controversy regarding the ensuing gunfight, which occurred on February 8, 1887. Short simply outdrew Courtright, then shot him in the heart and right shoulder.

Short fought his last gunfight on December 23, 1890, with Charles Wright, in yet another gambling-related argument, this one involving a shotgun. Short lost his left thumb and had pellets buried in this left leg, but survived to die of natural causes on September 8, 1893, at Geuda Springs, Kansas.

Selected Gunfights and Robberies
Leadville, Colorado, 1879
Short shot a man known only as Brown in a gambling argument. According to Bat Masterson, Short was confronted by a local gunman, but drew first, putting a bullet through the opponent's face. Incredibly, the man survived.
Tombstone, Arizona, February 25, 1881
Short killed well-known gambler Charlie Storms in a gambling argument. The gamblers had previously quarreled in Cheyenne, Wyoming, over a card game and in Leadville, Colorado, over a woman.
Fort Worth, Texas, February 8, 1887
In front of a shooting gallery adjoining the White Elephant Saloon, Courtright placed his hand on a pistol, prompting Short to pull his own Colt .45 from his pocket and shoot Courtright five times. Jim died within five minutes, after telling Officer John J. Fulford that "they finally got me." Later, Short contributed to a fund established for Courtright's destitute family. In this, one of the few documented face-to-face quick-draw gunfights between skilled practicioners in the Old West, there is no basis at all for the oft-told tale

that Courtright only lost because he caught his pistol on a watch chain.
Forth Worth, Texas, December 23, 1890

During a gunfight between Short and Charles Wright, arising from a gambling dispute, neither man was killed, but Short lost his left thumb.

Metz, *Encyclopedia,* 222; O'Neal, *Encyclopedia,* 284; DeArment, *Jim Courtright of Fort Worth,* 207, 226, 234.

Siringo, Charles (1855-1928)

A checkered-past cowboy-author, Siringo served twenty-two years as a Pinkerton Agency detective, starting in the 1890s. He tracked outlaws all over the West, notably Billy the Kid and Butch Cassidy. He died a pauper in Los Angeles after writing his memoirs.

A Texas native, he began working as a cowhand at age thirteen and remained so employed for the next nine years. Although he joined the hunt for Henry McCarty, more widely known as Billy the Kid, he also found time for the gambling tables along the way. Bad luck at the tables forced him out of the hunt for the Kid, or so the story goes.

While visiting Chicago several years later Siringo visited a fortune-teller who, he later related, changed his life by saying he should be a detective. During a stint at the Pinkerton Detective Agency he quickly made a name for himself as sly, proficient, and effective. Siringo joined the hunt for Harvey Logan (Kid Curry), an associate of Butch Cassidy and the Sundance Kid. This and other adventures prompted Siringo to write his memoirs in a series of books, dealing with his cowboy youth, his acquaintance with and pursuit of Billy the Kid, his twenty-two years with the Pinkerton Detective Agency, and the many outlaws he pursued. Despite publishing six books, which gained him much notoriety, Siringo died penniless on October 18, 1928, after moving close to his children in Altadena, California, in 1928.

O'Neal, *Encyclopedia,* 187; Tyler, *The New Handbook of Texas,* vol. 5, 1063-64; Metz, *Encyclopedia,* 223; Nash, 284.

Slaughter, John Horton (Texas John, Don Juan) (1841-1922)

Three months after his birth on October 2, 1841, infant John Slaughter was taken from his birthplace at Sabine Parish, Louisiana, by his family who set up home on a land grant in the Republic of Texas. Slaughter's formative years were spent on the family ranch near Lockhart. Beginning with the Civil War, Slaughter, as a "Minute Man of the Texas Rangers," was involved in numerous skirmishes with various Indian factions. Not particularly fearful of the Indians, Slaughter settled in the midst of them in what was known at the time as Apache country. Slaughter participated in routing renegades well into the 1890s. Married in 1871, Slaughter bossed a number of trail drives and poured nearly every cent into his own ranching enterprise, which by all accounts was quite successful.

Despite his Texas ties, he moved his family to Arizona. Along the way his wife contracted smallpox and died in Tucson. One year later in 1879, he remarried. He had his eye on a large parcel of land known as the San Bernardino Grant, which consisted of 65,000 acres stretching from Arizona to Mexico. Slaughter eventually bought the grant and soon was employing ten to twenty cowhands at any one time and nearly three dozen families to work and harvest the grain, hay, vegetables, and fruit orchards.

He served two terms as sheriff of Cochise County with the specific goal of cleaning up the towns of Galeyville and Tombstone. A successful rancher and entrepreneur, Slaughter eventually bought his neighbor and former business partner's spread, the Bato Rico, owned by George Lang. Slaughter owned a meatpacking house in California and a meat market in Charleston, Arizona. Slaughter won a seat in Arizona's territorial assembly but served only one year before returning his full attention to his many interests at home. By 1910, Slaughter owned two butcher shops in Bisbee, and later founded and managed the Bank of Douglas. Slaughter wasn't all business though. He frequently played high-stakes poker games, sometimes twenty-four hours at a sitting. John Slaughter died peacefully in his sleep at the age of eighty.

Selected Gunfights

South Spring Ranch, New Mexico, 1876

Slaughter was riding herd on a bunch of John Chisum's cattle when a drunken Barney Gallagher and an associate brandished a sawed-off shotgun and demanded cattle. Rather than fleeing, Slaughter galloped toward the unsuspecting adversary and fired a shot from his six-gun that smashed into the rustler's thigh. Gallagher's accomplice, a young man named Boyd, abandoned his partner and galloped away to safety. Gallagher was taken to town where he was treated at a local store. The bleeding could not be stopped, and he died about midnight.

Mexico, ca. 1880

Accompanied by two hands named John Swain and "Old Bat," Slaughter and several other cowhands rode into Mexico to retrieve some stolen cattle. On the trail back, the party was stalked by banditos who meant to keep the herd in Mexico. While most of Slaughter's party dashed for safety, Slaughter, Swain, and Old Bat kept their heads about them, drove the animals into a box canyon and put up a stalwart defense, driving off their attackers.

Fairbank, Arizona, 1887

By this time Slaughter was sheriff of Cochise County, and he and deputies Burt Alvord and Benjamin Franklin "Doc" Hall had tracked a killer and thief named Geronimo Baltierrez to a tent only one-half mile from town. Baltierrez was still inside the tent with his woman when the lawmen ordered his surrender. Baltierrez instead cut a slit in the tent and took off running, only to be stopped by a fence and more permanently stopped by two blasts of Slaughter's shotgun.

Cochise County, Arizona, May 1888

Slaughter, Alvord, and Cesario Lucero tracked three Mexican nationals who had robbed a train to a hideout in the Whetstone Mountains. The outlaws were taken by surprise while still half asleep in their bedrolls when the lawmen tried to arrest them. A gunfight broke out but lasted only until one of the train robbers was wounded, at which time all three gave up.

Cochise County, Arizona, June 1888

Using similar tactics while in pursuit of another group of bandits who sought refuge in the Whetstone Mountains, Slaughter, Alvord, and two Mexican nationals waited until first light to engage the bandits. When the time came, Slaughter ordered the bandits to surrender, then opened fire with his shotgun. One of the bandits was slightly injured by buckshot. The gang's leader, Guadalupe Robles, sprang to his feet holding his pistol, at which time Slaughter shot and killed him. Another outlaw, probably one Manuel, raced from the scene on foot but was thrown to the ground by another of Slaughter's shotgun blasts. Slaughter realized the fleeing man was only wounded and ordered his deputies to go after him and kill him. But the deputies couldn't find Manuel, and he got away.

San Bernardino Ranch, Arizona, September 19, 1898

This was a bad day for Peg-Leg Finney, a known thief, whom Slaughter observed moving about his property uninvited. Peg-Leg disappeared, and Slaughter, with four men, caught up to the outlaw asleep in the shade of a tree not far from the ranch house. All five men crept up on the dozing desperado, and Slaughter gingerly took up Peg-Leg's Winchester and tossed it away. The noise startled Finney from his slumber, and he sat straight with a pistol cocked and pointed right at Slaughter. Slaughter swung his own rifle into position and plugged Peg-Leg Finney with a bullet smashing through Finney's right hand before stopping in his chest. Two of Slaughter's men fired simultaneously, mortally wounding Finney, who died there.

San Bernardino Ranch, Arizona, ca. 1900

A gambler named Little Bob Stevens apparently attempted to improve his odds at the roulette table by simply taking all the money at gunpoint. Stevens then fled toward John Slaughter's San Bernardino Ranch. Little Bob Stevens's luck ran out for good on the San Bernardino when Slaughter caught and killed him.

Cochise County, Arizona, 1901

A ruthless ne'er-do-well robbed and murdered a mother, her son, and her daughter and came away with three hundred dollars of the family's money. He also came away with the outrage of a community. Slaughter readily joined the posse hunting the culprit. When they caught him, the murdering thief resisted arrest, or that's how the story goes, and he was riddled stem to stern.

Erwin, 27-34, 63, 112-116, 149-50, 212-16, 239-41, 256-61; O'Neal, *Encyclopedia,* 287-89; Metz, *Encyclopedia,* 225; Nash, 285-86.

Smith, Thomas C. (d. 1892)
Smith was born in Texas, probably in Fort Bend County, the son of

law officer Thomas Jefferson Smith. The elder Smith was born in 1808 and came to Texas with the Georgia Battalion in 1835. Published reports indicate that Thomas Jefferson Smith was present at the Goliad Massacre during the war for Texas independence from Mexico, but was spared because of his carpentry and gunsmith skills. He served as sheriff of Fort Bend County from August 2, 1852, until August 4, 1856.

Thomas Calton "Tom" Smith followed his father into law enforcement, initially serving as city marshal of Taylor, Texas. Tom was a deputy sheriff in Williamson County, Texas, by 1884. When his brother-in-law, J. T. Garvey, was elected sheriff of Fort Bend County in 1888, he chose Tom as his principal deputy. Garvey was a member of the "Woodpecker" faction of the Democrat party, then arrayed in an intramural campaign against their rivals in the "Jaybird" faction, which controlled most county government. On August 16, 1889, a gunfight erupted near the Fort Bend County courthouse, resulting in the death of Sheriff Garvey, another "Woodpecker" faction adherent, and one "Jaybird." Deputy Smith provided covering fire as Garvey and his allies were carried into the courthouse for protection.

Smith became a deputy U.S. marshal for the Western District of Arkansas on September 26, 1890. The following November he was employed by an association of Wyoming cattle barons to recruit Texas gunmen for the Johnson County War. That seething mess pitted established cattle barons against their hired cowboys, independent ranchers, and allies. The "cowboys" had two principal grievances. First, any cowboy who owned his own cattle was blacklisted from employment with the large ranchers. Second, maverick laws passed by the state legislature granted the Wyoming Stock Growers Association (WSGA) the exclusive right to conduct roundups and restricted the rights of small ranchers to acquire stray cattle in manners accepted by everyone until that time. A wage strike initiated by the cowboys and other issues prompted the powerful and politically connected large cattle growers to retaliate.

Tom Smith assembled and recruited some twenty Texans in Paris, Texas. The "Regulators" were told that their mission was to serve warrants on a number of "dangerous outlaws" who turned out to be nothing more than independent ranchers and cowboys. The recruits were promised five dollars a day, plus fifty dollars a head for each dangerous outlaw any Regulator was forced to kill. Despite grandiose plans to eliminate some thirty-four men, in the end, only Nick Ray and Nathan D. Champion were killed. Many of the Texans were quick to note that the warrants they were hired to serve never were provided. Even worse, the entire contingent, including Smith himself, were trapped at a ranch until rescued through the intercession of the state governor and others. Eventually, Smith and the other Texans were released, and no trial for the killings was ever scheduled.

Smith returned to Texas in 1892 and became a deputy U.S. marshal for the Eastern District of Texas stationed at Paris. He was killed on November 4, 1892, near Ardmore, Indian Territory, by a suspect on a passenger train. Three of his sons served as law officers, notably including Frank Smith who became an agent of the Federal Bureau of Investigation. Frank investigated the Osage Indian murders in Oklahoma, survived the Union Station massacre at Kansas City, Missouri, in 1933, and later assisted in the investigation of the Charles Urschel kidnapping in Oklahoma City.

Selected Gunfight
Powder River, Wyoming, November 1, 1891
Smith and three other "association detectives" rushed the cabin of Ross Gilbertson where an outspoken Nate Champion was staying. The plan failed when Champion wounded two attackers. The would-be assassins made a hasty retreat, leaving behind horses, clothing, and a rifle. Champion was killed on April 9, 1892, at the KC Ranch, along with Nick Ray, another "cowboy."

Smith, *War on Powder River,* 192, 201, 213; O'Neal, *Johnson County War,* 71, 73-75, 92, 97-98, 225-27, 231; O'Neal, *Encyclopedia,* 292-93; Metz, *The Shooters,* 172-77; Nash, 287-88; Ernst, *Deadly Affrays,* 337-38; Cordry, "Tom and Frank Smith"; Tise, 188.

Story, Tom (d. 1889)

A Texas outlaw, Story was killed by Deputy U.S. Marshal Bass Reeves. Story operated for five years, stealing horses in Indian Territory for sale in Texas. In 1889, Story and his partner, Peg Leg

West put the theft train in reverse, selling Texas horses in Indian Territory without benefit of title. Unhappy Texas resident George DeLaney reported one such theft to the U.S. marshal at Paris, Texas, then served as a one-man posse for Reeves in pursuit of the rustlers. After a four-day wait, Story crossed the Red River into Texas, leading two of Delaney's unsold prize mules. Story resisted arrest and was shot out of the saddle. West died prior to June 1896.

Burton, *Black Gun, Silver Star,* 14, 150, 318 n. 1.

Stoudenmire, Dallas (1845-82)

After serving with the Confederate Army during the Civil War, Dallas Stoudenmire farmed several years near Columbus, Texas, before enlisting in Company B of the Texas Rangers. After a few years of fighting Indians on the plains, Stoudenmire traded the badge for a

nail pouch and hammer in Alleyton, Texas. He ventured into sheep ranching and merchandising in and around Oldham and Llano Counties before taking the dangerous job of city marshal of El Paso, Texas, in 1881. Because of his heavy drinking, Stoudenmire was in and out of law enforcement. Having "retired" his commission at El Paso, he ran the Globe Restaurant, which was bequeathed to him by his brother-in-law. Then in July 1882, Stoudenmire was appointed a deputy U.S. marshal. Still his drinking and cavorting with women other than his wife, Belle,

Dallas Stoudenmire about the time he was city marshal of El Paso. (Courtesy of El Paso Public Library, Aultman Collection)

caused another early "retirement." Stoudenmire was shot to death in a saloon brawl at El Paso.

Selected Gunfights
Colorado County, Texas, 1876
Stoudenmire and a longtime antagonist approached each other on horseback, then dismounted and exchanged insults, then switched to bullets. The first shots missed their targets, but when they moved closer to each other Stoudenmire placed a fatal round in his opponent, thus ending the disagreement.

Alleyton, Texas, 1877
Stoudenmire was attending a party when a large brawl soon turned to gunplay. He was wounded during the clash but not before sending several of his opponents scurrying for cover. He was arrested, but when a guard fell asleep on watch, Stoudenmire escaped.

Near Alleyton, Texas, 1878
An argument over the ownership of a herd of cattle resulted in Stoudenmire and cronies engaging the Sparks brothers of Eagle Lake in a gun battle. When the smoke cleared, two of Sparks's men, Benton Duke and his son "Little Duke," were dead, and one of the Sparks brothers was seriously injured.

El Paso, Texas, April 14, 1881
Stoudenmire ran from a lunch table at the Globe Restaurant to aid Constable Gus Krempkau, who had just been mortally wounded by John Hale following a dispute. In the excitement, Stoudenmire fired a shot at Hale, but the shot went wild, mortally wounding an innocent bystander. When Hale peered from behind an adobe pillar, Stoudenmire shot him in the head. Hale's associate, George Campbell, saw what happened to Hale and claimed he was not a party to the fight. Mortally wounded Krempkau saw things differently and fired six rounds at Campbell from his prone position. One of the bullets broke Campbell's wrist, and another hit him in the foot. Stoudenmire also fired on Campbell with much more decisive accuracy, mortally wounding him with a gut shot.

El Paso, Texas, April 17, 1881
Stoudenmire and Samuel M. "Doc" Cummings, the marshal's brother-in-law, were patrolling the streets when Bill Johnson, the

former El Paso marshal-turned-drunk, sprang from ambush, firing a shotgun in the two men's direction and missing them both. Stoudenmire and Cummings simultaneously drew their six-guns and cut the would-be assassin down. Johnson had been cajoled into ambushing Stoudenmire by enemies of the lawman. Legend has it that others fired at Stoudenmire, who drove them off.

El Paso, Texas, December 16, 1881

Joe King ambushed the marshal from behind a garbage pile near the boardinghouse where Stoudenmire lived at about 3:00 A.M. The assailant was near enough to the marshal that the flashes from his gun temporarily blinded the lawman, but his shots missed nonetheless. Stoudenmire shot back, causing King to dash off into the darkness.

El Paso, Texas, July 29, 1882

Stoudenmire and brothers Frank, Jim, and George Felix "Doc" Manning had long been embroiled in a feud, which up until that time had been made up of insults and threats of retaliation. Friends of both parties arranged a meeting to bring about a truce between the parties. Doc and Jim met Stoudenmire at a saloon around five thirty that afternoon to discuss terms. Jim Manning left momentarily to find Frank Manning. Things rapidly turned ugly, and despite the best efforts of the saloon's coowner, J. W. Jones, guns flared.

Stoudenmire was instantly wounded in the chest but was still able to wrestle his opponent up and down the boardwalk outside the saloon. Stoudenmire produced a derringer and shot Doc in the arm, but that didn't end the fracas. Jim Manning ran to reinforce his brother. Jim's first shot from his .45 slammed into a barber pole, but the second found its way into the back of Stoudenmire's head behind the left ear. Stoudenmire collapsed, a dead man. Doc Manning, still reeling in anger, picked up Stoudenmire's derringer and pistol-whipped the dead man until Texas Ranger Jim Gillett pulled him off.

Metz, *Dallas Stoudenmire*, 1-126; O'Neal, *Encyclopedia*, 302-5; Tyler, *The New Handbook of Texas*, vol. 6, 116; Metz, *Encyclopedia*, 234; Hatley, *Bringing the Law to Texas*, 109-10; Sonnichsen, *Pass of the North*, 223-24, 238.

Sutton, William E. (Bill, Billy) (1846-74)

A product of Fayette County, Texas, he was born on October 20,

1846. Sutton served in the Confederate Army, settling in Clinton, DeWitt County, Texas, at the conclusion of the war where he was a deputy sheriff. Sutton agitated a conflict with the neighboring Taylor family by leading a posse that pursued and killed suspected horse thief Charley Taylor on March 25, 1868. This incident and others in 1868 prompted the Sutton-Taylor Feud, one of the bloodiest conflicts in Texas history. The Sutton-Taylor Feud lasted for about seven years, and was marked by numerous murderous ambushes. Sutton concluded his own part in the feud as an assassination victim on March 11, 1874, at Indianola, Texas.

Selected Gunfights
Bastrop, Texas, March 25, 1868

Deputy Sheriff Sutton and a posse pursued two members of a suspected gang of horse thieves. Suspected rustlers Charley Taylor and James Sharp resisted arrest, provoking a fierce gun battle in which Taylor was fatally wounded. Sharp survived the fight but not the ride back to town as he was shot and killed while allegedly trying to escape.

Clinton, Texas, December 24, 1868

William F. "Buck" Taylor and Taylor factionist Richard T. "Dick" Chisholm became entangled in a war of words on this particular Christmas Eve day with Bill Sutton, who was accompanied by a large contingent of friends and relatives. When the talks concluded, Taylor and Chisholm were killed in a gunfight.

DeWitt County, Texas, August 26, 1870

Brothers Henry and William Kelly were wanted for disturbing the peace in the town of Sweet Home the night of August 25. A posse led by Jack Helm, then captain in the Texas State Police, arrested Henry outside his home the following morning. The group then proceeded toward the home of William Kelly to place him in irons and was met by Sutton who rode with the posse. William rode out from his home to meet the posse after he heard gunshots coming from their direction. When William arrived, shots were fired, and both Henry and William were killed. Helm swore the two men had tried to escape, but the Texas State Police thought otherwise and fired him.

Cuero, Texas, April 1, 1873

Sutton was inside Bank's Saloon and Billiard Parlor when James Taylor and several Taylor supporters engaged him in a gunfight.

Although wounded, Sutton continued to lead his faction in the war with the Taylors. The attack was apparently prompted by the death in an ambush of young Taylor's father, Pitkin Taylor, the previous year.

Near Clinton, Texas, June 16, 1873

Sutton was driving to Clinton in a buggy, accompanied by John Meador, Ad Patterson, Doc White, and Horace French when the party was attacked by Taylor men. The Sutton faction soon drove off the attackers, but not before Meador took a round in the leg and French's horse was killed.

Cuero, Texas, December 1873

A large body of Taylor men swarmed Sutton and several friends shortly after they left Clinton. Riding fast and shooting faster, the Sutton contingent found refuge at the Gulf Hotel and traded shots with the opposing feudists for a day and a half. The Taylors were then surprised by a large posse of Sutton supporters. The frustrated citizens of Cuero finally confronted both factions and forced them to take their differences elsewhere.

Indianola, Texas, March 11, 1874

Sutton, his wife Laura, and Gabrielle Webster "Gabe" Slaughter all rode to the port town of Indianola in far South Texas for a steamboat trip to New Orleans. Unbeknown to any of them, Jim and Bill Taylor also were in Indianola. Sutton, Laura, and Slaughter blithely walked up to the ticket counter to purchase their passage aboard the steamer as the Taylor brothers sprang from hiding. Neither Sutton nor Slaughter had time to defend themselves. Sutton was cut down with bullets to the head and heart as his wife watched. Slaughter took a bullet to the head and also died. The Taylors escaped, then joined their friend, the notorious John Wesley Hardin, on a cattle drive.

Tyler, *The New Handbook of Texas,* vol. 6, 162-63; O'Neal, *Encyclopedia,* 305-97; Hatley, *The Law Comes to Texas,* 73-74, 84; Eckhardt, 67, 77, 158.

Sylva, Nate (prom. 1890s)

A Gainesville, Texas, outlaw associated with Felix Young in a fabled April 9, 1894, train robbery in Oklahoma Territory, Sylva was a jockey, horse trader, and Texas prison alumnus suspected by some of selling stolen horses for the Dalton gang. Felix Young was a horse thief well known in Oklahoma Territory. The pair planned a robbery at Pond Creek, a bustling community whose future was seemingly assured by a Rock Island station and all the benefits of being the Grant County seat. Young and Sylva recruited "Will Wade," later identified as James C. "Big Jim" Bourland, and Bill Rhodes. John T. O'Connors, of Trinidad, Colorado, and Frank Lacy, who lived near Pond Creek, rounded out the crew.

On April 9, 1894, two gang members boarded the southbound Rock Island train with other passengers about 10:00 P.M. One mile south of Pond Creek, the engineer was forced to stop because a small bonfire obstructed the tracks. After the express car was opened with dynamite, Rhodes came through the door using the fireman and engineer as shields. Jake Harmon, the unfazed express car guard and a former Wichita policeman, blasted the bandit into oblivion, motivating the rest of the outlaw crew to depart without the loot. A posse quickly captured Wade, who had inexplicably slowed his escape by attempting to take Rhodes's horse with him. Wade's confession led to the arrest of O'Connors and Lacy several days later at Hennessey by Deputy U.S. Marshal Pat Murphy and others. The two suspects were spirited away to Wichita, thereby avoiding the untimely appointment with "Dr. Lynch," which had been openly discussed in the Hennessey streets. About one month later, Sylva and Young were captured at El Reno by deputy U.S. marshals Chris Madsen, Pat Murphy, Louis Eichoff, and others.

The fate of the gang speaks volumes about the casual nature of crime and punishment in the Territories. Felix Young was inexplicably released for lack of evidence, but rearrested on other charges and secured in the Pond Creek jail. Sylva, Young, and Bourland broke out of the Pond Creek jail on June 3, 1894, and fled to Indian Territory where, according to Madsen's memoirs, Young was killed years later in an unrelated dispute. Bourland fled from Indian Territory to Texas but was arrested and returned to Oklahoma Territory. After serving part of a prison sentence, Bourland became a special detective at Anadarko, where, according to Madsen, he was killed in a 1906 saloon brawl. Madsen also related that Sylva was arrested years later in Butler, Missouri, but escaped to obscurity. Meanwhile, once prosperous Pond Creek was supplanted as Grant County seat in 1908 then dwindled to a virtual ghost town.

Shirley, *West of Hell's Fringe*, 207-11; Shirley, *Six-Gun and Silver Star*, 120.

Taylor, Bill (prom. 1870s)

Creed Taylor and his brothers Pitkin, Rufus, William, and Josiah, were the patriarchs of the DeWitt County family whose sons battled William E. Sutton and his allies in the Sutton-Taylor Feud. Some have said the feud actually began decades earlier than the late 1860s when both families lived in Georgia. No matter, only the Texas hostilities have been recorded for history.

When his father, Pitkin, died of wounds six months after being shot by a member of the Sutton clan in the summer of 1872, Bill vowed revenge and intensified a bloody campaign that had prompted numerous attacks on the Sutton faction. Taylor finally succeeded in his effort to kill Bill Sutton on March 11, 1874, in Indianola, Texas. Sutton and his friend Gabe Slaughter were ambushed as they were purchasing tickets to board a steamer bound for New Orleans. Later, according to relatives, Bill Taylor moved to Indian Territory where he became a law officer.

Selected Gunfights
Cuero, Texas, April 1, 1873
Bill and Jim Taylor found Sutton inside Bank's Saloon and Billiard Parlor and started a gunfight. Sutton was seriously wounded but survived.
Indianola, Texas, March 11, 1874
John Wesley Hardin discovered Sutton's plans for a trip to New Orleans and informed Bill and Jim Taylor. The pair proceeded to Indianola, spotted Sutton, his wife Laura, and Sutton's friend Gabe Slaughter at the steamboat ticket counter and opened fire, killing both men as Mrs. Sutton looked on.

Sonnichsen, *I'll Die Before I Run*, 19-90; O'Neal, *Encyclopedia*, 307.

Taylor, Jim (1852-75)

Jim Taylor was the most prominent Taylor brother involved in the Sutton-Taylor Feud. His murder on December 27, 1875, marked a reduction in the violence caused by hostilities between the Taylors and Sutton factionists true to the memory of William E. Sutton. Jim and Bill ambushed and killed William E. "Bill" Sutton, in 1874, while Sutton, his wife, and Gabe Slaughter purchased steamboat tickets to New Orleans.

Selected Gunfights

Cuero, Texas, April 1, 1873

Sutton was inside a saloon in Cuero when Jim Taylor and others became aware of his location. The Taylor faction fired at Sutton, wounding him critically before fleeing. Sutton, however, survived the attack.

DeWitt County, Texas, June 1873

While on patrol searching for Sutton factionists Taylor and his band came upon Jim Cox and other riders whom they began firing upon. When the smoke cleared, Cox and W. S. "Jake" Christman were dead.

Albuquerque, Texas, July 1873

According to one source, Taylor and John Wesley Hardin were at a blacksmith shop when they noticed Jack Helm and others approaching. Helm, seeing Taylor inside, boldly walked toward the shop only to get a blast of buckshot in the chest fired by Hardin. Taylor then walked up to the prone Helm and emptied his six-gun into the man's head. Seeing this incident, Helm's six hard cases turned and scampered away.

Indianola, Texas, March 11, 1874

Having received word from John Wesley Hardin that Sutton and Gabe Slaughter were planning to board a steamer for New Orleans, Jim and Bill met the travelers at the dock and ambushed them. The Taylors made a clean getaway after killing both men.

Clinton, Texas, December 27, 1875

Jim Taylor and a few supporters rode into Clinton. There they handed the reins of their horses to Martin King, who inexplicably allowed the horses to escape, perhaps in treachery. Suddenly a large Sutton party raced into town. Cut off and on foot, Jim Taylor and associates Mace Arnold and A. R. Hendricks scrambled through Martin's home toward a cabin in an orchard. Their path was blocked by Kit Hunter, a Sutton supporter, whom Taylor unsuccessfully attempted to shoot. Hunter returned fire, striking Taylor in the arm. Taylor, Arnold, and Hendricks made a run for the cabin but were all killed in a hail of gunfire.

Taylor, Phillip (Doboy)

Phillip and his brother Hays were cousins to Jim and Bill Taylor. Phillip's father was Creed Taylor, brother to the murdered Pitkin. Phillip, known as Doboy, involved himself early on in the struggles with the Sutton faction but was killed in an unrelated argument in Kerrville, Texas, in November of 1871.

Selected Gunfights

Mason, Texas, November 1867

Doboy and his brother Hays got into a quarrel with soldiers stationed at nearby Fort Mason. When the ensuing gunplay ended, both the soldiers were dead. This incident put the Taylor boys at odds with the law and gave an advantage to the Sutton faction, many of whom were law officers.

DeWitt County, Texas, August 23, 1869

Jack Helm, an aggressive leader of the Sutton Regulators, planned an ambush of Doboy and Hays Taylor near their father's farm. As the two unsuspecting soldier killers rode up to the Creed Taylor place, Helm and his men opened fire. After a ferocious gun battle, Hays was killed, and Doboy was wounded but managed to escape.

Near Pennington, Texas, September 7, 1869

Doboy, along with his friends Kelleson and Cook, was visiting the William Connor Ranch along the Neches River. They were surprised by Regulators around dawn in an ambush that left Kelleson dead and Doboy and Cook wounded. Doboy and Cook later surrendered but slipped away to freedom just as night fell.

Kerrville, Texas, November 1871

Doboy died in a senseless act of defiance when he called Sim Holstein into the street for battle after Holstein got a job Doboy wanted. When Holstein emerged into the street unarmed, Doboy pulled his pistol and fired. Undaunted, Holstein jumped a low gate and tackled the surprised Doboy. During the wrestling match, Holstein wrested the gun away from Doboy and shot him. Doboy fell but promptly rose to his feet, and Holstein plugged him again. Defiantly Doboy rose up again, and again Holstein shot him. This time Doboy rose and tried to stagger away, but Holstein shot him a fourth and final time. Even so, Doboy refused to die for six hours.

O'Neal, *Encyclopedia,* 309-31; Metz, *Encyclopedia,* 237; Hatley, *The Law Comes to Texas,* 45, 52, 68, 73, 75, 84; Eckhardt, 67-69, 72, 77, 158; Tyler, *The New Handbook of Texas,* vol. 6, 162-63.

The "Texas Invaders" (prom. 1891)

A group of some twenty Texans recruited to fight for the large ranchers were organized as the Wyoming Stock Growers Association (WSGA) in the 1890s. Texas participants included Tom Smith, Frank Canton, William Armstrong, Robert Barling (Barlin), J. K. Barling, J. M. Benford (Buford, Beuford), D. E. Booker, Jim Dudley (Gus Green), Buck Garrett, J. A. Garrett, Alex Howerton (Hamilton), J. C. Johnson, William Little, Alex Lowther, M. A. McNally, Jeff D. Mynett, K. Pickard (Rickard), B. C. Schultz, S. S. Tucker, George R. Tucker, Bill Wiley (Wille, Willey), and W. A. Wilson.

The group was assembled on April 5, 1892, at Cheyenne, then transported to Northern Wyoming under the nominal leadership of former Union major Frank E. Wolcott, who delegated de facto supervision of the group to former bandit Joe Horner, a stock detective operating under the alias Frank Canton. Three days after their departure from frosty Cheyenne, the Texans and other recruits found themselves moving through a gale to a Northern Wyoming cabin occupied by small ranchers ("rustlers") Nick Ray and locally popular Nate Champion. These "rustlers" had started their own competing group called the Northern Wyoming Farmers and Stock Growers Association (NWFSGA), an audacious and fatal decision.

Leadership of the small competing organization was promptly liquidated by the Texans, who killed both Ray and Champion, but soon found themselves trapped in a barn about ten miles from Buffalo, Wyoming, surrounded by unhappy citizenry led by local sheriff William "Red" Angus. Eventually, the army was rescued by the cavalry, taken to Cheyenne, but released when the county ran out of funds to maintain the prosecution, or so state officials said at the time.

Smith, *War on Powder River,* 183-242; Metz, *Encyclopedia,* 135.

Texas Jack (of California) (prom. 1850s)

A presumed Lone Star native, Texas Jack was associated with Tom Bell, an escaped San Quentin convict who led some thirty road agents working between the King's River and Marysville, California. On September 30, 1856, near Folsom, fugitives Texas Jack, Tom Bell, and Ned Conway encountered a posse led by Placer County sheriff John C. Boggs. Conway opened fire and was killed instantly when the posse responded. Bell and Texas Jack made their escape in the confusion, allowing four days of freedom for Tom Bell, who was captured and lynched, leaving only Texas Jack to tell the tale in places yet unknown.

Boessenecker, 17-19.

Thomas, Henry Andrew (Heck) (1850-1912)

Perhaps the most distinguished and authentically heroic of the deputy U.S. marshals riding for Judge Parker in Indian Territory, Thomas was born on January 6, 1850, at or near Oxford Georgia. Following Confederate war service as a boy in the Thirty-fifth Regiment of Georgia Volunteers and marriage to the daughter of an Atlanta minister, he migrated to Texas, where he worked as a railroad guard and detective. He was first employed by the Texas Express Company in Dallas, then, as now, a boomtown.

On March 18, 1878, Thomas was the express messenger aboard a train stopped at Hutchins, Texas, by the Sam Bass gang. Since his brother Jim, also an express messenger, had been robbed by the same gang less than a month earlier, Heck had anticipated trouble and hid about $4,000 (some say $22,000) from the gang. He was injured by a shotgun blast fired by a train employee.

While working for a detective association, he pursued cattle rustlers Jim and Pink Lee to the Strother Brown farm near Dexter, Texas, in early September 1885, with Deputy U.S. Marshal Jim Taylor. Both Lees were killed. The pair of lawmen supposedly split a $2,500 reward. Thomas became a deputy U.S. marshal stationed at Fort Smith, Arkansas. His wife left him shortly thereafter, and he married Mattie Mowbray, daughter of the pastor of the First Methodist Church in Tulsa. Thomas worked with Bill Tilghman and others in Wharton (now Perry), Oklahoma Territory, a place that seemingly had as many saloons as houses. He died on August 11, 1912, at Lawton, where he had been police chief.

Selected Gunfights
Hutchins, Texas, March 18, 1878

While employed as a railroad guard, Thomas fooled the Sam Bass gang who were robbing a train he was guarding. Wounded in the neck and just below one eye, Thomas had the foresight to hide money sacks in a stove. The thieves made off with decoy sacks containing what they thought was a treasure trove of currency but which actually contained only about $89.

Near Dexter, Texas, September 6, 1885

Finding a pair of murderous brothers near Dexter, Texas, about twenty miles north and west of Gainesville, Thomas and Deputy U.S. Marshal Jim Taylor ordered Pink and Jim Lee to throw up their hands in surrender. The Lee brothers opened fire, which Thomas and Taylor returned. Pink Lee dropped to the ground with blood oozing from his head and ears. Jim lasted long enough to fire three rounds at his pursuers but was felled by a round to the throat. Thomas and Taylor commandeered a wagon and hauled the bodies back to Gainesville, the Cooke County seat.

Snake Creek, Indian Territory, June 27, 1888

Heck Thomas and Burrell Cox, Hank Childers, and Jim Wallace found the Purdy gang of train robbers they had been trailing, then gave the bandits the customary chance to surrender. Aaron Purdy was first to draw, and he hit Thomas once in the right wrist, breaking it, and once in the side where an eight-inch gash opened him up. Fellow possemen returned fire, killing Purdy before he could cause any more damage. The other outlaws quickly surrendered.

Near Tahlequah, Indian Territory, 1889

Thomas was but one of many who would attempt to bring in the notorious Cherokee, Ned Christie. Sneaking up on Christie's home fifteen miles southeast of Tahlequah, Thomas, L. P. "Bones" Isbel, and a deputy named Salmon tried to flush him out. After a lengthy, but fruitless, gun battle, Thomas managed to set fire to the home. Christie's wife and son were inside with him. They ran from the burning home, and the boy was shot in the hip and lung. He and his mother nonetheless crawled to safety as the lawmen awaited Christie's appearance. Christie burst onto the scene firing and running when a bullet from Thomas's rifle tore through Christie's nose. The wound made an ugly mess of his face, but he managed to join his family in the safety of nearby woods. He was marred for life, and the once attractive Cherokee outlaw never forgave Thomas for his disfigurement.

Indian Territory, January 20, 1890

Outlaw Jim July jumped bail following a charge of train robbery, and Thomas set out to bring him back to face the charge. When the two did meet up, July attempted to resist the lawman, who simply shot him to death.

Orlando, Oklahoma Territory, November 29, 1892

On the trail of outlaw Oliver "Ol" Yantis, deputy U.S. marshals Heck Thomas, Chris Madsen, and Tom Hueston found their man at his sister's farm just outside of town. Yantis was carrying a revolver as he emerged from the house to feed cattle. Once again, Thomas presented himself and called for the outlaw to surrender. And once again, his command was met with bullets. Thomas dove for cover, as Madsen and Hueston killed Yantis.

Near Bartlesville, Indian Territory, July 1895

This time Thomas wasn't able to bring in his man, but he did find two of his fingers. Thomas and two Osage Indian scouts, Spotted Dog Eater and Howling Wolf, caught up to outlaw Little Bill Raidler. Little Bill had taken refuge in a cave near town, but the posse found his hiding place. Raidler didn't wait for Thomas's usual warning, but instead, he opened up on the three men. Thomas fired back, sending a bullet through Raidler's hand. Raidler scampered off into the woods and, despite their best efforts, the posse only came out with two of the mangled fingers Raidler had apparently amputated as a result of the bullet from Thomas's rifle.

Lawton, Oklahoma Territory, August 25, 1896

Perhaps learning from previous near misses, Thomas chose to surprise Bill Doolin at night on a road near the home of his father-in-law. Nonetheless, Doolin immediately opened fire with his Winchester. Thomas and his posse returned fire and shot Doolin to death.

Near Sapulpa, Indian Territory, November 1896

Dynamite Dick Clifton was a wanted man hiding near Sapulpa,

located about fifteen miles southwest of Tulsa. Clifton was with two other desperados when Thomas, his son Albert, and two Dunn brothers came up on them. After a vigorous gun battle all the lawmen laid claim to was some baggage and one horse.

O'Neal, *Encyclopedia,* 312-15; Smith, *Daltons,* 167; Nash, 300-301; Shirley, *Heck Thomas,* 1-98.

Thompson, Ben (1842-84)

Born on November 11, 1842, in Knottingley, England, Thompson immigrated with his family to Austin in 1851. Shooting incidents in Austin and New Orleans apparently prompted his enlistment in the Confederate Army, where he refined his gambling skills. A wartime romance with well-to-do Austin debutante Catherine Moore blossomed into a lifelong marriage and family.

Ben spent the early Reconstruction years in Texas, gambling and saloon keeping. Eventually he departed for the cow towns of Kansas, the home away from home to many a Texas cattleman. There he opened an Abilene saloon. Later, slowed but not defeated by a Kansas City wagon accident that severely injured his wife and son, Thompson sold his interest in the Bulls Head Saloon, then returned to Texas. By 1873, he was seeking his fortune in Ellsworth, Kansas, with his violence-prone younger brother Billy. Involved in numerous gunfights, he died with John King Fisher on March 11, 1884, in an alcohol-fueled row at Jack Harris's Vaudeville Saloon and Theater, in San Antonio, Texas.

Selected Texas Gunfights

Austin, 1859

A hunting party on the Colorado River degenerated into a shotgun duel between Ben and another wayward teenager, who was wounded.

Laredo, 1864

While off duty, Ben and Billy Thompson played monte with two Mexican soldiers, whom they killed.

Near Austin, 1865

Ben and several associates killed an indeterminate number of Federal occupation troops near Austin, for reasons unknown.

Austin, 1880

Splendidly attired Ben was mistaken for an Eastern dandy by several San Saba youths. Ben played along until his new hat was targeted by the miscreants, whom he drove off with gunfire.

San Antonio, March 11, 1884

Ben and John King Fisher visited Jack Harris's Vaudeville Saloon and Theater, the very locale where Thompson had killed Jack Harris in a quarrel almost two years earlier over a gambling debt. Revenge motivated certain assailants to kill the fabled pair. Suspects included a vaudeville performer and even the bartender. No one was ever prosecuted.

Selcer, 129-30; O'Neal, *Encyclopedia,* 315.

Thompson, Irvin (Blackie) (1893-1933)

A shoemaker born to parents from Wheeler County, Texas, Thompson may have been born in Arkansas or Oklahoma. He operated in both Oklahoma and Texas. He was a key witness in the Osage County, Oklahoma, Indian murder trials. He testified against Ernest Burkhart on June 4, 1926, in the murder of W. E. Smith.

A 1920 automobile theft in Osage County had earned him a five-year sentence, but he was paroled in 1922. Suspected of a Grady County bank robbery, he was captured on December 22, 1923, in Joplin, Missouri, convicted, and sentenced. He was paroled to work as an informant for federal agents investigating the Osage Indian murders, but his work proved unsatisfactory to say the least. He organized the "Thompson gang," which ambushed and killed Drumright police officer U. S. Lenox, on July 2, 1924, following a $1,500 robbery of the First State Bank of Avery.

Selected Additional Robberies and Gunfights

Skedee, Oklahoma, August 22, 1924

Henry Cornett, "Buster" Holland, and Blackie Thompson robbed the bank. During the holdup Blackie managed to shoot Holland four times.

Hoffman, Oklahoma, December 19, 1924

Blackie, Jeff Duree, and others were suspected of robbing the Security State Bank of $3,000 in currency and $5,000 in county bonds (today $54,260) by simply loading the 2,600-pound safe into a stolen truck.

Bartlesville, December 25, 1924

Thompson was surrounded by a posse led by U.S. Marshal Alva McDonald and surrendered without incident.

McAlester, Oklahoma, August 30, 1933

After convincing an incredibly gullible guard he just wanted to go fishing at the prison farm lake, Thompson escaped the McAlester State Prison with two other prisoners. Recaptured in 1934 following several Texas bank robberies, he escaped Huntsville Prison with R. A. Hamilton, who soon rejoined the Barrow gang.

Amarillo, Texas, December 6, 1934

Observed by Police Chief W. R. McDowell in a stolen car, Blackie sped eastward on Route 66, but was forced off the highway by gunfire and killed at point blank range by Deputy Sheriff Roy Brewer.

Koch, 12, 15, 334-35; Cordry, *Alive If Possible, Dead If Necessary,* 87.

Thompson, William (Texas Billy) (1845-97)

A younger brother of Ben Thompson, Billy participated in four gunfights, hiding in Indian Territory from 1868 until 1872. He was rather rough on his friends, leaving at least two of them, a soldier named Billy Burke and Deputy Sheriff C. B. Whitney, dead in his wake. Billy died of a stomach ailment in Houston on September 6, 1897.

Gunfights

Austin, Texas, September 2, 1868

Following a night of revelry together, U.S. Army sergeant William Burke suddenly threatened to drive the besotted and sleeping Thompson outside in his nightshirt (if any). Thompson mortally wounded Burke and fled.

Ellsworth, Kansas, August 15, 1873

Thompson accidentally shot his friend Sheriff C. B. Whitney, proclaiming as he escaped that on that particular evening he would have shot "Christ himself" (*sic*).

Near Austin, October 26, 1876

Billy was captured by Texas Rangers without a shot about thirteen miles northeast of town.

Ogallala, Nebraska, June 26, 1880

Fellow Texan Jim Tucker sprayed Billy with five slugs in a quarrel over a lady of joy. Thompson barely escaped a lynching due to the quick thinking of Bat Masterson.

Miller and Snell, 3, 219, 409, 506-7, 635-39; O'Neal, *Encyclopedia*, 321; Metz, *Encyclopedia*, 246-47.

Tilghman, William (Bill) (1854-1924)

Bill Tilghman was a deputy U.S. marshal, who, with Chris Madsen and Heck Thomas, comprised the "Three Guardsman" of Indian Territory days. He was born to a sutler at Fort Dodge, Iowa, on July 4, 1854. Bill's parents migrated to the Atchinson, Kansas, area about 1856. Bill became a buffalo hunter. One authority states that Tilghman met Wild Bill Hickock at an early age and emulated his gun style.

Tilghman visited Texas infrequently, but became familiar with many a Lone Star cowboy after becoming the deputy sheriff of Ford County, Kansas, whose county seat was and is Dodge City. Serving in law enforcement while running a saloon, he tracked a horse thief named George Snyder into Texas and later participated in two bitter county seat wars in Kansas. Along the way, he became acquainted with the Earp brothers and Doc Holliday.

He made the Oklahoma 1889 Land Run with Jim Masterson (brother of Bat), settling at Guthrie, and helped tame "Hell's Half Acre" at Wharton (now Perry). He became a deputy U.S. marshal in 1892, then served as Lincoln County sheriff, Oklahoma City police chief, and a state senator.

Selected Gunfights

Petrie, Indian Territory, June 25, 1874

Tilghman and fellow buffalo hunters, including Hurricane Bill, confronted "Blue Tooth" (known by no other name) and others who were holding the dead body of fellow buffalo hunter Pat Conger. Shots were exchanged, and the hunters retrieved the body for burial.

Near Mead City, Kansas, October 4, 1879

A posse including Bill Tilghman, Wyatt Earp, and Jim Masterson intercepted and wounded Texas cattleman James Kennedy who had accidentally killed Fannie Keenan, also known as Dora Hand, while trying to kill Dodge City mayor James H. "Dog" Kelley.

Near Pawnee, Oklahoma Territory, 1894

Tilghman and law officer Steve Burke found Cattle Annie (Anna McDougal) and Little Britches (Jennie Stevens) at a farmhouse. Stevens attempted to escape, and Tilghman pursued her, shooting her horse to end the chase, or so the story goes.

Cromwell, Oklahoma, November 1, 1924

Tilghman was killed attempting to arrest Wiley Lynn, a federal prohibition officer, whom Tilghman perceived to be intoxicated. Earlier, according to some, Tilghman had caught some Lynn associates with a plane load of narcotics near Cromwell.

Shirley, *Guardian of the Law,* 79, 294; Samuelson, *Shoot from the Lip,* 30-40, 117-27; O'Neal, *Encyclopedia,* 323-26.

Tomlinson, Joseph (Captain Joe) (1834-74)

Tomlinson (Tumlinson) was a lieutenant in the Jack Helm contingent, which served the Sutton faction in the Sutton-Taylor war. These men operated under color of Texas State Police authority. Tomlinson had lived in Texas since the days of the Republic. Described as about forty in 1874, he settled near Yorktown, Dewitt County. Eventually, he crossed the Taylors, setting off years of difficulties. Although he habitually carried about four weapons on his person, he narrowly escaped death in a June 1873 ambush in DeWitt County, between Helena and Yorktown, which claimed James W. Cox and W. S. "Jake" Christman. Tomlinson died of natural causes on November 23, 1874.

Wilkins, *The Law Comes to Texas,* 20; Sonnichsen, *I'll Die Before I Run,* 19-90.

Vermillion, Texas Jack (Texas Jack Tipton) (prom. 1880s)

Texas Jack was a mysterious shootist who wandered through Kansas, Colorado, and New Mexico. He encountered and associated himself with Doc Holliday and Wyatt Earp, then followed them to

Tombstone, Arizona. Although Vermillion did not participate in the O.K. Corral gunfight, one source places him among the Earp cohort that sought revenge following the March 18, 1882, pool hall murder of Morgan Earp by suspected assassins Pete Spence, Frederick Bode, and Cochise County deputy sheriff Frank Stilwell.

Stilwell experienced a fatal encounter with the Earp faction at the Tucson train yards on March 20, 1882. The group then pursued Spence to a campsite near Tombstone, only to learn from the county sheriff that Spence had already been taken into custody, leaving another suspect, Florentino "Indian Charlie" Cruz to face the deadly music.

Vermillion moved on to Denver where he worked as a confidence man, then arrived in Guthrie, Oklahoma Territory, in time for the 1889 land rush. Holliday biographer Karen Holliday Tanner revealed that Vermillion apparently spent his golden years in Stone Gap, Virginia, as a revivalist.

Metz, *Encyclopedia,* 73, 256; Tanner, *Doc Holliday,* 179, 183-84, 290 n. 4.

Wallace, William Alexander Anderson (Bigfoot) (1817-99)

Born in Virginia in 1817, Wallace was about nineteen years old when he relocated to La Grange County, Texas, to avenge the deaths of a brother and a cousin slain in the 1836 Mexican-led Goliad Massacre. Wallace traveled northward, stopping at Travis County and then San Antonio between 1840 and 1842, killing members of the Mexican male population as he went. He ended that spree finally and joined the Texas Rangers, seeing action in the Mexican War. Wallace was rewarded for his shooting, tracking, and leadership abilities and in 1858 was appointed a captain in the Rangers. He also rode shotgun on the San Antonio-El Paso stagecoach lines, thwarting many attempts of would-be robbers to help themselves to whatever was on board. In his retirement, Wallace purchased a ranch in Frio County and lived to the age of eighty-two until his death on January 7, 1899.

Utley, *Lone Star Justice,* 44, 93; Hatley, *The Law Comes to Texas,* 20, 29; Stone, 4-5, 862; Nash, 310-11.

Walker, Joe (ca. 1850-98)

Joe Walker never knew his father, a Texas rancher, who died when Joe was still an infant. His mother turned over cattle operations to her brother who managed the Walker ranch and his own before combining the two in about 1870 and then moving the entire herd to Arizona. The brother, a Dr. Whitmore, soon died in a clash with Indians there, and his wife and two sons left Arizona for Utah. After the death of Walker's mother, he traveled to Utah intent on reaching a settlement with the Whitmores on the value of the Walker family cattle that had been commingled with theirs. But the Whitmores coolly denied any relationship to their deceased aunt's son and denied him the right to any proceeds from the cattle. One source also characterizes him as a prospective suitor of a Whitmore daughter.

Walker took revenge for real or imagined slights by joining Butch Cassidy's Wild Bunch and rustling Whitmore cattle on more than one occasion. Walker was eventually tracked down by a posse who shot him at first light during the month of May in 1898. The posse also shot a man camping with Walker whom they initially believed was Butch Cassidy, but in fact was cowboy Johnny Herring, who had merely spent the night in Walker's camp.

Selected Gunfights

Price, Utah, summer 1895

Walker became a wanted man after he got drunk and shot up the town. Although no injuries were reported, he caused enough property damage to draw an arrest warrant.

Robbers Roost region, Utah, 1896

On the road near Granite, Walker encountered a five-man posse of bounty hunters. A chase ensued with both sides trading shots, but Walker was far enough ahead of his pursuers that he was able to find sanctuary some fifteen miles later at Robbers Roost.

Mexican Bend of the San Rafael River, Utah, 1897

Walker and fellow rustler, C. L. Maxwell, had just conducted another successful raid on the Whitmore place where they made off with a large herd of horses. The pair of outlaws secluded their spoils at a corral and cabin along the San Rafael River at Mexican Bend. The bandits began arguing with one another for reasons now unknown. Maxwell left camp and headed straight for the Whitmores to tell them where they could find their horses.

The Whitmores alerted the authorities, and Sheriffs C. W. Allred and Azariah Tuttle took up the hunt. They came up on their prey at the river's edge. When Walker saw the lawmen he realized he was cut off from the cabin. He then waded across the river and climbed the canyon wall on the opposite side. About halfway up, he pulled his pistol. As the two lawmen galloped toward him he shot Tuttle in the leg, knocking him from his horse. The lawmen took cover behind some boulders and traded shots with Walker. Allred went for help, and Tuttle kept Walker pinned down with rifle fire, but after about two hours the lawman asked Walker for some water. He agreed to fetch a pail of water, but only if Tuttle tossed out all his guns. Tuttle complied, and Walker provided him with water and walked away until he found a loose horse and rode off.

Pointer, 111, 120; O'Neal, *Encyclopedia*, 333-34; Nash, 309-10.

Webb, Jim (prom. 1900s)

A Texas cowboy and foreman, Webb killed black preacher William Steward for failure to contain a grass fire that migrated to the adjoining Washington-McLish Ranch that Webb managed. Bass Reeves and his posse arrested Webb shortly thereafter in the southern Chickasaw Nation. Ranch hand Frank Smith interfered in the arrest, and Reeves mortally wounded him with a pistol shot, while throttling Webb with the other hand. Later, Webb was released on bond, which he forfeited.

In June 1904, Reeves tracked Webb to a general store owned by Jim Bywater at Woodford, a community near Sacred Heart Mission. Webb quickly spotted Reeves on horseback and started a gunfight, shooting Reeves's reins from his hands, the last mistake he ever made. Reeves shot Webb three times with his Winchester, terminating Webb's career. The outlaw claimed to have killed eleven men, four in Indian Territory. Before dying, Webb presented Reeves with his weapon, which Reeves kept as a souvenir.

Burton, *Black Gun, Silver Star,* 82-86.

Webb, L. A. (Lew) (prom. 1890s)

Reportedly a Victoria, Texas, native, Webb was an associate of the Tisdales and other small ranchers in the Johnson County War. Webb was prominent on the "death list" of troublesome small ranchers apparently prepared by Frank Canton and others for large ranchers, published by the *Chicago Herald* on April 19, 1892. Webb was also a member of the North Wyoming Farmers and Stock Growers Association of "rustlers," and as such, reportedly encouraged young Martin Tisdale, the son of murder victim John A. Tisdale, to assassinate Frank Canton, who many believed was responsible for killing the elder Tisdale. Canton returned to Buffalo, Wyoming, in 1900, but had heard of the plot and avoided the confrontation with young Tisdale.

DeArment, *Alias Frank Canton,* 241-42.

Weightman (Waightman), George (Red Buck) (d. 1896)

Horse thief Red Buck Weightman was as ruthless as they came in Texas. His reputation quickly spread into Indian Territory, when he became a member of the Bill Doolin gang. His Texas legacy included the killings of Fred Hoffman, who served both as Dewey County, Texas, treasurer, and as a U.S. commissioner, known today as a United States magistrate. Red Buck's troublesome ways became too much for Doolin after an incident in Oklahoma Territory. Having just robbed a train near Dover, on April 3, 1895, gang member Tulsa Jack Blake was shot and killed by a local posse. Weightman's horse was shot out from under him, and he leaped onto the mount ridden by Bitter Creek Newcomb.

When the gang came to a pasture where some horses were grazing, Red Buck jumped from the haunches of Bitter Creek's horse, climbed a fence, and prepared to ride off with a stolen steed. Just then the owner, an elderly preacher, came out from his house in protest. Red Buck turned his mount back toward the preacher and shot him dead. Doolin expelled Red Buck from the gang, or so the story goes. Red Buck put together a gang of his own after the preacher incident in Dover. They were followed to a hideout by pursuing Texas Rangers. In the gunfight that followed, Weightman was wounded, but he and his ragtag bunch managed to escape.

A few months later Weightman and George "Hookey" Miller were found by lawmen in an Oklahoma dugout. Weightman was killed on March 4, 1896, near Arapahoe, Oklahoma Territory, by "D" County deputy Joe Ventioner, assisted by officers Womble, Shahan, Duckworth, and Lewis Williams of Washita County. Contrary to some reports, Chris Madsen was not involved. Rumored by some to be willing to kill for $150, Weightman was understandably unpopular with other Doolin gang members.

O'Neal, *Encyclopedia,* 335-36; Smith, *Daltons,* 164, 166; Samuelson, *Shoot from the Lip,* 77; Shirley, *Temple Houston,* 256-58; Hanes, 62; Shirley, *West of Hell's Fringe,* 139.

West, Richard (Little Dick) (ca. 1865-98)

Perhaps born in or near Decatur, Texas, Dick was reputedly an orphan who preferred to always sleep and dine "al fresco," that is to say, outdoors. He was said to have been "discovered" washing dishes in Decatur, Texas, in 1881, then worked at the H. H. Ranch in Oklahoma Territory.

Dick joined the Doolin Gang, participated in their Southwest City, Missouri, robbery, a robbery at Dover, Oklahoma Territory, and perhaps others. Late in his career, he joined the spectacularly unsuccessful Al Jennings gang, only to be killed on April 13 (or April 7), 1898, near Guthrie, Oklahoma Territory, by a posse led by Deputy U.S. Marshals Bill Tilghman and Heck Thomas. Bat Masterson reportedly considered him the worst criminal in the territory other than Doolin.

Nix, 58; Hanes, 63-64; Shirley, *West of Hell's Fringe,* 186.

Wilson, George (Texas George)

An alumnus of California's San Quentin prison, Wilson turned to stagecoach robbing in 1876. Two holdups liberating Wells Fargo cargo boxes caught the attention of that venerable institution, which promptly hired legendary lawman Steve Venard to track the road agents. By January 28, 1876, Venard had returned Wilson to San Quentin for a twelve-year time out.

Boessenecker, 53-55.

Yarberry, Milton J. (John Armstrong) (1849-83)

A gunfighter, rustler, and law officer, Yarberry was born at Walnut Ridge, Arkansas, as John Armstrong. He left there when a Sharp County sheriff put a $200 price tag on his head for a murder he supposedly committed. A short time later, Armstrong was implicated in another murder, this time at Helena, Arkansas. Eventually Armstrong joined cattle rustlers Mysterious Dave Mather and Dave Rudabaugh near Fort Smith, Arkansas. The trio was suspected of having murdered a prominent rancher, but were never charged. This may have accounted for Armstrong's observable nervousness after the killing. On one occasion, Armstrong supposedly turned on a man who was walking behind him down a Texarkana, Texas, street and shot him dead. Armstrong claimed he thought the man was a detective hired to arrest him. The truth was, the man was just a citizen walking behind Armstrong down a city street.

In 1876 and 1877, Armstrong was in Decatur, Texas, running a saloon as John Johnson. He reportedly killed a man in Decatur and soon after left Texas all together. By 1879, Armstrong had arrived in Las Vegas, New Mexico, as Milton J. Yarberry. According to one source he became part of "the Dodge City Gang." One of its most notable supposed members was John Henry "Doc" Holliday.

With a resume that included several suspected murders, other unexplained deaths, and cattle rustling, it is no wonder that the good citizens of Albuquerque appointed Yarberry chief of police. Chief Yarberry killed a rival over a woman on March 27, 1881. He pleaded self-defense and was acquitted. Less than three months later, on June 18, Yarberry shot and killed another man, again claiming self-defense. This time, however, the jury sentenced the police chief to death by hanging. Despite a temporary jailbreak, Yarberry was hanged at Albuquerque at about 3:00 P.M. on February 9, 1883, at the command of his close friend, Sheriff Perfecto Armijo.

Selected Gunfights

Albuquerque, New Mexico, March 27, 1881

Yarberry and another lawman, Harry Brown, were competing for the affections of a lovely divorcée named Sadie Preston. The competition must have been quite intense that day, as the rivals met outside a restaurant. Yarberry pulled his six-shooter and shot Brown several times, killing him on the spot.

Albuquerque, New Mexico, June 18, 1881

Constable Yarberry investigated a gunshot apparently fired by Charles D. Campbell whom Yarberry promptly shot in the back, according to examining physicians. Yarberry put himself at the mercy of his peers by claiming self-defense. This time the jury wasn't convinced since Campbell's pistol was never found. Yarberry was convicted of first-degree murder and sentenced to hang. He was hanged on February 9, 1882, at about 3:00 P.M. after playing a rousing fiddle tune.

DeMattos, 23, 24; Metz, *Encyclopedia,* 268; Thrapp, *Encyclopedia,* I, 176, 957; DeArment, *Deadly Dozen,* 52-65.

Young Brothers (prom. 1930s)

Oklahoma-raised Harry and Jennings Young were small-time car thieves and burglars who perpetrated the largest massacre of law enforcement officers in one incident in United States history, on January 2, 1932, near Springfield, Missouri. Brothers Paul (b. 1896), Jennings (b. 1898), and Harry (b. 1903) were born in Christian County, Missouri, to upstanding, honest J. D. Young and his wife Willie Florence (*sic*), who participated in the Oklahoma Territory land lottery in 1902 and moved the family to a farm about two miles east of Frederick, Oklahoma, in about 1909. Hard times convinced them to return to Missouri in 1917. Less than a year later, the family moved to a substantial, two-story farmhouse on ninety-eight acres of high-quality farmland about five miles east of Springfield near the community of Brookline.

While most of the Youngs were (and are) honest folk, as teenagers Jennings, Paul, and Harry were suspected of several burglaries in and near Frederick. The return to Missouri did little to change their reputations or habits. Paul somehow managed to attend Phillips University at Enid, Oklahoma, in 1916. Nevertheless, neighbors considered the young trio to be "afternoon farmers," with little enthusiasm for agricultural pursuits. Instead their passion seemed to be reserved for driving automobiles of questionable provenance, which they adorned with fancy accessories, using money of unknown origin. By December 1918, Paul and Jennings were charged with burglarizing three stores in Ozark and Nixa, small communities near Springfield. Each of the boys pled guilty to burglary on May 31, 1919, and found a new home in the Missouri State Prison at Jefferson City. They were soon released and returned to a life of crime, breaking the heart of their honest father, who died in November 1921.

April of 1924 found Harry in a Texas prison. Younger brother Oscar and mother Willie were charged by railroad detective R. E. Truman with filching Oklahoma-bound goods from a boxcar at Nichols Junction, a community since incorporated into Springfield. Truman, curiously enough was a first cousin and close friend of future president Harry S Truman. Oscar and "Ma" Young escaped incarceration, but Jennings was sentenced to three years at Leavenworth.

Brother Paul avoided Truman's wrath, but went to Missouri State Prison on other charges, was released in 1922, arrested in Texas for burglary some two years later, and upon his second release went straight. He died in Houston, Texas, on December 31, 1986, an eighty-something newlywed with a new home.

Harry and Jennings were not as smart. Harry mortally wounded Republic, Missouri, city marshal Mark Noe on June 2, 1929, while resisting arrest for public drunkenness. The unsuspecting city marshal had accepted Harry's seemingly kind invitation to drive them both to the Republic justice of the peace, but was instead killed and dumped in a ditch outside town. Harry fled to Houston, where Jennings was engaged in the moonlight car business. There, the two brothers set in motion the events that would lead to the death of eight more people.

After returning to Springfield through Oklahoma in a stolen Ford roadster, they borrowed a rifle and shotgun from their unsuspecting brother Oscar, then removed to the Young farmhouse, where their younger sisters Vinita and Lorena were recruited to sell the stolen car at the Medley used car lot in Springfield. Savvy, suspicious Mr. Medley stalled the sisters and later called police, who eventually arrested and interrogated them. After learning that Jennings and

Harry were at the Young farm near Brookline, outside of Springfield city limits, Sheriff Marcel Hendrix arranged for a raid on the Young farm the afternoon of January 2, 1932, by a combined force of city and county law enforcement. Sheriff Hendrix also asked a motorcycle patrolman to acquire some "medicinal" whiskey from popular Dr. Max Fitch for "nerve calming" after the raid. On his way out the door, Hendrix also told a local reporter about the pending arrest of notorious Harry and Jennings Young.

Instead, within an hour, six of the ten officers would be dead and three wounded. Approaching the house about 4:00 P.M. (some say 5:00 P.M.), they inexplicably assembled and strategized on the front porch, according to one source, perhaps within earshot of Harry and Jennings. When no one responded to several invitations to come out, Sheriff Hendrix and Deputy Sheriff Wiley Mashburn went to the back door, where they obtained access using a foot warrant. The instant the door was opened, Hendrix and Mashburn were met with shotgun fire and died almost immediately. Soon thereafter, patrolman Charley Houser and chief of detectives Sid Meadows were each killed in the front yard while peering from behind trees. Posseman Ollie Crosswhite was killed while seeking the cover of a storm cellar at about the time Detective Tony Oliver met death returning to his patrol car. The remaining officers, three of whom were wounded, returned to Springfield, while Harry and Jennings escaped, stealing a car along the way. Ben Bilyeu insisted years later that the two Young brothers had been assisted by Fred Barker, whom Bilyeu recognized from newspaper photographs. He also speculated that Charles Arthur "Pretty Boy" Floyd participated in the murders.

The ever protective Willie, confronted with the death of six law officers, told a newspaper reporter that young Harry didn't even drink, much less kill people. She also said something she would later regret, that is, if her boys were responsible for the murders, they should shoot themselves.

Harry and Jennings were in Houston by January 4, where they rented a room in a residence at 4710 Walker Avenue. Their landlord recognized their photograph in a newspaper and notified police, who surrounded the house on the morning of January 5. According to the most reliable version of events, three policemen went to the front door, removed and handcuffed an unemployed carpenter looking for work, and were then met with gunfire from inside the house. They responded with a shotgun. Soon, they heard four shots from the bathroom, which heralded the end of Harry and Jennings, who had mortally wounded each other, just as the Houston newspapers reported their mother had asked. One of the dying pair, probably Harry, ended this tragedy with a grisly invitation to the officers in the hallway, "We're dead, come on in." And they nearly were. Jennings was already gone, and Harry soon died in a nearby hospital.

Barrett and Barrett, 2-6, 9, 12, 16, 20, 24-28, 32-36, 44-46, 54, 75-80, 90, 108; Davis, 27-29, 40-43, 71-73, 75, 85, 97, 180, 183, 309, 311.

Younger, James (Jim) (1848-1902)

Born on January 15, 1848, in Lee's Summit, Missouri, Jim followed his brother Cole into the Quantrill irregulars in the spring of 1864, working first as a scout. Present when Quantrill was mortally wounded near Louisville, Kentucky, in May 1865, he was captured and transported to the military prison at Alton, Illinois. Released at the conclusion of the war, he returned to farming on the home place in Jackson County, Missouri. In 1808, Cole, Jim, John, Bob, and their mother moved to Dallas County, Texas.

Joining Cole and the James brothers in the April 1872 robbery of a Columbia, Kentucky, bank and perhaps two prior robberies, he returned to Texas in the winter of 1872-73. He became a Dallas policeman, but was accused of robbery on the testimony of accomplice J. J. L. Hollander, prompting Jim to strike out for Missouri. Then Jim joined brother John in a gunfight on March 16, 1874, with Pinkerton agents at Monegaw Springs, Missouri, following a train robbery. John Younger, Deputy Sheriff Ed Daniels, and Pinkerton agent Louis J. Lull were all killed, but Jim Younger and Agent John Boyle rode away.

Later, Jim was not so fortunate. On September 21, 1876, he received a disfiguring and disabling wound while pursued and captured following the ill-fated Northfield, Minnesota, raid. Restricted to a near-liquid diet during his prison term, he was paroled in 1901, then partnered with brother Cole in the tombstone business. After falling in love with journalist Alice "Alix" Miller, he became despondent when parole restrictions kept him from marrying or even selling valid life insurance policies. Jim killed himself in a St. Paul hotel on October 19, 1902.

Smith, *Last Hurrah of the James-Younger Gang,* 31, 37, 180, 209-10; O'Neal, *Encyclopedia,* 341-43; O'Neal, *Encyclopedia,* 314-43; Metz, *The Shooters,* 55, 60; Nash, 321, 323.

Younger, John (1851-74)

Born in 1851, in Lee's Summit, Missouri, and younger brother of James-Younger gang leader Cole Younger, John moved with his family to Dallas County, Texas, in 1868. Eventually, John became a dry goods clerk in Dallas, then killed Col. Charles H. Nichols, who was described in a contemporary newspaper account as acting sheriff of Dallas County in January 1871. Following his January 1874 participation in a train robbery at Gads Hill, Missouri, some hundred miles south of St. Louis, John and Jim Younger were hiding out with friends at Monegaw Springs, Missouri. Pinkerton agents Louis J. Lull and John Boyle and Deputy Sheriff Ed Daniels stopped at the residence to ask directions on March 16, 1874. When Jim and John followed the pair, a gunfight ensued. Lull shot John in the throat before Jim mortally wounded Lull and Daniels, then fell to the ground dead himself.

Smith, *Last Hurrah of the James-Younger Gang,* 180; Shirley, *Belle Starr,* 92; O'Neal, *Encyclopedia,* 343-44.

Selected Gunfights

Independence, Missouri, January 1866

Fifteen-year-old John Younger was slapped in the face with a fish by a Mr. Gilcrease. When Gilcrease turned, Younger coolly produced a revolver from his wagon and mortally wounded him. Younger was acquitted on the grounds of self-defense.

Dallas, Texas, January 15, 1871

According to one source, John used a slow-witted saloon patron named Russell for a firearms demonstration, shooting a pipe right out of his mouth, and thus drawing the attention of local authorities. The next day, Dallas County deputy sheriff John McMahon squeezed off a round that hit John in the throat. John let loose both barrels of his shotgun. McMahon, accompanied by Deputy Sheriff Charles Nichols, a wartime acquaintance of the Youngers, made the fatal mistake of arresting John, yet giving him just enough freedom of movement to start a gunfight. Younger and Tom Porter (Tom McDaniels) left Nichols mortally wounded and posseman James McMahon dead on the floor. Other sources confirm that John Younger engaged in such a gunfight, although the identity of the other participants is uncertain.

Near Denver, Colorado, 1871

John was on a return trip by train to Missouri from California when he wound up arguing with passengers somewhere near Denver. Shots rang out, and while no one was injured, Younger believed testimony would not be in his favor, so he left the train and hiked to Denver.

Monegaw Springs, Missouri, March 16, 1874

Following the Gads Hill train robbery on January 31, 1874, John and Jim Younger, the two main suspects, hid at a house at Monegaw Springs owned by a friend named Snuffer. Pinkerton detectives Louis J. Lull and John Boyle had been doggedly pursuing the outlaw brothers and eventually learned of the pair's whereabouts. The detectives enlisted the aid of Deputy Sheriff Ed Daniels, and the trio set out to entrap the Youngers by posing as lost cattle buyers in need of directions. They rode to the Snuffer home and asked directions, while John and Jim were hiding in another room.

When the bogus cattle buyers left, the Younger brothers followed and took them off guard on Chalk Level Road. The outlaws demanded to know their real identities and purpose for being in the area. When Pinkerton agent Lull went for his concealed pistol, John fired his double-barreled shotgun, mortally wounding Lull and killing Deputy Sheriff Daniels. When Lull attempted to escape, John chased him down and killed him, before falling dead to the ground. Only Pinkerton agent John Boyle and Jim Younger escaped the gunfight alive.

O'Neal, *Encyclopedia,* 343-44; Metz, *The Shooters,* 55; Hatley, *Bringing the Law to Texas,* 56; Nash, 321, 323; Drago, 93-94; Smith, *Last Hurrah of the James-Younger Gang,* 36; Yeatman, 116.

Younger, Robert (Bob) (1853-89)

Baby brother to the deadly Youngers, Robert was born in October 1853 at Lee's Summit, Missouri, too late to participate in the Civil

War. He left Texas with Cole in 1870 to enroll at William and Mary. By July 1873, he had joined the James-Younger gang in the derailment and robbery of a Chicago, Rock Island and Pacific Railroad train near Adair, Iowa. Although his brother Jim was troubled by the accidental death of hapless engineer John Rafferty during the derailment, Bob had no problem dividing Jim's share with the rest of the gang, or so the story goes. Although the trail is far from clear, one authority places Bob in a James-Younger stagecoach robbery between Malvern and Hot Springs, Arkansas, in mid-January 1874. During that robbery, the perpetrators exempted Confederate soldiers from the pilfering, then lectured the passengers on the perfidy of Northern interests. Bob may have been with John Younger and others during a train robbery at Gad's Hill, Missouri, on January 31, 1874.

Clever use of the "border shift" when wounded during the Northfield, Minnesota, raid, on September 7, 1876, allowed Bob to escape the town, only to be captured two weeks later near Madelia, Minnesota. Left to their fate by the James boys, Bob, Cole, and Jim were shot up and captured by a posse. Samuel Wells (Charlie Pitts) was killed on the spot.

During his sojourn at Stillwater Prison, Bob studied medicine, but succumbed to the prisoner's curse, tuberculosis, on September 16, 1889.

Smith, *Last Hurrah of the James-Younger Gang,* 208-9; O'Neal, *Encyclopedia,* 345-46.

Selected Gunfights
Columbia, Kentucky, April 29, 1872

Bob and four members of the James-Younger gang botched an attempt to rob the Columbia Deposit Bank. They succeeded only in wounding Judge James Garnett in the hand and killing cashier R. A. C. Martin, before they hurriedly leaped on waiting horses and galloped out of town.

Northfield, Minnesota, September 7, 1876

Northfield was the last hurrah of the infamous James-Younger gang. A similar scenario would befall the Dalton Gang in Coffeyville, Kansas, during a raid on that town's two banks in

October 1892. In Northfield, as in the Coffeyville raid some sixteen years later, the citizens came together quickly once they learned that the town's bank was under siege and fought back valiantly. Bob was badly wounded and might have died that day, but for the effort of his brother, Jim Younger, who caught a horse for him. A bank employee, A. E. Bunker, was wounded as he ran out of the bank. Another employee, Joseph Lee Heywood, was shot and killed in cold blood as the bandits raced outside to their horses.

Near Madelia, Minnesota, September, 21, 1876

A relentless posse overtook Cole, Bob, and Jim Younger, with Samuel Wells (Charlie Pitts), near Madelia. The hell-raising gunfight that followed resulted in three lawmen being wounded and in Wells's death. Amazingly, none of the Youngers were killed despite some very serious wounds. Cole received eleven gunshot wounds, Jim had five, and Bob was shot once in the chest, but none was fatal. Bob was shot one more time as he attempted to surrender. With hands raised Bob came out from cover and declared, "They're all down, except me," at which point another shot was fired, striking Bob in the cheek. Bob died in prison at Stillwater, Minnesota, on September 16, 1889, after suffering a debilitating bout of tuberculosis.

Smith, *Last Hurrah of the James-Younger Gang,* 85-225; O'Neal, *Encyclopedia,* 345-46; Metz, *The Shooters,* 51, 57, 59-60; Nash, 321-22.

Younger, Thomas Coleman (Cole) (1844-1916)

Born on January 15, 1884, in Lee's Summit, Missouri, Cole was the son of Henry Washington Younger, a self-made dry goods merchant and farmer with property in Jackson and Cass Counties, Missouri. Like many Missourians, Henry was a slaveholder, but against secession. He was robbed of a large sum of money and murdered near Lee's Summit in July 1862. Cole immediately assumed the worst and joined Confederate irregulars. Within months, it was discovered that the atrocity had been carried out by one "Captain Walley" and Federal militia he commanded. Walley was arrested by regular Federal forces, who reported that Walley confessed to the crime. A court martial had been disbanded in spite of the confession because corroborating Federal militia witnesses had been ambushed on the way to the trial by Confederate irregulars presumably led by Cole Younger.

Cole Younger was an effective guerilla who participated in the Lawrence, Kansas, massacre, yet later decried the wanton murder which occurred there. However, Younger denied participation in the murders of unarmed Union forces at Centralia in which he was supposed to have fired a single bullet through a file of fifteen Union soldiers.

He saw service as a bushwacker in Arkansas, Louisiana, and Texas. Returning home after the surrender, he may have participated with his wartime colleague Frank James in the first recorded daylight bank robbery of record, at Liberty, Missouri, on Tuesday, February 13, 1866.

The generally accepted James-Younger body of work included at least four train robberies, two stagecoach robberies, eleven bank robberies, and a profitable raid on the Kansas City State Fair. There is credible evidence that Cole and other gang members periodically hid in Indian Territory between jobs, but apparently committed no overt crimes there.

Cole led his family to Dallas County, Texas, in 1868 and returned from time to time until about 1872, having acquired cattle operations there. In 1870 Cole and his brother Bob even became Federal census officials, allowing Cole to learn about the area adjoining the family operations in Texas.

The good times came to an end in Northern climes. Following his 1876 capture in the aftermath of the disastrous Northfield, Minnesota, raid, Cole founded the first prison newspaper in the United States, the *Prison Mirror,* at Stillwater, Minnesota, in 1887. Ironically enough, Cole was first employed following his release from prison selling tombstones. Then he took a job selling coal oil burners in Muskogee and other Indian Territory venues.

Later, during his career giving testimonials against the life of crime, his wallet was once stolen while giving a lecture. Younger also partnered with Frank James in a 1903 traveling Wild West show. During his final years in Lee's Summit, he delighted in lecturing young people, including this writer's great aunt, about the benefits of clean living. He died peacefully in Lee's Summit, Missouri, on February 21, 1916.

Smith, *Last Hurrah of the James-Younger Gang,* 29-33, 210-13; Brant, 87-96.

Bibliography

Books

Adams, Ramon. *Burs Under the Saddle: A Second Look at Books and Histories of the West.* Norman: University of Oklahoma Press, 1964.

———. *More Burs Under the Saddle.* Norman: University of Oklahoma Press, 1979.

Alexander, Bob. *Dan Tucker, New Mexico's Deadly Lawman.* Silver City, NM: High-Lonesome Books, 2001.

———. *Desert Desperadoes: The Banditti of Southwestern New Mexico.* Silver City, NM: Gila Books, 2006.

———. *Fearless Dave Allison, Border Lawman.* Silver City, NM: High-Lonesome Books, 2003.

———. *John H. Behan: Sacrificed Sheriff.* Silver City, NM: High-Lonesome Books, 2002.

Banasik, Michael E. *Cavaliers of the Brush: Quantrill and His Men.* Iowa City: Camp Pope Bookshop, 2003.

Barra, Allen. *Inventing Wyatt Earp: His Life and Many Legends.* New York: Carroll and Graff Publishers, Inc., 1999.

Barrett, Paul W. and Mary H. *Young Brothers Massacre.* Columbia: University of Missouri Press, 1988.

Barrow, Blanche Caldwell, edited by John Neal Phillips. *My Life With Bonnie and Clyde.* Norman: University of Oklahoma Press, 2004.

Block, Lawrence, ed. *Gangsters, Swindlers, Killers and Thieves: The Lives and Crimes of Fifty American Villains.* New York: Oxford University Press, 2004.

Boessendecker, John. *Badge and Buckshot: Lawlessness in Old California.* Norman: University of Oklahoma Press, 1988.

Boswell, Evault. *Quantrill's Raiders in Texas.* Austin, TX: Eakin Press, 2003.

Brant, Marley. *The Outlaw Youngers.* Lanham, MD: Madison Books, 1992.

Burke, Bob. *From Oklahoma to Eternity: The Life of Wiley Post and the Winnie May.* Oklahoma City: Oklahoma Heritage Association, 1998.

Burrough, Bryan. *Public Enemies, America's Greatest Crime Wave and the Birth of the FBI, 1933-1934.* New York: Penguin Press, 2004.

Burrows, Jack. *John Ringo: The Gunfighter Who Never Was.* Tucson: The University of Arizona Press, 1987.

Burton, Art. *Black Gun, Silver Star: The Life and Legend of Frontier Marshal Bass Reeves.* Lincoln: University of Nebraska Press, 2006.

————. *Black, Red and Deadly: Black and Indian Gunfighters of the Indian Territory, 1870-1907.* Austin, TX: Eakin Press, 1991.

Butler, Ken. *Oklahoma Renegades.* Gretna, LA: Pelican Publishing, 1997.

Carlson, Chip. *Tom Horn: Blood on the Moon: Dark History of the Murderous Cattle Detective.* Glendo, WY: High Plains Press, 2001.

Castel, Albert and Goodrich, Thomas. *Bloody Bill Anderson: The Short Savage Life of a Civil War Guerilla.* Mechanicsburg, PA: Stackpole Books, 1998.

Colcord, Charles Francis. *The Autobiography of Charles Francis Colcord, 1859-1934.* Tulsa, OK: Privately Published, 1970.

Cordry, Dee. *Alive If Possible, Dead If Necessary.* Mustang, OK: Tate Publishing, LLC, 2005.

Crouch, Barry A. and Brice, Donaly E. *Cullen Montgomery Baker, Reconstruction Desperado.* Baton Rouge and London: Louisiana State University Press, 1997.

Davis, Bruce. *We're Dead, Come On In.* Gretna, LA: Pelican Publishing Company Inc., 2005.

DeArment, Robert K. *Alias Frank Canton.* Norman: University of Oklahoma Press, 1996.

————. *Bat Masterson: The Man and the Legend.* Norman: University of Oklahoma Press, 1979.

————. *Bravo of the Bravos: John Larn of Fort Griffin, Texas.* Norman: University of Oklahoma Press, 2002.

————. *Deadly Dozen: Twelve Forgotten Gunfighters of the Old West.* Norman: University of Oklahoma Press, 2003.

———— .*George Scarborough: The Life and Death of a Lawman on the Closing Frontier.* Norman: University of Oklahoma Press, 1992.

————.*Jim Courtright of Fort Worth: His Life and Legend.* Fort Worth, TX: TCU Press, 2004.

————. *Knights of the Green Cloth: The Saga of the Frontier Gamblers.* Norman: University of Oklahoma Press, 1982.

DeArment, Robert K., ed. *Life of the Marlows: A True Story of Frontier Life of Early Days.* Denton, TX: University of North Texas Press, 2004.

DeMattos, Jack. *Mysterious Gunfighter: The Story of Dave Mather.* College Station, TX: Creative Publishing Company, 1992.

Drago, Harry Sinclair. *Outlaws on Horseback.* New York: Dodd, Mead and Co., 1964.

Eckhardt, C. F. *Tales of Bad Men, Bad Women, and Bad Places: Four Centuries of Texas Outlawry.* Lubbock, TX: Texas Tech University Press, 1999.

Ernst, Donna. *Women of the Wild Bunch.* Souderton, PA: Wild Bunch Press, 2004.

Ernst, Robert. *Deadly Affrays: The Violent Deaths of the United States Marshals 1789-2004.* Phoenix, AZ: Scarlet Mask Enterprises, 2006.

Erwin, Allen A. *The Southwest of John Horton Slaughter, 1841-1922.* Glendale, CA: A. H. Clark Co., 1965.

Frost, Gordon H. and Jenkins, John H. *I'm Frank Hamer: The Life of a Texas Peace Officer.* Austin: Pemberton Press, 1968.

Garza, Phyllis de la. *Death for Dinner: The Benders of (Old) Kansas.* Honolulu: Talei Publishers, Inc., 2003.

Gillett, James B. *Six Years with the Texas Rangers, 1875 to 1881.* New Haven, CT: Yale University Press, 1925.

Girardin, G. Russell with William J. Helmer. *Dillinger, The Untold Story.* Bloomington and Indianapolis: Indiana University Press, 1994.

Hamilton, Stanley. *Machine Gun Kelly's Last Stand.* Lawrence: University of Kansas Press, 2003.

Hanes, Col. Bailey C. *Bill Doolin, Outlaw, O. T.* Norman: University of Oklahoma Press, 1968.

Hardin, John Wesley. *The Autobiography of John Wesley Hardin.* (first published in 1896). College Station, TX: Creation Books, 2000.

Harkey, Dee. *Mean as Hell: The Life of a New Mexico Lawman.* Santa Fe, NM: Ancient City Press, 1989.

Harman, S. W. *Hell on the Border.* Muskogee, OK: Indian Heritage Association, 1971.

Hatley, Allen G. *Bringing the Law to Texas: Crime and Violence in Nineteenth Century Texas.* LaGrange, TX: Centex Press, 2002.

————. *Texas Constables: A Frontier Heritage.* Lubbock, TX: Texas Tech University Press, 1999.

Helmer, William J. and Mattix, Rick. *Public Enemies: America's Criminal Past, 1919-1940.* New York: Facts on File, Inc., 1998.

Hickey, Michael M. *John Ringo: The Final Hours: A Tale of the Old West.* Honolulu, HI: Talei Publishers, Inc., 1995.

Hutton, Harold. *Doc Middleton: Life and Legends of the Notorious Plains Outlaw.* Chicago, IL: Sage Books, The Swallow Press, Inc., 1974.

Jameson, W. C. *Billy the Kid: Beyond the Grave.* Dallas, TX: Taylor Trade Publishing, 2005.

Johnson, David. *The Mason County "Hoo Doo" War, 1874-1902.* Denton, TX: University of North Texas Press, 2006.

Kelly, Charles. Outlaw Trail: *A History of Butch Cassidy and His Wild Bunch.* New York: Bonanza, 1959.

Knight, James R. with Jonathan Davis. *Bonnie and Clyde: A Twenty-First Century Update.* Austin, TX: Eakin Press, 2003.

Koch, Michael. *The Kimes Gang.* Bloomington, IN: Author House, 2005.

Kohn, George C. *Dictionary of Culprits and Criminals.* Metuchin, NJ: Scarecrow Press, 1986.

Maccabee, Paul. *Dillinger Slept Here.* St. Paul, MN: Minnesota Historical Society Press, 1995.

Marohn, Richard C. *The Last Gunfighter: John Wesley Hardin.* College Station, TX: Creative Publishing Co., 1995.

Martin, Jack. *Border Boss: Captain John R. Hughes, Texas Ranger.* Austin, TX: State House Press, 1990.

McCorkle, John. *Three Years with Quantrill: A True Story Told By His Scout John McCorkle.* Reprint, Norman: University of Oklahoma Press, 1992.

McCullough, Harrell. *Seldon Lindsey, U.S. Deputy Marshal Also Gunslinger, Cowboy, Outlaw, Indian Fighter.* Oklahoma City: Paragon Publishing, 1990.

Metz, Leon Claire. *Dallas Stoudenmire: El Paso Marshal.* Norman: University of Oklahoma Press, 1979.

————. *Encyclopedia of Lawmen, Outlaws and Gunfighters.* New York: Checkmark Books, 2003.

————. *John Selman, Gunfighter,* 2d ed. Norman: University of Oklahoma Press, 1980.

————. *John Wesley Hardin: Dark Angel of Texas.* Norman: University of Oklahoma Press, 1998.

————. *Pat Garrett, The Story of a Western Lawman.* Norman: University of Oklahoma Press, 1974.

————. *The Shooters, A Gallery of Notorious Gunmen from the American West.* El Paso, TX: Managean Books, 1976.

Miller, Nile H. and Snell, Joseph W. *Why the West Was Wild: A Contemporary Look at the Antics of Some Highly Publicized Kansas Cowtown Personalities.* Norman: University of Oklahoma Press, 1993.

Miller, Rick. *Sam Bass and Gang.* Austin, TX: State House Press, 1999.

Milligan, James C. *The Choctaw of Oklahoma.* Durant, OK: Choctaw Nation, 2003.

Milner, E. R. *The Lives and Times of Bonnie and Clyde.* Carbondale and Edwardsville: Southern Illinois University Press, 1996.

Morgan, R. D. *The Tri-State Terror: The Life and Crimes of Wilbur Underhill.* Stillwater, OK: New Forums Press, 2005.

Nash, Jay Robert. *Encyclopedia of Western Lawmen and Outlaws.* New York: DeCapo Press, 1994.

Newton, Willis and Joe. *The Newton Boys: Portrait of an Outlaw Gang.* Austin, TX: State House Press, 1994.

Nix, Evett Dumas. *Oklahombres: Particularly the Wilder Ones.* St. Louis, MO: Eden Publishing House, 1995.

Nolan, Frederick. *The West of Billy the Kid.* Norman: University of Oklahoma Press, 1998.

O'Neal, Bill. *Encyclopedia of Western Gunfighters.* Norman: University of Oklahoma Press, 1979.

————. *The Bloody Legacy of Pink Higgins: A Half Century of Violence in Texas.* Austin, TX, Eakin Press, 1999.

————. *The Johnson County War.* Austin, TX: Eakin Press, 2004.

Owens, Ron. *Oklahoma Heroes: A Tribute to Fallen Law Enforcement Officers.* Paducah, KY: Turner Publishing Company, 2000.

————. *Oklahoma Justice, The Oklahoma City Police: A Century of Gunfighters, Gangsters and Tourists.* Paducah, KY: Turner Publishing Co., 1995.

Parsons, Chuck. *John B. Armstrong, Texas Ranger and Pioneer*

Ranchman. College Station, TX: Texas A&M University Press, 2007.

Parsons, Chuck and Little, Marianne E. Hall. *Captain L. H. McNelly, Texas Ranger: The Life and Times of a Fighting Man.* Austin, TX: State House Press, 2001.

Peterson, Paul R. *Quantrill of Missouri: the Making of a Guerilla Warrior—The Man, the Myth, the Soldier.* Nashville, TN: Cumberland House, 2003.

Phillips, John Neal. *Running with Bonnie and Clyde: The Fast Years of Ralph Fults.* Norman: University of Oklahoma Press, 1996.

Pointer, Larry. *In Search of Butch Cassidy.* Norman: University of Oklahoma Press, 1988.

Poulsen, Ellen. *Don't Call Us Molls: Women of the John Dillinger Gang.* Little Neck, NY: Clinton Cook Publishing Corp., 2002.

Preece, Harold. *Lone Star Man: Ira Aten, Last of the Old Time Texas Rangers.* New York: Hasting House, 1968.

Ramsey, Winston G., ed. *On the Trail of Bonnie and Clyde Then and Now.* London: Battle of Britain International, Ltd., 2003.

Rasch, Phillip J. *Trailing Billy the Kid.* Stillwater, OK: Western Publications, 1995.

Recko, Corey. *Murder on the White Sands: The Disappearance of Albert and Henry Fountain.* Denton, TX: University of North Texas Press, 2007.

Reed, Nathaniel. *Life of Texas Jack.* Tulsa, OK: Privately Published, 1936.

Robinson, Charles M. III. *The Frontier World of Fort Griffin: The Life and Death of a Frontier Town.* Spokane, WA: The Arthur H. Clark Company, 1992.

———. *The Men Who Wear the Star: The Story of the Texas Rangers.* New York: Random House, 2000.

Rosa, Joseph G. *The Gunfighter: Man or Myth?* Norman: University of Oklahoma Press, 1969.

Rosa, Joseph G. and Koop, Waldo E. *Rowdy Joe Lowe: Gambler with a Gun.* Norman: University of Oklahoma Press, 1989.

Samuelson, Nancy B. *The Dalton Gang Story.* Dexter, MI: Thomson-Shore, 1992.

———. *Shoot from the Lip.* Eastford, CT: Shooting Star Press, 1998.

Selcer, Richard, ed. *Legendary Watering Holes: The Saloons That Made Texas*

Famous. College Station, TX: Texas A&M University Press, 2004.

Settle, William A. *Jesse James Was His Name.* Columbia, MO: University of Missouri Press, 1966.

Shirley, Glenn. *Belle Starr and Her Times: The Literature, The Facts, and The Legends.* Norman: University of Oklahoma Press, 1990.

———. *The Fighting Marlows: Men Who Wouldn't Be Lynched.* Fort Worth: Texas Christian University Press, 1994.

———. *Guardian of the Law: The Life and Times of William Matthew Tilghman (1854-1924).* Austin, TX: Eakin Press, 1988.

———. *Heck Thomas, Frontier Marshal.* Norman: University of Oklahoma Press, 1981.

———. *Henry Starr: Last of the Real Badmen.* New York: David McKay Company, 1965.

———. *Law West of Fort Smith.* Lincoln: University of Nebraska Press, 1971.

———. *Marauders of the Indian Nations: The Bill Cook Gang and Cherokee Bill.* Stillwater, OK: Barbed Wire Press, 1994.

———. *Purple Sage: The Exploits, Adventures, and Writings of Patrick Sylvester McGeeney.* Stillwater, OK: Barbed Wire Press, 1989.

———. *Shotgun for Hire.* Norman: University of Oklahoma Press, 1970.

———. *Six-Gun and Silver Star.* Albuquerque: University of New Mexico Press, 1955.

———. *Temple Houston: Lawyer with a Gun.* Norman: University of Oklahoma Press, 1980.

———. *The Fourth Guardsman.* Austin, TX: Eakin Press, 1997.

———. *They Outrobbed Them All: The Rise and Fall of the Vicious Martins.* Stillwater, OK: Barbed Wire Press, 1992.

———. *Thirteen Days of Terror.* Stillwater, OK: Barbed Wire Press, 1996.

———. *Toughest of Them All.* Albuquerque: University of New Mexico Press, 1953.

———. *West of Hell's Fringe.* Norman: University of Oklahoma Press, 1978.

Simmons, Lee. *Assignment Huntsville: Memoirs of a Texas Prison Official.* Austin: University of Texas Press, 1957.

Sinise, Jerry. *George Washington Arrington: Civil War Spy, Texas Ranger,*

Sheriff and Rancher. Burnet, TX, Eakin Press, 1979.

Smith, Helena Hunnington. *The War on Powder River.* Lincoln: University of Nebraska Press, 1966.

Smith, Robert Barr. *Daltons! The Raid on Coffeyville, Kansas.* Norman: University of Oklahoma Press, 1996.

————. *Last Hurrah of the James-Younger Gang.* Norman, University of Oklahoma Press, 2001.

Sonnichsen, C. L. *I'll Die Before I Run.* New York: Harper and Brothers, 1951.

————. *Pass of the North.* El Paso: Texas Western Press, 1968.

————. *Roy Bean: Law West of the Pecos.* Lincoln: University of Nebraska, Bison Book Edition, 1991.

Steele, Phillip. *Starr Tracks: Belle and Pearl Starr.* Gretna, LA: Pelican Publishing, 1987.

Steele, Phillip and Scoma, Marie Barrow. *The Family Story of Bonnie and Clyde.* Gretna, LA: Pelican Publishing, 2000.

Sterling, William Warren. *Trails and Trials of a Texas Ranger.* Norman: University of Oklahoma Press, 1959.

Stiles, T. J. *Jesse James: Last Rebel of the Civil War.* New York: Vintage, 2002.

Stone, Ron. *The Book of Texas Days.* Austin, TX: Eakin Press, 1997.

Tanner, Karen Holliday. *Doc Holliday: A Family Portrait.* Norman: University of Oklahoma Press, 1998.

Tanner, Karen Holliday and John D., Sr. *Last of the Old-Time Outlaws: The George Musgrave Story.* Fallbrook, CA: Runnin' Iron, 2003.

Tefertiller, Casey. *Wyatt Earp: The Life Behind the Legend.* New York: John Wiley and Sons, Inc., 1997.

Thrapp, Dan L. *Encyclopedia of Frontier Biography.* Spokane, WA: Arthur H. Clark Co., 1990.

Tise, Sammy. *Texas County Sheriffs.* Albuquerque, NM: Oakwood Printing, 1989.

Tyler, Ron, ed. *The New Handbook of Texas,* 6 Vols. Austin: Texas State Historical Association, 1996.

Utley, Robert M. *Billy the Kid: A Short and Violent Life.* Lincoln: University of Nebraska Press, 1989.

————. *High Noon in Lincoln: Violence on the Western Frontier.* Albuquerque: University of New Mexico Press, 1987.

————. *Lone Star Justice: The First Century of the Texas Rangers*. New York: Oxford University Press, 2002.

————. *Lone Star Lawmen: The Second Century of the Texas Rangers*. New York: Oxford University Press, 2007.

Wallis, Michael. *Billy the Kid: The Endless Ride*. New York: W. W. Norton & Co., 2007.

Webb, Walter Prescott. *The Texas Rangers: A Century of Frontier Defense*. 1935. Austin: University of Texas Press, 1997.

Wilkins, Frederic. *Defending the Borders: The Texas Rangers, 1848-1861*. Austin, TX: State House Press, 2001.

————. *The Law Comes to Texas: The Texas Rangers, 1870-1901*. Austin, TX: State House Press, 1999.

————. *The Legend Begins: The Texas Rangers, 1823-1945*. Austin, TX: State House Press, 1996.

Wood, Fern Morrow. *The Benders: Keepers of the Devil's Inn*. Chelsea, MI: BookCrafters, 1992.

Yeatman, Ted P. *Frank and Jesse James: The Story Behind the Legend*. Nashville, TN: Cumberland House, 2000.

Articles

Ahlquist, Diron Lacina. "Tom Horn's Indian Territory Manhunt." *Oklahombres Journal,* Vol. VIII, No. 3, Spring 1997.

Burton, Jeffrey. "Tom Ketchum and His Gang." *Wild West Magazine,* February 2002.

Butler, Ken. "The Troublesome Stevenson Brothers." *Oklahombres Journal,* Vol. XV, No. 1, Fall 2003.

Cordry, Dee. "Tom and Frank Smith." *Oklahombres Journal,* Vol. VIII, No. 2, Winter 1997.

Kirkwood, Kevin. "Corner Saloon." *Oklahombres Journal,* Vol. XI, No. 4, Summer 2000.

May, John D. "The Most Ferocious of Monsters: The Story of Outlaw Crawford Goldsby, Alias Cherokee Bill." *Chronicles of Oklahoma,* Vol. 77, No. 3, Fall 1999.

Samuelson, Nancy. "Bill Power and Dick Broadwell: Members of the Dalton Gang." *Oklahoma Outlaws Lawmen History Association Journal.* Vol. III, No. 3, Fall 2006.

————. "Who Really Robbed the Longview Bank?" *Oklahoma Outlaws Lawmen History Association Journal,* Vol. 3, No. 4, Winter 2006.

Smith, Robert Barr. "The Bad Christian Brothers, Black Jack and Bob." *Wild West Magazine,* December 2000.

————. "The Cook Gang: Plaguing Indian Territory." *Wild West Magazine,* August 2006.

Tower, Michael. "Fred Tecumseh Waite: The Outlaw Statesman." *Chronicles of Oklahoma,* Vol. 76, No. 2, Summer 1998.

Williams, Nudie E. "United States vs. Bass Reeves: Black Lawman on Trial." *Chronicles of Oklahoma,* Vol. 68, No. 2, 1990.

Letter

Letter from Mr. Dorman Holub, Chairman, Young County (Texas) Historical Commission, to author regarding Thomas B. Collier, 6 March 2007.

Interviews

Interview with Candy Moulton, *Wild West Magazine,* Vol. 16, Issue 2, August 2003.

Interview, *Tulsa World,* January 1, 2000.

Newspapers

Lincoln (Nebraska) *Journal Star*
Osage County (Oklahoma) *News*
Tulsa (Oklahoma) *World*

Index

302   200 TEXAS OUTLAWS